EUCHARISTIC MIRACLES

"And whilst they were at supper, Jesus took bread, and blessed, and broke: and gave to his disciples, and said: Take ye, and eat. This is my body. And taking the chalice, he gave thanks, and gave to them, saying: Drink ye all of this. For this is my blood of the new testament, which shall be shed for many unto remission of sins."

—Matthew 26:26-28

Consecrated Hosts stolen from the Basilica of St. Francis in Siena in the year 1730, then found, and now venerated in the same church. The Hosts have remained fresh and incorrupt for over 250 years, in contrast to the deterioration of unconsecrated hosts kept under the same conditions. The Hosts have been recognized by many popes and adored by many distinguished pilgrims, including St. John Bosco and Pope John XXIII. (See chapter 16.)

EUCHARISTIC MIRACLES

AND

EUCHARISTIC PHENOMENA
IN THE LIVES OF THE SAINTS

By

Joan Carroll Cruz

"I am the living bread which came down from heaven. If any man eat of this bread, he shall live for ever; and the bread that I will give, in my flesh, for the life of the world."

—John 6:51-52

TAN BOOKS AND PUBLISHERS

Nihil Obstat   Rev. John H. Miller, C.S.C.
                    Censor Librorum

Imprimatur   ✠ Philip M. Hannan
                    Archbishop of New Orleans
                    April 25, 1986

Library of Congress Catalog Card No.: 86-50850

ISBN: 978-0-89555-303-4

Cover design by Chris Pelicano.

Printed and bound in the United States of America.

TAN BOOKS AND PUBLISHERS

1987

"The Jews therefore strove among themselves, saying: How can this man give us his flesh to eat? Then Jesus said to them: Amen, amen I say unto you: Except you eat the flesh of the Son of man, and drink his blood, you shall not have life in you. He that eateth my flesh, and drinketh my blood, hath everlasting life: and I will raise him up in the last day. For my flesh is meat indeed: and my blood is drink indeed."

—*John* 6:53-56

*This book is dedicated to
the School Sisters of Notre Dame—
with appreciation, affection, and admiration.*

CONTENTS

—Part One—
EUCHARISTIC MIRACLES

ix

—Part Two—
EUCHARISTIC PHENOMENA
IN THE LIVES OF THE SAINTS

AUTHOR'S PREFACE

The greatest treasure in the Catholic Church is, without question, the Holy Eucharist—in which Jesus Christ humbly assumes the appearance of bread. Whether retained in simple chapels or grand basilicas, the Eucharist remains a sign of the Heavenly Father's unwillingness to be physically separated from His children.

His children, on the other hand, have not always appreciated this presence and, as painful as it is to consider, many have abused the gift by receiving it unworthily, by doubting the Real Presence of God in the sacred Host, or by treating the Sacrament with indifference. For these reasons the Saviour has seen fit at times to prove His presence by performing Eucharistic miracles of various kinds.

In order to learn of these miracles and to determine their approximate number, I have examined numerous books on the Eucharist, but only two volumes mentioned Eucharistic miracles, and these gave only one or two reports. Since miraculous happenings were excluded from the vast majority of these scholarly works, it seems that they were deemed unnecessary to prove the points made by the authors, or were perhaps little regarded by them. However, if a picture is worth a thousand words, surely miracles of the altar—in which the species are still preserved or the event is well documented—will encourage a keen awareness and appreciation of the Sacrament and will prove what many pages of print expound, namely, that Jesus is truly present in the Holy Eucharist.

Since the books mentioned have already dealt with the theological aspects of the Blessed Sacrament, this present work will be primarily a compilation of miracle accounts. These accounts were gleaned from various sources, and were, in turn, authenticated by the churches involved—through correspondence and from materials which they generously provided. There also have been many other such miracles, but research would be endless if an attempt were made to include every single one.

It is hoped that the reader, after reflecting on the contents of this volume, will be blessed with a deeper reverence for this Holy Sacrament and will repair as much as he is able the abuses that are directed to this Heavenly Presence that was given to us by a loving Creator and Saviour.

—Joan Carroll Cruz

INTRODUCTION

The Catholic Teaching on the Holy Eucharist

The holy Catholic Church teaches that at the moment of the Consecration of the Mass, the bread and wine on the altar truly become the Body and Blood of Jesus Christ. The bread and wine cease to exist, though the appearances and properties, or *accidents,* of bread and wine remain. This momentous change is known as *transubstantiation*—change of substance.

The consecrated Host and the Precious Blood under the form of wine are given the adoration that is reserved for God alone, since they are, indeed, Almighty God Himself. This highest form of veneration is known as *latria.* The opinions that Christ is only in the Eucharistic elements as in a sign, or that Christ is received only spiritually, were condemned by the Council of Trent. (Trent, Session XIII, canons 1, 6, 8, Oct. 11, 1551).

Both the bread and wine become the whole Jesus Christ—His Body, Blood, Soul and Divinity, so that the recipient receives Christ whole and entire under either form. Furthermore, the tiniest particle of a consecrated Host or the smallest drop of consecrated "wine" *is* Christ. Yet Christ is not divided, He remains one.

Our Lord is present as long as the appearances of bread and wine remain. When a consecrated Host is digested or dissolved in water, and no longer has the appearance of bread, it is no longer Jesus. Thus Our Lord is present in a communicant for about 15 minutes, and one should adore Him within oneself as long as He is sacramentally present. A famous story is told about St. Philip Neri, who saw a woman who had received Holy Communion leave the church right after Mass, disregarding Christ within her. The saint sent two altar boys with lighted candles to accompany her, as she was still a living tabernacle of the All-Holy God.

While it is true that God is everywhere, as the Creator and Sustainer of all things, and that He is present by sanctifying grace in all souls in the state of grace, these are *spiritual* presences. The

Eucharistic presence of Christ—Body, Blood, Soul and Divinity— is entirely unique, and it alone is referred to as *the Real Presence*.

To receive Holy Communion worthily one must be in the state of grace, that is, free of having committed a mortal sin that has not been confessed and absolved in the Sacrament of Penance. To receive Holy Communion in the state of mortal sin is itself a mortal sin of sacrilege. A person who has committed a mortal sin must first cleanse his soul in the Sacrament of Penance before receiving Communion. St. Paul declares (*1 Cor.* 11:29) that anyone who would receive the Eucharist unworthily eats and drinks judgment to himself. (The sin of sacrilegious Communion is of course forgivable in the Sacrament of Penance.)

The communicant must also, in addition to being in the state of grace, have a right intention and perform the required fast. The current requirement is to fast from all food and drink (except water and true medicine) for one hour before the actual time of receiving. Fasting for a longer time—for example, for three hours or from midnight—is an excellent preparation.

The serious Catholic will also strive to purify his soul from venial sin in order to provide a worthy dwelling place in his heart for Our Lord. The best immediate preparation for Holy Communion is praying the Mass devoutly.

Catholics must receive Holy Communion at least once a year, during the Easter season (in the United States, from the first Sunday of Lent through Trinity Sunday, the 8th Sunday after Easter).

The special sacramental effects of the Eucharist are an intrinsic union of the recipient with Jesus Christ (and also with the other members of His Mystical Body); the spiritual nourishment of the soul, preserving and increasing the supernatural life of sanctifying grace (an effect comparable to the nourishment of our bodies by food); and a pledge of heavenly bliss and the resurrection of the body.

By receiving Holy Communion, a Catholic obeys Our Lord's command to eat His Body and drink His Blood. He performs an act most pleasing to God, who longs to come into his heart. And in turn, his desire to receive *Him* will increase. Each reception of Holy Communion brings an increase of sanctifying grace in the soul; this takes place to the degree that the recipient has opened himself to Our Lord by emptying his soul of sin and worldly desires, and in accord with the dispositions of his immediate preparation, reception, and thanksgiving.

Sanctifying grace is the very life of Christ in the soul; a spiritual reality difficult to describe, it can be imagined as pure water or as light. Sanctifying grace renders the soul holy and pleasing to God, and gives it a supernatural beauty which far surpasses the greatest natural loveliness. A person must be in the state of sanctifying grace at the moment of death in order to be saved. Every visit of Jesus Christ in the Eucharist is a promise of eternal life for those who remain in His grace by obeying His commandments.

In Holy Communion Our Lord brings graces to enable us to keep His commandments. Frequent Holy Communion has long been urged by the Church as a means to overcome sin, including habitual sins—and in particular, habitual sins of impurity. The frequent reorienting of oneself toward Jesus Christ which is entailed in frequent devout Holy Communion is a most fruitful spiritual exercise, weakening the sensual and worldly impulses in the soul and awakening an appreciation for the things of God, thus disposing the soul to derive much spiritual profit from Holy Communion. St. John Bosco, the "Friend of Youth" and reclaimer of wayward boys, often spoke of three "springs" to the spiritual life: Confession, Holy Communion, and devotion to the Blessed Virgin Mary.

From earliest times the Church has venerated the Eucharistic "bread" and "wine" as the actual Body and Blood of Jesus Christ, since this was the teaching of Christ Himself. Our Lord knew the depth of faith which would be required for acceptance of this doctrine, so He first prepared His followers by the miraculous multiplication of loaves and fishes. (*Matt.* 14:15-21). Then He foretold that He would give His very flesh and blood as food and drink. This was the turning point for many of His followers: "Many therefore of his disciples, hearing it, said: This saying is hard, and who can hear it? . . . After this many of his disciples went back; and walked no more with him." (*John* 6:61, 67). These had not misunderstood Him; they simply would not accept what He was saying. But Our Lord did not offer an explanation to soften His words or to give them a symbolic meaning. Rather, "Then Jesus said to the twelve: Will you also go away?" (*John* 6:68).

The actual institution of the Holy Eucharist came after the Last Supper. It is described thus by St. Matthew: "And whilst they were at supper, Jesus took bread, and blessed, and broke: and gave to his disciples, and said: Take ye, and eat. This is my body. And taking the chalice, he gave thanks, and gave to them, saying: Drink ye all of this. For this is my blood of the new testament, which shall be shed for many unto remission of sins." (*Matt.* 26:26-28). This momentous event is also recounted by St. Mark (*Mk.* 14:22-24), St. Luke (*Lk.* 22:17-20), and St. Paul (*1 Cor.* 11:23-26). These words of Our Lord have ever been, and are now, accepted in their true and literal sense by the whole of Catholic Christendom.

St. Ignatius of Antioch (d. 170), who was a disciple of the Apostle John, wrote the following concerning the heretics of those early times: "They have abstained from the Eucharist and prayer, because they do not confess that the Eucharist is the flesh of our Saviour Jesus Christ." St. Ephrem (d. 373) said: "But if anyone despise it or reject it or treat it with ignominy, it may be taken as a certainty that he treats with ignominy the Son, who called it and actually made it to be His Body." And St. Justin (d. 165) declared:

> We call this food "Eucharist," of which no one should partake who does not believe in the truth of our doctrine, who has not been cleansed by the regeneration and remission of his sins and whose life is not in conformity with the precepts of Jesus Christ. Because we do not partake of this as ordinary food and drink, and since in virtue of the word of God, Jesus Christ incarnate takes flesh and blood for our redemption. We know also that this food which in the natural order would become our flesh and blood, being consecrated in the prayer which contains His own divine words, is the flesh and blood of the same Jesus made man.

The saints of later ages, too, have consistently and eloquently professed faith in the real presence of Jesus within the humble consecrated Host. St. Francis of Assisi (c. 1181-1226), in one of his few extant letters, wrote that "Everything in man should halt in awe. Let all the world quake and let Heaven exult when Christ the Son of the living God is there on the altar in the hands of the priest." The saint deemed no dignity greater than that of the priesthood, "because of its sublime privilege of consecrating the Body and Blood of Christ." St. Anthony of Padua (1195-1231) affirmed:

> We must firmly believe and declare openly that the same
> body that was born of the Virgin, which was hung on the
> cross, lay in the tomb, rose on the third day and ascended to
> the right hand of the Father, was given in food to the Apos-
> tles, and now the Church truly consecrates and distributes it
> to the faithful.

The great 13th century philosopher and theologian, St. Thomas
Aquinas (c. 1225-1274), has been called "the Eucharistic Doctor," not only for his inspiring theological writing on the Eucharist
in his *Summa Theologica,* but also for his Eucharistic hymns and
his composition of the Proper of the Mass for the feast of Corpus
Christi. St. Thomas, considered by many to equal Plato and
Aristotle as one of the greatest philosophers of all time, declared
on his deathbed regarding the Eucharist:

> If in this world there be any knowledge of this Mystery
> keener than that of faith, I wish now to affirm that I believe
> in the Real Presence of Jesus Christ in this Sacrament, truly
> God and truly man, the Son of God, the Son of the Virgin
> Mary. This I believe and hold for true and certain.

The first American-born canonized saint, Elizabeth Ann Seton
(1774-1821), while still an Episcopalian, attended Mass while on
a visit to Italy. When her Catholic companion whispered at the
elevation of the Host, "This is the Body of Christ," the future saint
became deeply agitated and later wrote to her sister-in-law:

> How happy we would be if we believed what these dear
> souls believe, that they possess God in the Sacrament and
> that He remains in their churches and is carried to them
> when they are sick! Oh, my! When they carry the Blessed
> Sacrament under my window, while I feel the loneliness and
> sadness of my case, I cannot stop my tears at the thought: My
> God, how happy I would be, even so far away from all so
> dear, if I could find You in the church as they do . . . The
> other day, in a moment of excessive distress, I fell on my
> knees without thinking when the Blessed Sacrament passed
> by, and cried in an agony to God to bless me if He was there,
> that my whole soul desired only Him.

After the blossoming of Elizabeth's faith and her eventual conversion, it seems she could hardly contain herself when she exclaimed, "God is everywhere, in the very air I breathe—yes, everywhere, but in His Sacrament of the altar He is as present actually and really as my soul within my body; in His Sacrifice daily offered as really as once offered on the cross."

This holy Sacrament, given to men by a loving God as a perpetual presence among His children, while keenly adored by the saints and by the faithful members of the Church throughout the ages, has on the other hand been doubted by many, neglected and ignored by others, received unworthily by some, and even desecrated by a few. For these reasons, and others known only to God, the Lord has seen fit at times to manifest His presence by extraordinary Eucharistic miracles. One of the first to mention such a miracle was St. Cyprian, who wrote about the year 258:

> If you do not fear future punishment, at least fear those of the present. How many apostates do we behold who have met an unhappy end? One is struck dumb, another possessed by a demon becomes his own executioner. This one, attempting to communicate amongst the faithful, is seized by horrible convulsions. That one, striving to open the tabernacle in which the body of the Lord was preserved, sees flames issuing forth.

Other Eucharistic miracles have taken different forms. On many occasions Hosts have bled, or a Host has been transformed into flesh and the Eucharist "wine" into perceptible blood. On other occasions Hosts have levitated, or have been preserved for long periods of time. These miracles have resulted in a resurgence of faith in the Real Presence, as well as in conversions to the Catholic faith. They have been followed by acts of reparation and increased devotion for the "Sacrament of Christ's love." In this way these prodigies have strengthened the faith of thousands, and even of millions, because many Eucharistic miracles have endured for centuries.

We, too, are privileged to witness these wonders, even if only through words and pictures. They remain a testimony by God to one of the most basic truths and most exalted mysteries of the Catholic religion: *"And the Word was made flesh, and dwelt among us"*—not only in Bethlehem, but in every Catholic tabernacle and in every faithful Catholic heart.

ACKNOWLEDGEMENTS

Gratitude is extended to my brother, Daniel J. Carroll, Jr. for his help in editing the galleys of this volume, to Mrs. Andreé Avcalade for assisting with the French translations, Mr. Carlos Mazier, who helped with the Spanish translations, Mrs. Rosalinde Rettich Wax for the German translations, and Mrs. Sabina Carimi for the Italian translations. Many thanks also to Mrs. Carol Shaw, Arthur N. Hoagland, M.D., Sr. M. Barbara Anne, F.M.S.C., and Rev. Louis V. Scagnelli, O.C.D. A particular mention should also be made of the 19th-century book entitled *Legends of the Blessed Sacrament*, by Emily Mary Shapcote, which was the source for most of the woodcuts found herein.

The following are those who kindly answered my queries about the miracles mentioned in this book. Their generosity in supplying books, papers and photographs has placed me profoundly in their debt. My deepest appreciation goes to them all.

Austria: Röm.-Kath-Pfarramt, Seefeld.

Belgium: J. Michiels, Louvain; R. Bois Sawreye, Brussels; De Pastoor Parochie Sint-Quintinus, Hasselt; Sister Geneviève Simons, Antwerp.

Czechoslovakia: Anna Vanecková, Slavonice.

France: Vicaire Episcopal Adolphe-Marie Hardy, Paris; Rev. A. Marsolet, Rouen; The Sister Secretary, Paray Le Monial; Prof. Michel Grivelet, Dijon; Jean Ancien, Braine; Jean Pardon, Braine; le Curé A. Marion, Faverney; Pere M. Louis Bourgeois, Blanot; Abbé Jean-Claude Veissier, Bordeaux; Soeur Claudine Ferrier, Labrede; Father Jacques Lanuc, Bordeaux.

Germany: Dr. Hilda Thummerer, Augsburg; Dr. Paul Mai, Regensburg.

Italy: P. Antonio Giannini, Siena; Il P. Rettore, P. Carlo Vincenti, Cascia; Basilica Di S. Francesco, Siena; Suor Chiara, O.S.A., L'Aquila; Don Carlo Lella, Ferrara; Sanctuario S. Rita, Cascia; Il rettore Basilica Catterdrale, Orvieto; Frati Minori Conventuali, Lanciano; Sac. Eugenio De Angelis, Morrovalle; Mons. Otello Gentili, Macerata; P. Ulderico Pallottini, Lanciano; Fr. Luigi Giobbio, S.d.B., Turin; Sac. Ambrogio Constantini, Alatri; Don Desiderio Sozzi, Florence.

The Netherlands: Deacon J. C. Suidgeest, Amsterdam.
Portugal: Church of the Holy Miracle, Santarem.
Spain: El cura Parroco Emilio Allonza Canfranc, Daroca; The Jesuit Fathers, Alcalá de Henares.

—Joan Carroll Cruz

GLOSSARY

Chalice—The vessel used at Mass to contain the Precious Blood of Christ. It is usually several inches in height with a wide base, a stem with a knob midway and a cup.

Ciborium—The vessel which contains the small Hosts used for the Communion of the faithful. It is similar to a chalice, but has a larger cup and usually has a matching cover.

Corporal—A small, square, white linen cloth, about the size of a man's handkerchief, on which the sacred Host and the chalice are placed during Mass.

Eucharist—The Sacrament in which, under the appearances of bread and wine, the Body and Blood of Christ are truly, really and substantially present as the grace-producing food of our souls. More specifically, the consecrated Host and the consecrated "wine," that is, the Precious Blood.

Host—The wafer of unleavened bread which becomes the Body and Blood of Christ at the moment of Consecration in the Mass. (One large Host for the priest and many small Hosts for the congregation are consecrated at Mass.) The word derives from the Latin *hostia,* or "victim," since in the Holy Sacrifice of the Mass Jesus Christ offers Himself to God the Father as the victim and propitiation for our sins. (Thus each Mass is the renewal of the one Sacrifice of Calvary.)

Lunette—A crescent-shaped device or a double circle of gold or metal gilt by means of which the Host is held securely and upright when exposed in a monstrance.

Monstrance—A vessel usually made of gold or precious metal which is used for the exposition of the Blessed Sacrament. The principal part is a circular glass through which the consecrated Host can be viewed. Surrounding this circular glass is a metal sunburst of golden "rays." A cross might surmount the vessel, which stands on a pedestal and is supported by a circular base.

Ostensorium—Monstrance.

Paten—A plate of precious metal on which the Host is placed during Holy Mass.

Pyx (Pronunciation: pix)—A flat circular container usually about the size and shape of a man's pocket watch in which the Host is carried to the sick. This term is also used for a small round vessel with a removable lid in which the Host is kept in a tabernacle.

Reliquary—A case intended to contain and expose a sacred relic. It can be of any size and often resembles a small ostensorium. In some European churches they are very large and elaborate and sometimes immovable.

Tabernacle—The box-like receptacle wherein the Blessed Sacrament is reserved on an altar. It can be made of any sturdy material and in any shape, although preferably with a dome. It is covered with a veil. The interior is lined with silk, a corporal is folded on its floor, and the small Hosts for Communion are kept there in a ciborium. A pyx containing Hosts for the sick and a capsula (round metal vessel with a short stem and a stand) which contains a large Host for the purpose of Exposition and Benediction may also be kept there.

Transubstantiation—The word officially approved by the Council of Trent to express the changing of the entire substance of bread and wine into the Body and Blood of Christ. After the Consecration only the appearances, or "accidents" (color, taste, smell, quantity, etc.) of bread and wine remain.

Viaticum—The Holy Eucharist when it is given to those in danger of death.

—PART ONE—

EUCHARISTIC
MIRACLES

Chapter 1

THE MIRACLE OF LANCIANO, ITALY

8th Century

In about the 700th year of Our Lord, in a monastery then named for St. Longinus, the Roman centurion who pierced the side of Christ with a lance, a priest-monk of the Order of St. Basil was celebrating the Holy Sacrifice of the Mass according to the Latin Rite. Although his name is unknown, it is reported in an ancient document that he was "... versed in the sciences of the world, but ignorant in that of God." Having suffered from recurrent doubts regarding transubstantiation (the change of the bread and wine into the Body and Blood of Christ), he had just spoken the solemn words of Consecration when the host was suddenly changed into a circle of flesh, and the wine was transformed into visible blood.

Bewildered at first by the prodigy which he had witnessed, he eventually regained his composure, and while weeping joyously, he spoke to the congregation: "O fortunate witnesses, to whom the Blessed God, to confound my unbelief, has wished to reveal Himself visible to our eyes! Come, brethren, and marvel at our God, so close to us. Behold the flesh and blood of our Most Beloved Christ."

The congregation rushed to the altar, marveled at the sight, and went forth to spread the news to other townspeople who, in turn, came to the church to witness the Eucharistic miracle for themselves.

The flesh remained intact, but the blood in the chalice soon divided into five pellets of unequal sizes and irregular shapes. The monks decided to weigh the nuggets. On a scale obtained from the Archbishop, it was discovered that one nugget weighed the same as all five together, two as much as any three, and the smallest as much as the largest.

3

The Host and the five pellets were placed in a reliquary of artistic ivory. Over the years they have been in the keeping of three different religious orders. At the time of the miracle, the Church of St. Longinus was staffed by Basilian monks, but it was abandoned by them at the close of the 12th century. The property passed quickly to the Benedictines, and then to the Franciscans—who had to demolish the old church because of damage incurred during earthquakes. The new church that was built on the site was named after their founder, St. Francis of Assisi.

History records that after the miracle was certified, a document telling the details of the miracle was written on parchment in both Greek and Latin and was safeguarded by the monks between two tablets. We are told that in the first years of the 16th century, when the monastery was in the possession of the Franciscans, the document was shown to two visiting monks of the Order of St. Basil. Wishing, perhaps, to save their order the disgrace of having the weak faith of one of its members live on in history, they left with the document during the night; and despite many investigations, the Franciscans " . . . have never been able to find out whither the two fugitives had fled."

The ivory reliquary was replaced in 1713 by the one which now exhibits the two relics. This is a monstrance of finely sculptured silver and crystal. The flesh is enclosed in the way a Host is usually enclosed in a monstrance, and the nuggets of blood are held in a chalice of artistically etched crystal, which some believe might be the actual chalice in which the miraculous change occurred.

In 1887 Archbishop Petrarca of Lanciano obtained from Pope Leo XIII a plenary indulgence in perpetuity for those who visit the Church of the Miracle during the eight days preceding the annual feast day, the last Sunday of October.

In February of 1574, Monsignor Rodrigues verified in the presence of reputable witnesses that the combined weight of the five pellets of congealed blood was equal to the individual weight of any of them, a fact that was later memorialized by being chiseled on a marble tablet, dated 1636, which is still located in the church. During subsequent authentications of the blood, however, this prodigy was not repeated.

A number of these authentications have been performed throughout the centuries, but the last verification, in 1970, is the most scientifically complete, and it is that examination which we will now consider.

Performed under strict scientific criteria, the task was assigned to Professor Doctor Odoardo Linoli, university professor-at-large in anatomy and pathological histology, and in chemistry and clinical microscopy, head physician of the united hospitals of Arezzo. Professor Linoli availed himself of the services of Doctor Ruggero Bertelli, a professor emeritus of normal human anatomy at the University of Siena. Dr. Bertelli not only concurred with all of Professor Linoli's conclusions, but also presented an official document to that effect.

Assembled in the sacristy of the Church of St. Francis on November 18, 1970 were the Archbishop of Lanciano, the Bishop of Ortona, the Provincial of the Friars Minor Conventual, the chancellor of the archdiocese, the reverend secretary of the Archbishop and the entire community of the monastery, together with Professor Linoli.

On examining the ostensorium, it was observed that the lunette containing the flesh was not hermetically sealed and that the particles of "unleavened bread" in the center of the flesh, that had remained for many years, had by then entirely disappeared. The flesh was described as being yellow-brown in color, irregular and roundish in shape, thicker and wrinkled along the periphery, becoming gradually thinner as it reached the central area where the tissue was frayed, with small extensions protruding toward the empty space in the middle. A small sample was taken from a thicker part for examination in the laboratory of the hospital in Arezzo.

On examining the five pellets of blood, it was noted that the prodigy regarding the weight of the pellets was no longer evident, as it was last noted in 1574. The five pellets were found to be quite irregular in form, finely wrinkled, compact, homogeneous and hard in consistency, being a yellow-chestnut color and having the appearance of chalk. A small sample was taken from the central part of one pellet for microscopic examination and scientific study. Later, after all the studies were completed, the fragments of both relics were returned to the church.

The conclusions reached by Professor Linoli were presented on March 4, 1971 in detailed medical and scientific terminology to a prestigious assembly, including ecclesiastical officials, the provincials and superiors of the Friars Minor Conventual, and representatives of religious houses in the city as well as civil, judicial, political and military authorities, representatives of the medical staffs of the city hospitals, various religious of the city and a number of the city's residents.

The professor's conclusions were later discussed by the Very Rev. Father Bruno Luciani and Professor Urbano, the chief analyst of the city hospital of Lanciano and a professor at the University of Florence. A copy of the detailed report and the minutes of the meeting and discussions are kept in the archives of the monastery. Authentic copies were sent to various officials of the Catholic Church and to superiors of the Order, while another was delivered to His Holiness Pope Paul VI during a private audience.

As a result of the histological (microscopic) studies, the following facts were ascertained and documented: The flesh was identified as striated muscular tissue of the myocardium (heart wall), having no trace whatsoever of any materials or agents used for the preservation of flesh. Both the flesh and the sample of blood were found to be of human origin, emphatically excluding the possibility that it was from an animal species. The blood and the flesh were found to belong to the same blood type, AB. The blood of the Eucharistic miracle was found to contain the following minerals: chlorides, phosphorus, magnesium, potassium, sodium in a lesser degree, and a greater quantity of calcium. Proteins in the clotted blood were found to be normally fractionated, with the same percentage ratio as those found in normal fresh blood.

Professor Linoli further noted that the blood, had it been taken from a cadaver, would have altered rapidly through spoilage and decay. His findings conclusively exclude the possibility of a fraud perpetrated centuries ago. In fact, he maintained that only a hand experienced in anatomic dissection could have obtained from a hollow internal organ, the heart, such an expert cut, made tangentially—that is, a round cut, thick on the outer edges and lessening gradually and uniformly into nothingness in the central area. The doctor ended his report by stating that while the flesh and blood were conserved in receptacles not hermetically sealed, they were not damaged, although they had been exposed to the influences of physical, atmospheric and biological agents.

The ostensorium containing the relics was previously kept to the side of the altar in the Church of St. Francis, but it is now situated in a tabernacle atop the main tabernacle of the high altar. A stairway at the back of the altar enables the visitor to approach very close to the tabernacle, which is open in the back, so that he can clearly see the reliquary containing the flesh and blood.

The visitor will notice that the Host appears rosy in color when it is backlighted. As he gazes, he must undoubtedly reflect upon the countless numbers of others who have looked upon this awesome miracle during its more than 1200 years of existence.

Ostensorium with the miraculous Eucharist of Lanciano—the Host which turned to flesh and the wine which turned to visible blood in the eighth century. A wax seal can be seen to the right of the crystal chalice. This reliquary dates back to 1713, although the chalice itself is thought by some to be the very one in which the miraculous change occurred.

The flesh of the Eucharistic miracle of Lanciano. The circle of flesh appeared around the Host. Over the centuries the "unleavened bread" of the Host has pulverized and disappeared, but the flesh remains intact. At scientific examinations made in 1971 the flesh was found to be human striated muscular tissue of the myocardium (heart wall), type AB, and to be absolutely free of any agents used for preserving flesh.

The blood of the Eucharistic miracle of Lanciano; this blood has divided into five irregularly shaped pellets. At scientific examinations conducted in 1971 these pellets were found to be human blood, type AB, with proteins normally fractionated and present in the same percentage ratio as those in normal fresh blood.

The stairway behind the altar leading up to the miraculous Eucharist in the tabernacle.

The altar of the Church of St. Francis. The upper tabernacle holds the miraculous Eucharist, which can be approached from the stairway behind the altar.

The interior of the Church of St. Francis. One can see here the two tabernacles, as well as a stained-glass window above the altar honoring the Blessed Eucharist.

Above: Another view of the interior of the Church of St. Francis, where the miraculous Eucharist is enshrined.
Below: Exterior of the Church of St. Francis. The square and surroundings are visible here.

The entrance to the Church of St. Francis. The present church is built on the site of the original church in which the miracle occurred.

An outside view of Lanciano's church of St. Francis showing the bell tower, which rises above the surrounding buildings.

A painting in the Church of St. Francis depicting the miracle. The priest displays to the amazed people the Eucharistic elements which have become visible flesh and blood.

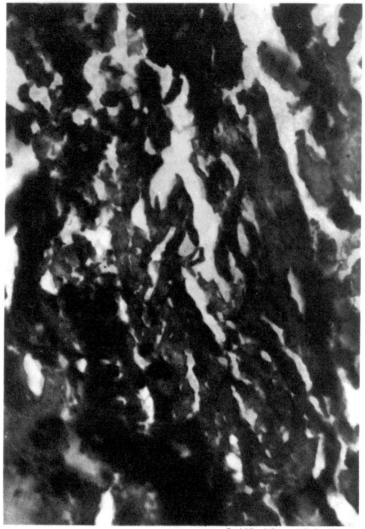

Photograph of a fragment of the Eucharistic flesh of Lanciano as examined by Doctors Linoli and Bertelli in Siena, Italy in 1971. This photo gives an enlarged view of the tissue, which is seen to be composed of muscle fibers, isolated and in fascicles of various sizes; the structure is syncitial. Drs. Linoli and Bertelli concluded that the flesh was striated muscular tissue of the myocardium (heart wall), of human origin.

Chapter 2

THE MIRACLE OF BRAINE, FRANCE

1153

At the time of the Eucharistic miracle of Braine, a great many non-Catholics lived in that city, which is located in the archdiocese of Soissons. Agnes of Braine, a countess who lived in a castle of the city, tried to convert many of these non-Catholics and singled out a beautiful Jewish girl on whom to concentrate her efforts. The girl steadfastly refused to believe in the Holy Eucharist and remained skeptical despite the zeal of the countess. Apparently determined to win the girl to the Faith, the countess went so far as to use force to remove her to the castle, where she was eventually engaged as a chambermaid and a lady-in-waiting.

In 1153 the Archbishop of Soissons, Anculphe de Pierrefonds, arranged for a solemn High Mass and a procession around the city of Braine in observance of the feast of the Holy Spirit. Attending the ceremonies were all the people of Braine, including the non-Catholics, who attended out of respect for the Archbishop and out of curiosity about the elaborate activities that were planned.

During the Holy Sacrifice of the Mass celebrated by the Archbishop, at the time of the Elevation, the people saw, instead of the Host, a small child. Descriptions are not available, nor is it known how long the vision lasted, but it was apparently so magnificent and impressive that the non-Catholics, now filled with the Holy Spirit, *demandèrent le baptême*—demanded Baptism. It is speculated that among those who asked for Baptism was the young Jewish girl whom the countess had attempted to convert.

Following the miracle Countess Agnes of Braine founded a monastery, where the miraculous Host was kept for centuries.

It is known that 80 years after the miracle, in 1233, Cardinal Jacque de Vitry visited and worshiped the miraculous Host. In 1718, more than 550 years after the miracle, Dom Martene saw the Host, which was still entire and which was described as being the size of a large coin. However, 15 years after this visit an historian of Valois by the name of Carlier discovered that the Host, in the normal fashion, had been reduced to a little dust. The Host had been kept in a tabernacle, together with the chalice that had been used during the Mass of the miracle.

The ivory box in which the Host had been kept was regarded as a treasure. When the monks abandoned the abbey during the French Revolution (which began in 1789), they entrusted the ivory box to the safekeeping of Lambert, the Chief of Police. It was returned to the church of Braine in 1839, where it was kept in the sacristy for a long time.

Not only had the Host and chalice been faithfully kept, but also the vestments used during the Mass of the miracle. The chasuble, the outer large vestment the priest wears at Mass, was of fine silk richly embroidered with liturgical symbols, including the face of an angel on the front panel, and an Agnus Dei on the back. Around the neck of the vestment was a band of gold, which was embellished with fine pearls and a few precious stones. Because of the beauty and value of the vestment and the fact that it had been worn during the historic Mass, it was held in high regard by the people.

As a result of a difference of opinion between the monks and Heduin, a member of the National Guard, an inventory of the abbey was made between April 21-24, 1790, just one year after the start of the French Revolution. It was discovered that the precious chasuble of the miracle was not in its place. Heduin took advantage of the situation to complain to the city authorities, who initiated an investigation. It was learned that during the preceding year the prior of the monastery had actually sold the chasuble to a merchant of Lyon to satisfy the needs of the abbey and the church. The merchant refused to negotiate a return of the vestment, but did offer to donate the pearls that had been removed from it.

One report has it that all the articles used in the Mass of the miracle were preserved in the church, including the tools employed in the making of the hosts. This seems to be confirmed by the inventory made during the French Revolution, which specifically lists all the articles that were utilized during the Mass of the miracle. This inventory list is still preserved in the archives of the Departement de l'Aisne at Laon; however, the articles themselves have since been dispersed or destroyed.

The present cure' of Braine confirms that the Eucharistic miracle did occur and that processions were held in its honor for many years, but the annual observances are no longer held.

Chapter 3

THE MIRACLE OF FERRARA, ITALY

1171

An ancient tradition dating from the year 454 A.D. speaks of a place called a *capital,* where a Byzantine image of the most Holy Virgin was venerated. Later, the increasing number of fervent believers brought about the building of a small church where the *capital* once stood. This church, built about the year 657, was constructed on the ford of the river and was appropriately named S. Maria del Vado, i.e., St. Mary of the Ford. It was in this small church, a little more than 500 years later, that a spectacular Eucharistic miracle occurred.

It was Easter Sunday, the 28th of March, 1171. The Mass of the festival was being celebrated by Padre Pietro de Verona, who was assisted by Padre Bono, Padre Leonardo and Padre Aimone, all members of the order of Canons Regular Portuensi. At the moment when the consecrated Host was broken into two parts, all those present were startled to see a stream of blood spurting from it. The movement of the blood was so violent and abundant that it sprinkled a semi-circular vault that was situated slightly behind and above the altar. Not only did the witnesses see the blood, they also saw that the Host had turned to flesh.

News of the miracle was promptly shared with those outside the church, and these quickly spread the word throughout the parish and the surrounding areas, arousing incredible enthusiasm.

Bishop Amato of Ferrara and Archbishop Gherardo of Revenna rushed to the scene. They, too, saw the proof of the miracle: the blood and the Host which had turned to flesh. They were in agreement that the blood was "the real miraculous blood of Our Lord."

The earliest known document giving details of the miracle is entitled *Gemma Ecclesiastica,* and was written in 1197 by Geraldo Cambrense. This manuscript was discovered in 1981 by Mons.

22

Antonio Samaritani, a historian living in Ferrara. The original document is now kept in London; a copy is in the Vatican. The document attests that in Ferrara, on Easter Sunday, the Host changed into flesh.

Another document, dated March 6, 1404, was written by Cardinal Migliorati, who acknowledged the prodigy, while Pope Eugenio IV officially recognized it in a Papal Bull of April 7, 1442. Additionally, Pope Benedict XIV (1740-1758) recognized the miracle, as did Cardinal Nicolo Fieschi in 1519.

Of all the visitors to the altar of the miracle, the most distinguished of all was Pope Pius IX, who journeyed to the church in 1857. Pointing to the drops of blood, he exclaimed, "These drops are like the ones on the corporal in Orvieto!" (See chapter 11, on the miracle of Bolsena-Orvieto.)

In 1500, the little church was enlarged, improved, embellished and transformed into the present basilica. During this construction the marble vault, spotted with the miraculous, still-crimson drops of blood, was detached from the place where the miracle occurred and was removed to a side chapel, where it was placed in a splendid setting. The double-tiered shrine contains an altar on the ground floor; the vault is located on the second level. Staircases on either side of the altar permit the observer to draw close to the vault for a reverent inspection. The holy blood is still visible to the naked eye and is admired and revered as an exceptional relic.

Since 1930 the basilica has been in the care of the Missionaries of the Most Precious Blood, the spiritual sons of St. Gaspar del Bufalo, the great apostle of devotion to the Blood of the Saviour— a situation that seems very appropriate.

A year-long celebration was observed in 1970, commemorating the eighth centennial of the miracle.

Above: Artistic depiction of the Eucharistic miracle which took place in the Church of Santa Maria del Vado in Ferrara, Italy in 1171. At the moment when the consecrated Host was broken into two parts, blood spurted forth from it, sprinkling a semicircular marble vault behind the altar. Moreover, the Host turned to flesh.

Right: Close view of the vault and Latin inscription commemorating the miracle.

Side chapel in the Church of Santa Maria del Vado. The blood-spattered vault is situated on the second tier of this shrine, and staircases permit visitors to draw close for a reverent inspection of the blood stains. A painting at the ground level shows the astonished priest and people at the moment of the miracle.

The nave of the Church of Santa Maria del Vado. The shrine of the miraculous Eucharist is off to the side. In 1981 a scholar discovered an historic document from 1197 describing the Eucharistic miracle of Ferrara.

Chapter 4

THE MIRACLE OF
AUGSBURG, GERMANY

1194

The history of this miracle begins with a woman of Augsburg who conceived the idea of reserving a consecrated Host in her home. For this purpose she received Holy Communion one morning, clandestinely removed the Host from her mouth, and conveyed it to her home. There she fashioned two pieces of wax, placed the Host between them and sealed the edges, thereby creating a crude reliquary. In this manner she kept the Blessed Sacrament for five years; but during that time her conscience was so troubled that in 1199 she was at last compelled to bring the matter to the attention of a parish priest, who immediately visited her home and returned the Host to the Church of the Holy Cross.

Among the priests of the parish was one known as Berthold, a choir director who was considered a very holy man. Father Berthold was assigned to open the wax reliquary, and it was he who first noticed that part of the Host had changed into what appeared to be flesh, with clearly defined red streaks. All the priests of the community who witnessed the opening of the wax case were amazed. They discussed the subject at length, and then decided that they could better determine the identity of the specimen if it could be divided into two parts. To their bewilderment, it could not be separated, because it was held together with threadlike veins. It was then decided that the specimen was the flesh of Jesus Christ.

Some of the priests were speechless at the spectacle, others were frightened, and some suggested that the transformation be kept a secret. The sacristan, however, voiced the opinion that such an occurrence should be reported to the Bishop, so it was brought to his attention without further delay.

In the presence of Bishop Udalskalk, who carefully examined

the miraculous Host, many people of the parish and priests from other areas also viewed the miracle. The Bishop then ordered that the miraculous Host be returned to its reliquary of wax for transfer to the cathedral. While at the cathedral, the Host was exposed from Easter until the feast of St. John the Baptist. During this time a second miracle took place: the Host was seen to swell in size until it cracked its wax casing and separated from it. This separation of the blood-red Host from its wax covering was effected without any sort of human intervention.

On the suggestion of the Bishop, the miraculous Host and the pieces of wax were then placed in a crystal container, which was returned to the Church of the Holy Cross. In this church the miraculous Host has been kept under glass in perfect condition for over 780 years.

Bishop Dekret, on May 15, 1199, decreed that special services should be held each year in commemoration of the miracle. This yearly observance was to be called *Fest des Wunderbarlichen Gutes,* i.e., Feast of the Wonderful Miraculous Treasures. Every year on May 11 this feast is observed with solemn Masses and the wearing of special vestments.

Through the years, other churches began to observe the feast, among them the college church of St. Moritz; then in 1485 the cloister church of St. George; in 1496 the Domkirche; and by 1639 it was known to have been celebrated each year in the whole diocese of Augsburg, as the newer churches adopted the traditional services. Many healings are known to have taken place during the celebrations that honor the holy miracles.

Soon after the events of 1199, the details of both occurrences were reported in documents that were widely distributed. And it is fortunate indeed that they were, since a fire in 1314 in the Hl. Kreuzklosters, the Holy Cross Cloister, destroyed all the original papers pertaining to the miracle. For centuries, German writers have depended upon the copies of those early papers. Much has been published since then about the miracle.

Chapter 5

THE MIRACLE OF ALATRI, ITALY

1228

A young lady of the city of Alatri was attracted to a handsome young man who had many admirers. Trying in vain to gain his attention and interest, she decided to search for someone who could provide her with a love potion and soon found a woman who had a reputation for knowing about such matters. The young lady was told to receive the Eucharist and, as soon as she could, before it became moist in her mouth, to remove it delicately into a cloth.

"After all," the woman declared, "what medicine could be more potent than one made with the divine body of the King of Hearts?"

The young lady did as she was instructed and was satisfied that no one noticed the removal of the Blessed Sacrament. Her conscience, however, was troubled almost immediately. During her walk home, and especially when she entered the house, she was so troubled she decided to soothe her conscience by hiding the Sacred Host. Placing the Blessed Sacrament in a small pouch, she looked for a secure hiding place, and decided upon a remote corner of the house where bread was kept.

Two days and two nights passed. During fitful sleep she was tormented by nightmares and imagined she heard voices of judgment that consigned her to eternal fire. On the third day, soon after dawn, she arose from her bed and retrieved the Host. While debating whether to give the Host to the woman who had given her such bad advice or to return it to the church, she opened the pouch and lifted the folds of the linen cloth. To her horror she saw that the Host was no longer like bread, but had turned the color of flesh—which she knew to be alive.

Her tears and sobs attracted the members of her family, who rushed to her, saw the miracle and quickly notified the neighbors. The news spread through the community and, through the efforts of messengers, was shared throughout the city.

When the parish priest was notified, he went to the house with other priests, took the pouch containing the Host, and covered it with a veil. While on the way back to his church, he decided instead to bring the Host to the Bishop, because of the enthusiasm and impatience of the great crowd of people who wanted to see the miracle for themselves.

It is said that among all the people who accompanied the priest, one person was missing—the woman who had suggested the potion. This woman later acknowledged that when she heard the news of the miracle, she hid in the darkness of her house, preparing her defense. She decided to say, among other things, that she was a good and honest person of prayer and that the young girl was a liar who had falsely accused her. After she was satisfied that she had enough reasons for her defense, she felt better and when the messengers summoned her before the Bishop, she readily accompanied them. When this woman realized that the crowd was not hostile toward her, she felt new sentiments, and decided to throw herself at the feet of the Bishop to beg forgiveness.

Meanwhile, in the cathedral, the Host had been placed upon the altar amid candles and flowers. The line of people who approached to examine the miracle seemed endless. The next day people from neighboring areas also displayed their curiosity. During this time Bishop Giovanni of Alatri was almost constantly occupied with meeting visiting ecclesiastical and civil personages who wanted to consult about the matter.

While all agreed that a grave sacrilege was involved, they were not sure what severe and exemplary penance should be imposed upon the two women. A letter was then composed by Bishop Giovanni to the Supreme Pontiff, Gregory IX, briefly describing the sacrilege and the wonder of the miracle which had followed it. The Holy Father was asked what penance should be inflicted upon the women, who had acknowledged their guilt and were sincerely repentant. Properly bearing the seals of the Bishop and the signatures of his associates, the letter was sent to Rome by a courier.

During Easter season of the same year, 1228, the Bishop of Alatri had the joy of showing the Pope's reply to the priests of his diocese. Dated March 13, the parchment bearing the Pope's signature is now carefully kept in the archives of the Cathedral of Alatri. After repeating the facts of the case, the Pontiff had stated:

...we should express our most heartfelt thanks to Him
who, while always operating in wonderful ways in all His
deeds, on some occasions works miracles and performs ever
new wonders in order to recall sinners to penance, convert
the wicked and confound the evil deeds of heretics by
strengthening the faith of the Catholic Church, supporting its
hope and enkindling its charity.

Therefore, dear brother, by this apostolic letter, we provide that you inflict a lighter penance on the girl who, in our
opinion, in committing such a serious sin, was driven more
by weakness than by wickedness, especially in consideration
of the fact that she certainly repented sincerely when confessing her sin. However, against the instigator who, with her
perversity, prompted the girl to commit the sacrilege, take
those disciplinary measures that you think more suitable;
also order her to pay a visit to all the neighboring bishops, to
confess her sin to them and to implore their forgiveness with
devout submissiveness.

The miraculous Host remained perfectly intact through the centuries until the year 1700, when Bishop Monsignor Guerra gave to
Cardinal Cybo a small portion of it, which was described as being
the size of a *cece,* a chick-pea. This small piece was placed in a
reliquary furnished by the Cardinal, who entrusted it to the
Church of S. Maria degli Angeli alle Terme in Rome, where he
wanted to be buried. However, when the monks who cared for this
church were transferred in later years, they removed the Host
elsewhere, perhaps having forgotten the bequest of the Cardinal
and his desire that it remain in this church. In recent years at-
tempts have been made to locate this small portion of the Host, but
without success.

The main part of the miraculous Host, which is kept in its own
chapel in the Cathedral of Alatri, is exhibited twice each year, on
the first Sunday after Easter and the first Sunday after Pentecost.
Because of its humble origin it is said to be the "Miracle of the
Poor."

In 1960, while celebrating his 25th episcopal jubilee, Bishop
Edoardo Facchini of Altari declared that he was "... well aware
of the profound faith of the people in the real presence of Jesus in
the Eucharist, which is confirmed by the miracle of the incarnate
Host whose relic is venerated and reserved in our basilica

cathedral." The Bishop deemed it opportune during this celebration to proceed with the canonical recognition of the sacred relic, which was conducted in the presence of another Bishop and many clergymen.

The reliquary was taken from its chapel to a room in the cathedral, where the seals were carefully inspected and found to be intact. The glass tube in which the Host is kept was removed from the reliquary, and the ribbon of red silk and the seal of Monsignor Pietro Saulini, Bishop of Alatri, were recognized. These were declared to be the same as that described in the minutes of the previous recognition, dated December 1, 1886.

After breaking the seal Bishop Facchini extracted the miraculous Host. He declared that it had the same appearance as in previous recognitions—that is, a piece of flesh which appeared to be slightly brown, ". . . which has taken the cylindrical form given to it by the tube and appears shiny in every part that was in contact with the tube."

After the consultation of the witnesses and their acknowledgment of satisfaction with the examination, the miraculous Host was returned to the glass tube and enclosed with a double seal. It was then placed in its silver and gold ostensorium, which is shaped like a cross with undulating rays of gold.

For the 750th anniversary of the miracle in 1978, special celebrations were observed and lectures were given. The lectures are preserved in booklets which provide details of the miracle. During the services for this 750th anniversary, Mons. Cesario D'Amato stated during his address that ". . . the miracle subsists. It is visible, indestructible, real."

The new ostensorium containing the glass tube in which the miraculous Host is kept.

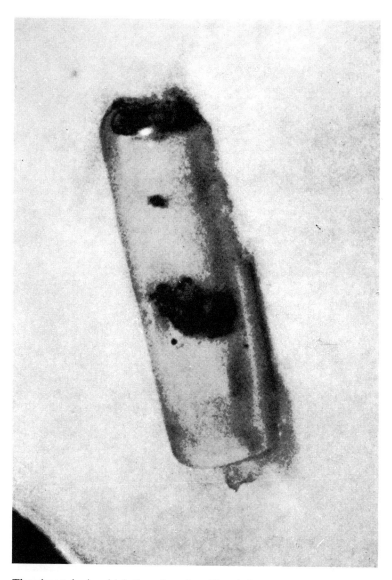

The glass tube in which the miraculous Host is kept. The dark area at the top is the official seal. A canonical recognition was conducted by Bishop Facchini of Alatri in 1960, and in 1978 special celebrations were held for the 750th anniversary of the miracle. This Host turned to flesh in the year 1228 after a young lady, in search of a love potion to attract a certain young man, had removed the Host from her mouth. The girl repented of her sin, as did the woman who advised her to commit the sacrilege.

The chapel enshrining the miraculous Eucharistic Host in the Cathedral of Alatri.

Two pages from the canonical recognition of the miraculous Host which was ordered by Bishop Ignazio Dani in 1584.

Chapter 6

THE MIRACLE OF SANTAREM, PORTUGAL

Early 13th Century

There lived in the village of Santarem, 35 miles south of Fatima, a poor woman who was made miserable by the activities of her unfaithful husband. In her extreme unhappiness she consulted a sorceress, who promised deliverance from her trials for the price of a consecrated Host. After many hesitations the woman finally consented, and visited the Church of St. Stephen. After receiving Holy Communion, she removed the Host from her mouth and wrapped it in her veil, intending to take it to the sorceress.

But within a few moments blood began to issue from the Host. The amount of blood increased so much that it dripped from the cloth and attracted the attention of bystanders. Seeing blood on the woman's hand and arm and thinking her injured, several witnesses rushed forward to help. The woman avoided them and ran to her home, leaving a trail of blood behind her.

Hoping to hide the bloody veil and its contents, she placed them in a chest; but during the night she was forced to reveal them to her husband when a mysterious light issued from the trunk, penetrating the wood and illuminating the whole house. Both knelt in adoration for the remaining hours until dawn, when the parish priest was summoned.

News of the mysterious event spread quickly and attracted countless people who wanted to contemplate the miracle. Because of the furor, an episcopal investigation was promptly organized.

The Host was taken in procession to the Church of St. Stephen, where it was encased in wax and secured in the tabernacle. Some time later, when the tabernacle was opened, another miracle was discovered. The wax that had encased the Host was found broken into pieces, and the Host was found miraculously enclosed in a crystal pyx. This was later placed in a gold and silver pear-shaped

38

monstrance with a "sunburst" of 33 rays, in which it is still contained.

After approbation by ecclesiastical authorities, who saw no reason to condemn or suppress reports of the miracle, the Church of St. Stephen was renamed "The Church of the Holy Miracle." It is here that the Host is still preserved and displayed for the admiration and veneration of pilgrims. In the nave of the church, high up on both sides, are ancient paintings depicting the miracle.

The Host is somewhat irregularly shaped, with delicate veins running from top to bottom, where a quantity of blood is collected in the crystal. In the opinion of Dr. Arthur Hoagland, a New Jersey physician who has observed the miraculous Host many times over a period of years, the coagulated blood at the bottom of the crystal sometimes has the color of fresh blood, and at other times that of dried blood.

This miracle, which occurred in the early part of the 13th century, has endured for over 700 years.

Dr. Hoagland

The bleeding Host of Santarem in its monstrance, held by Father Philip Higgins, an American priest stationed in Pennsylvania.

A closer view of the miraculous Host. It is somewhat irregularly shaped, with delicate veins running from top to bottom, where a quantity of blood is collected in the crystal.

Father Higgins holds up the miraculous Host, positioning a candle behind it for better visibility.

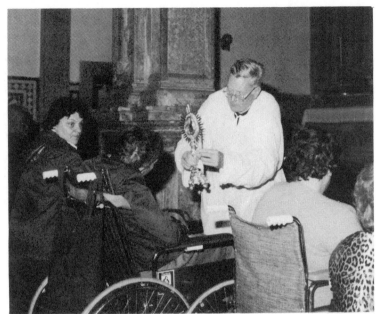

Above: The Church of the Holy Miracle, where the miraculous Eucharistic Host is enshrined.

Upper Left: Father Higgins blessing handicapped pilgrims with the miraculous Host.

Lower Left: The main altar of the Church of the Holy Miracle. Note the Latin inscription above the sanctuary: "Indeed, the Lord is in this place.—*Gen.* 28:16."

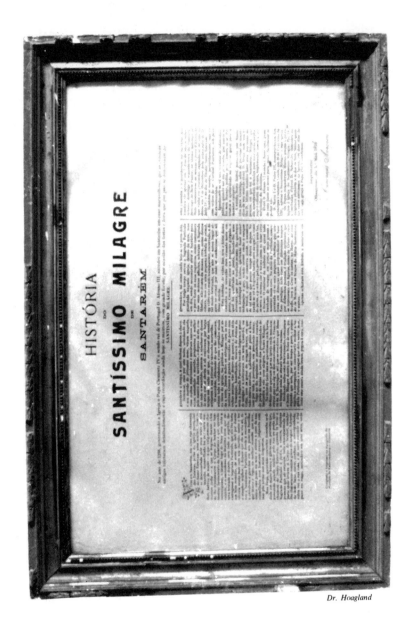

Dr. Hoagland

44

Above: Commemorative monument on the site of the trunk. On the second line of writing one can discern the words *Milagre anno 1266*— "Miracle year 1266."

Left: Plaque describing the miracle. The miracle occurred when a woman, distraught over the activities of her unfaithful husband, removed the Host from her mouth and wrapped it in her veil, intending to take it to a sorceress who had promised deliverance in return for a consecrated Host. Upon being removed from her mouth, the Host began to bleed. The woman hid her bloody veil at home in a trunk, but a mysterious light revealed its presence. This plaque is located in the woman's home.

Altar in the home where the woman hid the Host.

Chapter 7

THE TWO MIRACLES OF FLORENCE, ITALY

1230 and 1595

The Church of San Ambrogio, located in the center of the city of Florence, is privileged to have not one, but two Eucharistic Relics.

The first miracle occurred on December 29, 1230, and involved a priest by the name of Uguccione, who was then serving as the chaplain of the monastery of nuns who were affiliated with the Church of San Ambrogio.

One morning after celebrating Holy Mass, the priest absent-mindedly neglected to wipe the chalice dry, leaving a small amount of consecrated "wine" in the bottom of the golden vessel. The next morning, when he was preparing for the celebration of another Holy Mass, he was astonished to find at the bottom of the chalice a quantity of coagulated blood!

After 750 years, this blood is still perfectly preserved. In the Church of San Ambrogio, where the miracle is kept, the walls have been decorated by Cosimo Rosselli with paintings that portray a procession with the miraculous Eucharistic blood through the streets of Florence in 1340, when the city was afflicted with a pestilence.

The second miracle occurred on March 24, 1595, when the altar cloth of the main altar caught fire, damaging the altar and the tabernacle. A pyx containing consecrated Hosts fell to the floor and opened on impact. Those that fell onto the carpet at the foot of the altar twisted and curled, and they united together from the heat of the fire. Nevertheless, this collection of Hosts is still perfectly preserved after almost 400 years.

Today the two miracles are reserved in the same monstrance. At the very top is a receptacle held by a small golden angel, in which a recently consecrated Host can be placed. Beneath this, between two larger angels, is a crystal through which one can see the crystal vial and the coagulated blood of the miracle of 1230. Beneath this cylinder and behind a sheet of crystal is a receptacle in which the Hosts of 1595 can be clearly seen. This reliquary is kept in a chapel, in a beautiful tabernacle sculptured by Mino of Fiesole in 1481.

Every year the monstrance containing the two Eucharistic Relics is placed on display in the Church of San Ambrogio. According to the pastor of the parish, the miracles ". . . are a strong reminder of the real presence of Jesus in the Eucharist."

Above and preceding page: Ostensorium containing the two Eucharistic miracles of Florence. Between the two angels is a crystal vial containing the coagulated blood which was found in a chalice in the year 1230. Beneath this blood are the Hosts which underwent the fire of 1595 and which are still perfectly preserved. At the top of the ostensorium as pictured on this page is a receptacle held by a small golden angel, in which a recently consecrated Host can be placed.

Chapter 8

THE MIRACLE OF DAROCA, SPAIN

1239

The city of Daroca, located in northeastern Spain, is proud of its historical past and its importance during Roman times, when it was the ninth staging-post on the Roman military road from Laminium (in a district then called Carpetania) to Caesaraugusta (now called Zaragoza). Outside the city, the Roman Consul Quintus Cecilius Metelus and his legions were repulsed in 143 B.C. Beyond the town is the River Jiloca, on whose banks the chivalrous knight, El Cid, marched victoriously with his troops after a campaign against the Moors.

The city's past seems still alive in its Roman, Moorish and medieval walls, castles, towers, plazas and streets. In its churches and museums can be found priceless art treasures of Roman, Gothic and Renaissance influence.

But of all the ancient structures and valuable art treasures, Daroca's greatest pride is the relic of the *Sagrados Corporales,* the Sacred Corporals, dating back to 1239, the year of the miracle.

In that year, when the city of Valencia was under the reign of the Catholic King Don Jaime, the Saracen King Zaen Moro decided to recapture the city with fresh troops brought from the northern states of Africa. The Catholic king learned of the Saracen's intentions, and knowing that his own troops were greatly outnumbered, he ordered an outdoor Mass to be offered, encouraging his soldiers to receive the Holy Eucharist together with their captains. King Jaime assured his soldiers that if they were thus fortified they would be able to do battle without fear and with purity on their lips.

Immediately after the distribution of Holy Communion, the Saracens made a surprise attack. The priest was apparently bewildered and terrified by the sudden and fierce clash of arms; instead of consuming the six remaining Hosts, he placed them for safety between two corporals. To further ensure their safety, he quickly placed the cloths under rocks a short distance from the altar.

After the battle, as the Saracen troops retreated in disgrace, the Catholic soldiers returned and knelt before the altar to give thanks to God for their decisive victory. The priest, in the meantime, attempted to locate the Hosts in their hiding place and had great difficulty in doing so until divine inspiration finally assisted him.

After recovering the cloths, he unfolded them, but was amazed to find that the six Hosts had disappeared, leaving six blood stains. Wondering what motives God had had for bringing about such a miraculous occurrence, he at last decided that it was a sign of God's protection and love for the Catholic troops. The priest then took the bloodied corporals to the soldiers for their inspection and veneration.

Since the Mass had been offered in the field, well outside the city of Valencia, three towns—Teruel, Catalayud and Daroca—all claimed that the miracle had occurred within their jurisdictions. All three claimed that the holy corporals should be given to them for safekeeping. The matter was long debated until it was finally decided that the matter would best be settled by chance. All agreed that the cloths should be placed on the back of a mule and that the animal should be allowed to wander to whichever town nature would direct it. The mule made for the lower gate of the city of Daroca.

A church was soon built in Daroca as a repository for the blood-stained corporals. Enlarged in the 15th and 16th centuries, it is now known as St. Mary's Collegiate Church (the *Colegiata*). On the walls of the Holy Relics Chapel are scenes of the miracle, along with numerous multicolored alabaster statues in medieval poses. This shrine contains the corporals on which the stains of blood are still clearly visible.

The miracle is said to have been widely known in its day, and it is mentioned in many official documents—especially in documents of the year 1340. The miracle is said to have been ". . . the subject of much bibliography in the 15th century, and the story has been told by many a famous pen."

For more than seven centuries the *Sagrados Corporales* have been Daroca's revered and cherished possession.

The golden shrine of the holy corporals stained with blood from the six Hosts which lay wrapped up and hidden under rocks during a battle with the Saracens in 1239.

Chapter 9

THE MIRACLE OF
OLMÜTZ, CZECHOSLOVAKIA

1242

During the 13th century when the Tartars were overrunning various countries, dispensing cruelty and destruction, Jaroslas of Sternberg was charged with protecting the kingdom of Moravia, which was in danger of imminent attack. Gathering an army of 8,000 men from Bohemia and 4,000 Moravian citizens, he assembled them in the fortified city of Olmütz.

The enemy troops soon presented themselves in the land and promptly began burning villages and killing all who opposed them. Even the monastery of Gradie was not spared. After beheading the occupants, the Tartars burned the monastery buildings to the ground. Then, with the severed heads of the monks tied to their horses' tails, they brazenly approached the city, camping outside the very gates of Olmütz.

Appalled by what they saw, Jaroslas' men wanted to attack at once; but they were restrained by their leader, who thought it best to wait for a more advantageous time to engage the enemy. Interpreting the delay as a sign of cowardice, the Tartars relaxed their vigilance, with many leaving camp to forage around the countryside.

On the feast of St. John the Baptist, Jaroslas made a humble confession of his sins and received the Holy Eucharist. Following his example, his warriors also received the Sacraments, in preparation for the battle planned for the following night.

With some of the soldiers remaining behind to protect the city of Olmütz, the others assembled outside the city gates shortly after midnight in preparation for battle. Once again the warriors imitated the example of their leader, who dismounted and knelt in the dust beside his horse. When all the soldiers were on their knees, Jaroslas offered a prayer to the Mother of God and vowed to build

53

a church in her honor should they be victorious. After raising their voices in an Ave Maria, the soldiers mounted their steeds and rode from the fortified city toward the enemy.

Not only did they journey under the protection of the Mother of God, but they were additionally fortified with the real presence of the Eucharistic Saviour. Following the Communion of the soldiers the previous day, five consecrated Hosts had remained. Jaroslas had these enclosed in a ciborium which a priest on horseback carried into battle. Jaroslas likened this to the incident in the Old Testament when, by the command of God, the Ark of the Covenant was carried into battle by the Israelites. (*Josue* 6).

Under the cover of darkness the battle raged, bloody and costly in human life. The leader of the Tartars was killed and the enemy so crippled that it was obvious the Christians had won. Terrified by the great number of their dead and discouraged by the loss of their leader, the Tartars left Moravia for Hungary, where they regained strength to continue their wars of destruction.

The victory over the Tartars was attributed to the presence of the Eucharist on the battlefield—but this was only part of the miracle of which Olmütz is proud.

Following the battle, when the consecrated Hosts were returned to the church, the priest was amazed to find that each Host exhibited a clear, shining circle of a rosy color. When he presented the spectacle to the congregation, they praised Almighty God for the victory and for this prodigy which had so demonstrated His power and glory.

Opposite: The Blessed Sacrament borne by a priest on horseback in a victorious battle with the cruel and destructive Tartars. After the battle, each of the consecrated Hosts was found to bear a shining rose-colored circle.

55

Chapter 10

THE MIRACLE OF REGENSBURG, GERMANY

1257

For many years there were in Regensburg (formerly called Ratisbon) two chapels with the same name, St. Saviour, and both have interesting histories involving the Blessed Sacrament.

The oldest was founded in the year 1255. On March 25 of that year, which was Holy Thursday, a priest named Dompfarrer Ulrich von Dornberg was scheduled to bring the Blessed Sacrament to the sick members of his parish. On reaching a little stream called Bachgasse, the priest carefully set foot on the narrow plank that served as a bridge—and promptly slipped, dropping the ciborium he had been carrying. The Hosts spilled from the vessel onto the bank of the stream and it was with some difficulty that the priest collected them.

The parishioners, on hearing of the accident, decided to build a chapel on the site where the Hosts had been soiled, in reparation for the disrespect done to the Blessed Sacrament—even though the incident had been unintentional. The erection of a wooden chapel was started the same day and was completed three days later, on March 28. Bishop Albert of Regensburg called the little wooden structure St. Saviour's Chapel and consecrated it on September 8, 1255. The miracle of Regensburg occurred in this chapel two years later.

During the offering of the Holy Sacrifice, a certain priest (whose name is not given) wondered about the real Presence of Jesus in the Eucharist. All at once, the corpus on the large altar crucifix before him seemed to come alive. One of the hands of Our Lord detached itself from the cross, stretched forward, and removed the chalice from the hands of the priest! With shock and fear, he stepped backward, gazed intently at the miracle, and fervently repented of his doubt. It was only then that the chalice was restored to him.

After this miracle, great crowds visited the church, many traveling great distances. With the offerings that were generously given, the wooden chapel was replaced with a stone structure in 1260. Sometime after the stone chapel was completed, its name was changed from St. Saviour's Chapel to *Kreuzkapelle* or Cross Chapel in honor of the miraculous crucifix that was greatly venerated there.

In 1267 a monastery was built beside the stone chapel. It was entrusted to the Eremitical Augustinians, who maintained it until the year 1803. In 1855 the chapel fell into decay and was demolished. Since the people regretted the loss, another chapel was built in the area. During World War I, however, this chapel is said to have been profaned.

The history of Regensburg's second St. Saviour Chapel begins in 1476 with a 13-year-old boy who stole from the church of St. Emmeram a silver ciborium containing many consecrated Hosts. While running down the street, he threw the Hosts against a house. When the Hosts were found, they were collected with great solemnity and ceremoniously carried to the cathedral in the presence of Bishop Henry IV of Regensburg.

The owner of the house where the boy had discarded the Hosts was appalled at the sinful incident. With the help of his neighbors, he built a chapel the same year. This St. Saviour Chapel was located in Weissen-Hahnen-Gasse, the White Rooster Alley.

In 1542, four years before the death of Martin Luther, the chapel was confiscated by the Lutherans. For many centuries it has been used as an inn.

We are told that there are many traditional services and processions in Regensburg in honor of the Most Holy Eucharist.

Right: Miracle of the crucifix and chalice at Regensburg. A priest offering Mass wondered about the Real Presence of Our Lord in the Eucharist when suddenly one of the hands of Christ detached itself from the crucifix and removed the chalice from his hands.

Chapter 11

THE MIRACLE OF BOLSENA-ORVIETO, ITALY

1263

In 1263 a German priest, Peter of Prague, stopped at Bolsena while on a pilgrimage to Rome. He is described as being a pious priest, but one who found it difficult to believe that Christ was actually present in the consecrated Host. While celebrating Holy Mass above the tomb of St. Christina (located in the church named for this martyr), he had barely spoken the words of Consecration when blood started to seep from the consecrated Host and trickle over his hands onto the altar and the corporal.

The priest was immediately confused. At first he attempted to hide the blood, but then he interrupted the Mass and asked to be taken to the neighboring city of Orvieto, the city where Pope Urban IV was then residing.

The Pope listened to the priest's account and absolved him. He then sent emissaries for an immediate investigation. When all the facts were ascertained, he ordered the Bishop of the diocese to bring to Orvieto the Host and the linen cloth bearing the stains of blood. With archbishops, cardinals and other Church dignitaries in attendance, the Pope met the procession and, amid great pomp, had the relics placed in the cathedral. The linen corporal bearing the spots of blood is still reverently enshrined and exhibited in the Cathedral of Orvieto.

It is said that Pope Urban IV was prompted by this miracle to commission St. Thomas Aquinas to compose the Proper for a Mass and an Office honoring the Holy Eucharist as the Body of Christ. One year after the miracle, in August of 1264, Pope Urban IV introduced the saint's composition, and by means of a papal bull instituted the feast of Corpus Christi.

After visiting the Cathedral of Orvieto, many pilgrims and tourists journey to St. Christina's Church in Bolsena to see for themselves the place where the miracle occurred. From the north aisle of the church one can enter the Chapel of the Miracle, where the stains on the paved floor are said to have been made by the blood from the miraculous Host. The altar of the miracle, which is surmounted by a 9th-century canopy, is now situated in the grotto of St. Christina. A reclining statue of the saint is nearby.

In August of 1964, on the 700th anniversary of the institution of the feast of Corpus Christi, Pope Paul VI celebrated Holy Mass at the altar where the holy corporal is kept in its golden shrine in the Cathedral of Orvieto. (His Holiness had journeyed to Orvieto by helicopter; he was the first pope in history to use such a means of transportation).

Twelve years later, the same pontiff visited Bolsena and spoke from there via television to the 41st International Eucharistic Congress, then concluding its activities in Philadelphia. During his address Pope Paul VI spoke of the Eucharist as being ". . . a mystery great and inexhaustible."

Linen corporal bearing blood stains from the miracle of the year 1263. A German priest named Peter of Prague had barely spoken the words of Consecration when blood began to seep from the Host, trickling over his hands onto the altar and the corporal.

Another view of the reliquary, showing the panelled doors which close over the holy corporal.

Chapter 12

THE TWO MIRACLES OF PARIS, FRANCE

1274 and 1290

In the year 1274, during the reign of Philip III, a thief stole a pyx from the Church of St. Gervais in Paris and secretly carried it to the Champ du Landit near the Abbey of St. Denis. Here he opened the golden case to throw away the Host—but the moment the pyx was opened, the Host flew upward and began to flutter about his head. A number of peasants who saw the Host moving about the terrified young man hurriedly notified Mathieu de Vendome, the Abbot of St. Denis, who in turn notified the Bishop of Paris.

Both the Abbot and the Bishop, together with prelates from nearby churches, went quickly to the Champ du Landit, where all saw the Host fluttering in the air. When the priest who had consecrated the Host approached to examine what was taking place, the Host settled into his hands in the sight of a great throng of people. Many of these people escorted the priest and the sacred Host back to the church from which it had been stolen. This Host remained in good form until it disappeared during the fierce anti-Catholic vandalism of the French Revolution.

Following the miracle, the Bishop ordered that every Friday in the Church of St. Gervais a canticle should be sung in its memory, and that a special Office should be held on September 1. These services were observed for many years even after the Host disappeared.

A mere 16 years later, in 1290, Paris was honored with yet another, even more spectacular Eucharistic miracle. This second miracle involved a poor woman who had nothing of value except a dress, which she pawned to obtain a little money for living expenses. With the approach of Easter Sunday, she yearned to be well dressed for the festival, but since she did not have enough money to claim her dress, she visited the pawnbroker and asked if she could have it for just one day. The pawnbroker, described as being a non-Christian, was curious about the Host received by Christians at Holy Mass, and informed the woman that she could have her dress completely if she would bring him the consecrated wafer which the priest would give her in Holy Communion.

Consenting to this shameful proposal, the poor woman attended Holy Mass and received the Sacrament. After secretly removing the Host from her mouth, she delivered it to the home of the pawnbroker, who placed it on a table. Then, in the presence of the woman and of his own children, the man drew out a penknife and repeatedly stabbed the Host.

Suddenly, blood in great streams gushed from the cuts, splashing the woman and the children. Shocked by the flow of blood, the man threw the Host into a nearby fire, where it fluttered among the flames, completely unaffected by the fire or the heat. Then, thoroughly frightened, he snatched the Host from the fire, and in another effort to destroy it, he dropped it into a kettle of boiling water.

The water immediately began to turn red and bloody. Somehow the bloody water spilled over the kettle, fell onto the floor and coursed its way into the street, where it attracted the attention of passersby.

A woman standing outside was curious about its origin, entered the house, and witnessed a vision of our Saviour standing before the kettle. In a few moments the vision disappeared, but in its place the woman saw the Host suspended in the air. As the Host gradually descended, the woman snatched a nearby vase and received it into that receptacle. Then, with great care and reverence, the Host was taken to the Church of St. Jean-en-Grevè, where it was conserved as a precious treasure and was honored with special services, especially on the feast of Corpus Christi.

It is reported that at the sight of the bloody water the terrified pawnbroker quickly hid himself in a "coal-hole," but he was later arrested and convicted of the sacrilege.

King Philip IV (Philip the Fair) and the Bishop of Paris were informed of this miracle shortly after it had taken place and eventually the house in which it occurred was converted into a chapel.

In 1444 this miraculous event was the subject of a play, *The Mystery of the Holy Host.* It was again dramatized in 1533 on the feast of Corpus Christi.

This very extraordinary miracle was investigated by Father Giry, who recounted it in his book entitled *Fête du Tres-Saint Sacrement* (*Feast of the Most Blessed Sacrament*), in which he persuaded Catholics to observe the feasts inaugurated in commemoration of the miracle. The miracle was also investigated by Msgr. Guerin, the chamberlain of Pope Leo XIII. Msgr. Guerin recorded the facts regarding the event in his book *Vies des Saints*, and declared the miracle to be authentic.

The expiatory chapel that had been built in the house of the miracle was replaced by a church which was known by successive names: *La Maison ou Dieu fut bouilli* (the House where God was boiled), *L'eglise du Sauveur bouillant* (the Church where the Saviour was boiling), *La Chapelle du Miracle* (the Chapel of the Miracle)—and finally it is known by two names: the Church of St. Francis and the Temple of the Billettes. This church, built in the 14th century over the place where the miracle occurred, was constructed by the Brothers of Charity—who were also known as *Billettes* because the small rectangular scapulars they wore reminded the people of billets or handbills.

The Carmelites replaced the Brothers of Charity and completed the construction of the church in 1756, but in 1812 it became the property of the Lutherans.

Adjoining the church is the medieval *Cloitre des Billettes*, a cloister of simple grace that is excellently kept and often visited by tourists.

Chapter 13

THE MIRACLE OF
SLAVONICE, CZECHOSLOVAKIA

1280

The miracle of Slavonice is simply told. In the year 1280 a herdsman, tending his flocks in the fields outside the city, was surprised to see a mysterious fire burning atop bushes that had grown over a heap of stones. On approaching the spectacle, he saw within the blaze a Host that remained unaffected by the flames and heat. The priest who was called to the scene identified the Host as being the one in a precious vessel that had been stolen in the dead of night the year before. The culprit was never identified, but it was apparent that he had discarded the Host where it had just revealed itself.

The priest deposited the Host in a vessel he had brought with him and, together with several parishioners who had hurried to see the miraculous fire, proceeded toward the city only a short distance away. On approaching the city gates, it was noticed that the Host had disappeared from the vessel. It was again found in the flames atop the heap of stones. After retrieving it again, the priest and people once more made for the city. But the Host disappeared yet another time. Only after the priest and the people promised to establish a sanctuary on the place of the discovery did the Host remain in the vessel for its return to the parish church.

The promise was honored, and there arose above the stone heap a chapel that soon proved to be too small for the crowds that traveled great distances to adore the miraculous Host. For these pilgrims several indulgences were granted by Bishop Dietrich of Olmütz, and afterwards by Gregory, Bishop of Prague.

The chapel continued to be a great attraction until the early 15th century, when bands of Hussites swarmed the countryside spreading destruction and heresy. The privileged chapel was razed to the ground, although the little heap of stones remained undisturbed. Following the retreat of the Hussites, another chapel was built over the spot in 1476. This was consecrated by the Bishop of Olmütz, who named it the Church of Christ's Holy Body. Like the first chapel, this one proved to be too small for the pilgrims who continually journeyed there. It was subsequently enlarged until the church as it now stands was completed in the year 1491. Later, the Pope granted a plenary indulgence to all who would devoutly visit this church and with true penitence receive the Holy Eucharist. It is reported that on account of this indulgence the concourse of pilgrims became so great that several priests were required to distribute Holy Communion to the crowds who availed themselves of this privilege.

Of great interest in this church is the Altar of Grace, which was built over the stone heap that always remained in its original location. Here Holy Mass is still celebrated. This altar stands some distance in front of the high altar and is conspicuous in both its placement and its elaborateness. Atop the Altar of Grace is a sculpture of two angels adoring a Host surrounded by flames and rays. A bas-relief within the church depicts the herdsman pointing the way toward the flames in the field, while a procession, preceded by banners, emerges from the parish church.

The anniversary of the day on which the sacred Host was discovered in the flames is still observed and is known as *Bauern-Feuerfest,* or The Countryman's Fire Feast.

Fronleichnamskirche (Hl. Geist) in Zlabings

Church of Christ's Holy Body, built over the stone heap where a stolen Host was found in 1280.

Above: Sculpture of two angels adoring the miraculous Host, which is shown surrounded by flames and rays. This sculpture stands atop the Altar of Grace (inside the Church of Christ's Holy Body), erected over the stone heap, which has always remained in its original location.

Right: A bas relief within the church depicting the herdsman pointing the way toward the flames in the field, while a procession emerges from the parish church.

Chapter 14

THE MIRACLE OF OFFIDA, ITALY

1280

The Eucharistic miracle of Offida actually took place in the city of Lanciano, the site of the first miracle reported in this book. This second miracle, which is now kept in Offida some 60 miles north of Lanciano, did not happen to a doubting priest, like the former miracle; rather, it was occasioned by the discord in an unhappy household.

A woman named Ricciarella, the wife of Giacomo Stasio, deeply afflicted by her unhappy marriage, had tried everything at her disposal to win the love of her husband. Finally someone claimed to know of a way for her to achieve the harmony she desired. Ricciarella was advised to receive the Holy Eucharist, convey it to her kitchen, and heat it over the fire until a powder was obtained. This she was to put into the food or drink of her husband, who would then grow to love and respect her.

In desperation for relief from her sad situation, Ricciarella attended Holy Mass, received the Eucharist, and secretly let the Host fall from her mouth into the top of her dress. After taking it home she placed it on a *coppo,* a semi-circular tile shaped like that which is placed along the ridge or summit of a roof. She then placed the tile over a fire. As soon as the sacred Host was heated, instead of turning into powder it began to turn into a piece of bloody flesh. Horrified at what was taking place, Ricciarella attempted to stop the process by throwing ashes and melted wax onto the tile, but without success. The tile soon bore a huge smear of blood, and the flesh remained perfectly sound.

Frantic for a way to dispose of the evidence of her sacrilege, Ricciarella took a linen tablecloth decorated with silk embroidery and lace and wrapped it around the tile and the bloody Host. Carrying the bundle outside, she went to the stable and buried it in the place where garbage from the house and filth from the stalls were heaped.

That evening when her husband Giacomo approached the stable with his horse, the animal refused to enter, contrary to its usual docile behavior, and remained stubborn despite a severe beating from its master. At last it relented, but instead of proceeding directly, it entered sideways, facing the heap of garbage, until at last it fell on its knees. Giacomo became violent at the sight and accused his wife of placing a spell on the stable that made the animal fearful of entering it. Ricciarella, of course, denied everything and remained silent about the cause of the difficulty.

For seven years the Blessed Sacrament remained hidden beneath the garbage, and for that period of time the animals went in or out sideways, appearing to show respect for the heap of refuse.

Instead of the peace Ricciarella had attempted to gain from her sacrilege, she was instead tormented day and night with remorse for her sin. Finally she decided to confess what she had done to a priest from the monastery of St. Agostino in Lanciano, Prior Giacomo Diotallevi, a native of Offida.

Kneeling for confession, Ricciarella found herself unable to speak through her sobs, even though the priest encouraged her to be unafraid and to be at peace. Finally, still being unable to speak of the sacrilege, she asked for the help of the priest, who began to name various sins. At the end of this list, seeing that Ricciarella did not admit to any of them, Father Giacomo said, "I have told you all the sins that can be committed. I do not know what your fault could be unless you killed God."

"This is my sin!" she said. "I have killed God!" Ricciarella then related the story of her sacrilege.

Surprised at what was finally disclosed to him, Father Giacomo absolved Ricciarella, encouraged her to be at peace, and arranged to have the Host removed from the garbage pile without delay.

After vesting suitably, he journeyed to the stable and, unconcerned about disease or sickness, began to remove the garbage and filth. To his surprise, he discovered that the tile, the bloody Host, and the tablecloth were not contaminated, and looked as if they had been recently buried. Father Giacomo then carried the tile, the Host, and the tablecloth to his monastery.

A few days later, after obtaining permission from his superior, he went to his native Offida and showed the miracle to Father

Michele Mallicano and many illustrious citizens of the city. All agreed that the miraculous Host should receive maximum honor and that a special reliquary should be crafted for its enshrinement. For this reliquary a large amount of silver was donated. It was then decided that artisans in Venice would be entrusted with the responsibility of fashioning a reliquary in the shape of an artistic cross to contain not only the miraculous Host, but also a piece of wood from the cross of Christ.

Father Michele, along with another priest, carried the Host in a chalice to Venice. There he commissioned a jeweler to fashion the special reliquary, and swore the jeweler to secrecy regarding its purpose. After the jeweler accepted the chalice containing the Host, he developed a severe fever. He was in the state of mortal sin. But after he made a proper confession, the fever left him.

When the construction of the cross was completed, the jeweler sealed the piece of the true cross and the miraculous Host under separate crystals and entrusted the reliquary to the two priests, who soon left Venice for Offida. The jeweler, however, did not keep his oath of secrecy, but told everything to the doge, the chief magistrate of Venice, suggesting that the cross and its treasures should be taken away from the priests and kept in Venice. The doge agreed, and sent a ship to intercept the priests. But a storm at sea made navigation impossible, and the effort was abandoned.

When the priests arrived at Ancona, Venetian merchants told them of the doge's intention and of their apparently miraculous escape. Under the continued protection of God, the priests arrived safely at Offida with the precious cross.

At the time these events occurred, they were documented on parchment which, unfortunately, can no longer be found. However, an authentic copy, made by the notary Giovanni Battista Doria and dated April 18, 1788, is still preserved.

High atop the main altar of the Sanctuary of Saint Augustine in Offida, also known as the Sanctuary of the Miraculous Eucharist, is found an artistic arrangement which houses the silver cross containing the miraculous Host. The tile on which Ricciarella heated the Host, still showing the smear and splotches of blood, is kept in a rectangular glass-sided case. The tablecloth in which the tile and the bloody Host were wrapped is also kept under glass. Paintings depicting the events of the miracle can also be seen in the church. (They are reproduced here.)

In 1980, solemn services were observed in honor of the seventh centennial of the translation of the miraculous Host from Lanciano to Offida.

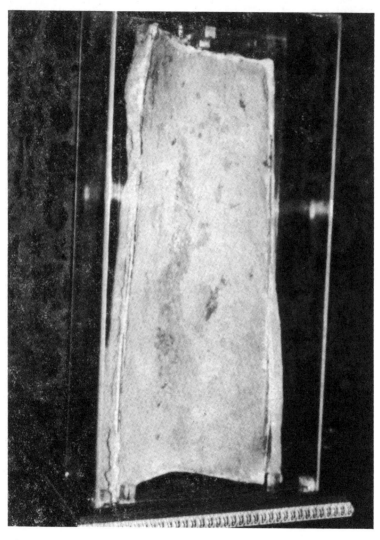

The tile on which Ricciarella heated the Host over a fire, hoping to obtain a magical powder with which to win the love of her husband. Instead, the Host turned into a piece of bloody flesh. The blood smear and drops of blood on the tile are clearly visible.

The tablecloth which Ricciarella wrapped around the bloody Host and tile before burying them beneath the garbage heap.

The silver reliquary containing the miraculous Host and a piece of the True Cross. The Host, the tile and the tablecloth are kept in the Sanctuary of St. Augustine in Offida, also known as the Sanctuary of the Miraculous Eucharist.

Giacomo Stasio mistreats his wife, Ricciarella.

Ricciarella is advised to receive Holy Communion and then to convey the Host to her kitchen, heat it over a fire until a powder is obtained, then put the powder into the food or drink of her husband, who would then supposedly grow to love and respect her.

The sacrilegious Communion of Ricciarella. She has allowed the Host to fall from her mouth, hiding it in the top of her dress.

The moment of the miracle. As the Host is heated on a tile over the fire, it turns into a piece of bloody flesh.

Ricciarella's husband's horse kneels before the garbage pile beneath which the bloody Host is hidden.

Seven years after the miracle, after being tormented day and night with remorse, Ricciarella confesses her sin to Father Giacomo Diotallevi. For a long time she was choked with sobs. Then she exclaimed, "This is my sin! I have killed God."

Ricciarella shows Father Giacomo the bloody tile and cloth.

The return of the priests to Offida from Venice where they had had a
special silver reliquary made for the miraculous Host.

Chapter 15

THE MIRACLE OF HASSELT, BELGIUM

1317

Constant Van der Straeten, a renowned historian who was for many years an officer of the cathedral of Hasselt, gives us a brief history of this miracle.

A priest from Viversel, helping the priests in the city of Lummen, was asked to bring the Holy Eucharist to a man of the village who was ill. Taking with him one Host in a ciborium, the priest entered the man's house and placed the ciborium on a table while he went to speak with the family in another room.

While the priest was absent, a man who was in mortal sin wandered into the room, removed the cover of the ciborium, touched the Host and then picked it up. At once the Host began to bleed. Frightened, the man dropped the Host into the ciborium and quickly departed. When the priest returned for the ciborium he found the cover removed, and he was astonished to see the Host spotted with blood.

At first undecided about what to do, the priest finally brought the ciborium and the Host to the pastor and related what had taken place. The pastor advised him to carry the miraculous Host to the church of the Cistercian nuns at Herkenrode, approximately 30 miles away.

This convent, founded near Liege in the 12th century, was the first foundation of the Cistercian nuns in Belgium. (An outstanding member of this community was the stigmatist St. Lutgarde, who lived from 1182-1246). Even during a time of decline in the Cistercian Order, this foundation continued to grow in size until it ranked among the most important convents in the Low Countries. Because of this venerable community's reputation for holiness, the pastor apparently felt that the miraculous Host would be more appropriately enshrined in the convent's church.

The priest journeyed to the Cistercian church, and as soon as he approached the altar and placed the Host upon it, a vision of Christ, crowned with thorns, was seen by everyone present. Our Lord seems to have thereby given a special sign of His willingness to be enshrined there. Because of this vision and the miraculous Host, Herkenrode quickly became one of the most famous places of pilgrimage in Belgium.

The Host was securely kept in the church at Herkenrode until 1796, during the French Revolution, when the nuns were expelled from their convent. During this dreadful time the Host was entrusted to the care of a succession of different families. It is said that it was once placed in a tin box and walled into the kitchen of a house.

In 1804 the Host was removed from hiding and taken during solemn services to the Church of St. Quentin in Hasselt. This picturesque church of Gothic architecture, dating from the 14th century, contains impressive paintings of the 16th and 17th centuries which recall events in the history of the miracle. But much more important, the Church of St. Quentin still guards the miraculous Eucharistic Host of 1317, which remains in splendid condition.

Chapter 16

THE TWO MIRACLES
OF SIENA, ITALY

1330 and 1730

The city of Siena, made famous by St. Catherine and St. Bernardino, was singled out for not one, but *two* Eucharistic miracles. The first occurred in 1330 and the second exactly 400 years later, in 1730. There is a great collection of documents attesting to the details of both miracles. The first was a bloody miracle, the second unbloody. Both are still preserved and both remain objects of great interest and devotion.

The miracle of 1330 concerns a priest of Siena who had under his care the faithful of a village on the outskirts of the city. A farmer of the village became grievously ill and sent for the priest. In great haste the priest removed a consecrated Host from the tabernacle, but instead of placing it in a pyx, he inserted the Host between the pages of his breviary. Positioning the book under his arm, he hurried to the bedside of the farmer.

After prayers were recited the priest opened the breviary to give the Host to the sick man, but discovered, to his amazement, that the Host was bloody and almost melted. Saying nothing about this, he closed the book and returned to Siena. It is said that neither the farmer nor anyone in the house was aware of the miracle at this time.

In a state of deep remorse, the priest went to the Monastery of St. Augustine, where he told the details of the miracle to Padre Simone Fidati, a man of deep spirituality, who was also a celebrated orator. (After Padre Simone's death, he was beatified by Pope Gregory XVI, who approved an Office and Mass in his honor.)

The priest showed Padre Simone the two pages stained with the blood of the Host, and entrusted the breviary to his care. After receiving absolution for his sinful handling of the consecrated

Host, the priest departed from the miracle's history, which continues with Padre Simone.

After a time, Padre Simone removed one of the bloody pages and made a gift of it to his confreres, the Augustinian priests in Perugia. This gift, unfortunately, was lost in 1866 during the suppression of religious orders.

The second page was enclosed in a silver vessel and, during another period of unrest, was taken to Padre Simone's hometown of Cascia, where it prompted ardent devotion among priests, the faithful, and civil authorities. The City Register of 1387, which is kept in the City Hall of Cascia, gives the details of a yearly feast of *Corpus Domini* ("The Body of the Lord"). During this celebration, the Mayor and members of the Council, together with the general populace, were instructed to gather in the church to honor the venerable relic with a procession and a solemn Mass. For this observance the city was to provide a 10-pound candle at its own expense.

The miracle was also honored by Pope Boniface IX, who officially approved the veneration accorded the relic in a bull dated January 10, 1401. His Holiness generously conceded the Indulgence of the Portiuncula to everyone who visited the Church of St. Augustine on the feast of Corpus Domini.

On June 7, 1408, Pope Gregory XII approved the continued devotion to the relic and added other indulgences for those who visited the church in which it was kept. The relic was also honored by Popes Sixtus IV, Innocent XIII, Clement XII and Pius VII.

In 1962 there was a thorough examination of the relic. The dimensions of the bloodstained paper were found to be 52 x 44 mm.; the diameter of the bloody stain is 40 mm. The color of the stain was described as light brown, but when viewed through a magnifying lens the color appeared redder, while particles of coagulated blood were clearly identified. The condition still persists.

Another phenomenon exists in that the stain, when viewed through a weaker lens, reveals the profile image of a man who is recognizably sad. The same image can also be seen in photographs of the stain.

In 1930 a Eucharistic Congress was held in Cascia, coinciding with the sixth centennial observance of the miracle. For this event a new ostensorium was blessed for the relic.

Thus the Basilica-Sanctuary of St. Rita in Cascia has within its blessed precincts three holy relics: the incorrupt body of St. Rita, the bones of Blessed Simone Fidati, and the relic of the Eucharistic miracle of 1330 that has been preserved for over 650 years.

*   *   *   *   *

The second Eucharistic miracle of Siena has roots in the 13th century when special services and festivities were introduced in honor of the feast of the Assumption of the Blessed Virgin Mary. These observances became traditional and were still conducted at the time of the miracle. So it was that on August 14, 1730, during devotions for the vigil of the feast, while most of the Sienese population and the clergy of the city were attending these services, thieves entered the deserted Church of St. Francis. Taking advantage of the friars' absence, they made for the chapel where the Blessed Sacrament was kept, picked the lock to the tabernacle and carried away the golden ciborium containing consecrated Hosts.

The theft went undiscovered until the next morning, when the priest opened the tabernacle at the Communion of the Mass. Then later, when a parishioner found the lid of the ciborium lying in the street, the suspicion of sacrilege was confirmed. The anguish of the parishioners forced the cancellation of the traditional festivities for the feast of Our Lady's Assumption. The Archbishop ordered public prayers of reparation, while the civil authorities began a search for the consecrated Hosts and for the scoundrel who had taken them.

Two days later, on August 17, while praying in the Church of St. Mary of Provenzano, a priest's attention was directed to something white protruding from the offering box attached to his prie dieu. Realizing that it was a Host, he informed the other priests of the church, who in turn notified the Archbishop and the friars of the Church of St. Francis.

When the offering box was opened, in the presence of local priests and the representative of the Archbishop, a large number of Hosts were found, some of them suspended by cobwebs. The Hosts were compared with some unconsecrated ones used in the Church of St. Francis, and proved to be exactly the same size and to have the same mark of the irons upon which they were baked. The number of Hosts corresponded exactly to the number the Franciscan friars had estimated were in the ciborium—348 whole Hosts and six halves.

Since the offering box was opened but once a year, the Hosts were covered with the dust and debris that had collected there. After being carefully cleaned by the priests, they were enclosed in a ciborium and placed inside the tabernacle of the main altar of the Church of St. Mary. The following day, in the company of a great gathering of townspeople, Archbishop Alessandro Zondadari carried the Sacred Hosts in solemn procession back to the Church of St. Francis.

During the two centuries that followed it has sometimes been wondered why the Hosts were not consumed by a priest during Mass, which would have been the ordinary procedure in such a case. While there is no definite answer, there are two theories. One explanation is that crowds of people from both Siena and neighboring cities gathered in the church to offer prayers of reparation before the sacred particles, forcing the priests to conserve them for a time. The other reason the priests did not consume them might well have been because of their soiled condition. While the Hosts were superficially cleaned after their discovery, they still retained a great deal of dirt. In such cases it is not necessary to consume consecrated Hosts, but it is permitted to allow them to deteriorate naturally, at which time Christ would no longer be present.

To the amazement of the clergy, the Hosts did not deteriorate, but remained fresh and even retained a pleasant scent. With the passage of time the Conventual Franciscans became convinced that they were witnessing a continuing miracle of preservation.

Fifty years after the recovery of the stolen Hosts, an official investigation was conducted into the authenticity of the miracle. The Minister General of the Franciscan Order, Father Carlo Vipera, examined the Hosts on April 14, 1780, and upon tasting one of them he found it fresh and incorrupt. Since a number of the Hosts had been distributed during the preceding years, the Minister General ordered that the remaining 230 particles be placed in a new ciborium and forbade further distribution.

A more detailed investigation took place in 1789 by Archbishop Tiberio Borghese of Siena with a number of theologians and other dignitaries. After examining the Hosts under a microscope, the commission declared that they were perfectly intact and showed no sign of deterioration. The three Franciscans who had been present at the previous investigation, that of 1780, were questioned under oath by the Archbishop. It was then reaffirmed that the Hosts under examination were the same ones stolen in 1730.

As a test to further confirm the authenticity of the miracle, the Archbishop, during this 1789 examination, ordered several unconsecrated hosts to be placed in a sealed box and kept under lock in the chancery office. Ten years later these were examined and found to be not only disfigured, but also withered. In 1850, 61 years after they were placed in a sealed box, these unconsecrated hosts were found reduced to particles of a dark yellow color, while the consecrated Hosts retained their original freshness.

Other examinations were made at intervals over the years, the most significant being that of 1914, undertaken on the authority of Pope St. Pius X. For this inquiry the Archbishop selected a distinguished panel of investigators, which included scientists and professors from Siena and Pisa, as well as theologians and Church officials.

Acid and starch tests performed on one of the fragments indicated a normal starch content. The conclusions reached from microscopic tests indicated that the Hosts had been made of roughly sifted wheat flour, which was found to be well preserved.

The commission agreed that unleavened bread, if prepared under sterile conditions and kept in an airtight, antiseptically cleaned container, could be kept for an extremely long time. Unleavened bread prepared in a normal fashion and exposed to air and the activity of micro-organisms would remain intact for no more than a few years. It was concluded that the stolen Hosts had been both prepared without scientific precautions and kept under ordinary conditions which should have caused their decay more than a century before. The commission concluded that the preservation was extraordinary, "... e la scienza stessa che proclama qui lo straordinario."

Professor Siro Grimaldi, professor of chemistry at the University of Siena and director of the Municipal Chemical Laboratory, as well as the holder of several other distinguished positions in the field of chemistry, was the chief chemical examiner of the holy particles in 1914. Afterward, he gave elaborate statements concerning the miraculous nature of the Hosts, and wrote a book about the miracle entitled *Uno Scienziato Adora* (*A Scientific Adorer*). In 1914 he declared:

The holy Particles of unleavened bread represent an example of perfect preservation . . . a singular phenomenon that inverts the natural law of the conservation of organic material. It is a fact unique in the annals of science.

In 1922 another investigation was conducted—this one in the presence of Cardinal Giovanni Tacci, who was accompanied by the Archbishop of Siena and the Bishops of Montepulciano, Foligno and Grosseto. Again the results were the same: the Hosts tasted like unleavened bread, were starchy in composition and were completely preserved.

In 1950 the miraculous Hosts were taken from the old ciborium and placed in a more elaborate and costly one, which caught the eye of another thief. Thus, despite the precautions of the clergy, another sacrilegious theft occurred on the night of August 5, 1951. This time the thief was considerate enough to take only the container and left the Hosts in a corner of the tabernacle. After counting 133 Hosts, the Archbishop himself sealed them in a silver ciborium. Later, after being photographed, they were placed in an elaborate container which replaced the one that had been stolen.

The miraculously preserved Hosts are displayed publicly on various occasions, but especially on the 17th of each month, which commemorates the day they were found after the first theft in 1730. On the feast of Corpus Christi the Sacred Hosts are placed in their processional monstrance and triumphantly carried in procession from the church through the streets of the town, an observance in which the whole populace participates.

Among many distinguished visitors who have adored the Hosts was St. John Bosco. They were likewise venerated by Pope John XXIII, who signed the album of visitors on May 29, 1954, when he was still the Patriarch of Venice. And although unable to visit the miraculous Hosts, Popes Pius X, Benedict XV, Pius XI and Pius XII issued statements of profound interest and admiration.

With a unanimous voice, the faithful, priests, bishops, cardinals and popes have marveled at and worshiped the holy Hosts, recognizing in them a permanent miracle, both complete and perfect, that has endured for over 250 years.

By this miracle the Hosts have remained whole and shiny, and have maintained the characteristic scent of unleavened bread. Since they are in such a perfect state of conservation, maintaining the appearances of bread, the Catholic Church assures us that although they were consecrated in the year 1730, these Eucharistic Hosts are still really and truly the Body of Christ. The miraculous Hosts have been cherished and venerated in the Basilica of St. Francis in Siena for over 250 years.

Above and left: The ostensorium containing the breviary page which became stained with blood in the year 1330 when a priest hastily inserted a consecrated Host in the book to take it to a sick man. In the blood stain one can see the profile image of a man; the drawing shown between the two angels provides a guide for discerning this image. The relic has been honored by many popes, and is now venerated in the Basilica of St. Rita in Cascia, Italy.

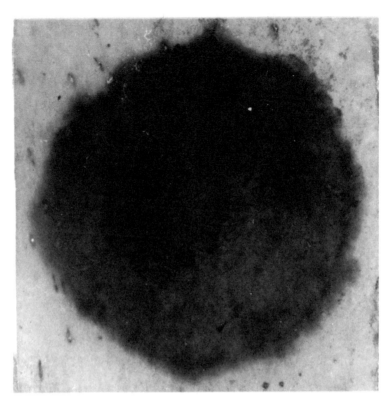

Above: The breviary page. The profile image is visible thereon.

Right: Consecrated Hosts stolen from the Basilica of St. Francis in Siena in the year 1730, then found, and now venerated in the same church. The Hosts have remained fresh and incorrupt for over 250 years, in contrast to the deterioration of unconsecrated hosts kept under the same conditions. The Hosts have been recognized by many popes and adored by many distinguished pilgrims, including St. John Bosco and Pope John XXIII.

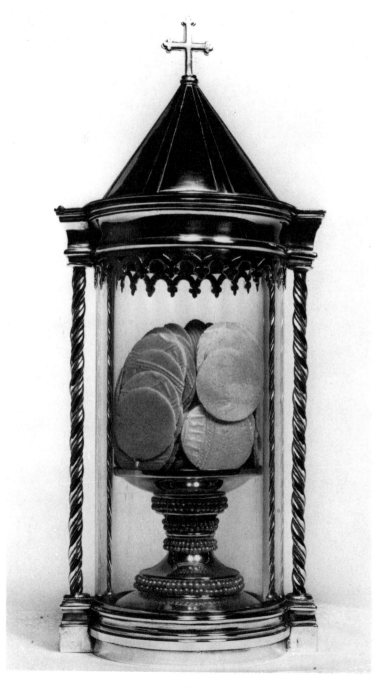

Grassi

Above and below: Archbishop Toccabelli of Siena transfers the miraculous Hosts to a new ostensorium on September 23, 1950.

Grassi

The elaborate monstrance in which the Hosts are carried in procession on the Feast of Corpus Christi.

Chapter 17

THE MIRACLE OF BLANOT, FRANCE

1331

The village of Blanot is situated in a long, narrow valley surrounded by picturesque mountains. Inconspicuous because of its location, it was nevertheless favored by God, who honored it with a Eucharistic miracle. The physical evidence of this event is still preserved in the church in which it occurred.

Before relating the miracle, it would be best to recall the manner in which Holy Communion was distributed in the 14th century (and in many places yet today). During Holy Mass, when the time approached for the distribution of Communion, the communicants would approach the altar railing which separated the body of the church from the sanctuary. Taking their places side by side along the length of the railing, they would kneel. At about the same time, two altar boys would approach the railing and take their places one at each end. Reaching down for a long linen cloth that hung the length of the railing on the side facing the sanctuary, each would take his end of the cloth and flip it over the top of the railing. The communicants would then place their hands beneath the cloth. The priest, holding the ciborium containing the consecrated Hosts, would approach one end of the railing and distribute the Hosts as he moved along its length. At the time of the miracle this was the way in which Holy Communion was received at Blanot.

The miracle occurred on Easter Sunday, March 31, 1331, at the first Mass of the day, which was offered by Hugues de la Baume, the vicar of Blanot. Because of the solemn occasion, two men of the parish named Thomas Caillot and Guyot Besson were also serving in addition to the altar boys. At Communion time the two men approached the altar railing, took their places at each end and turned the long cloth over the railing. The parishioners took their places, held their hands under the cloth and waited for the approach of the priest.

One of the last to receive was a woman named Jacquette, described as being the widow of Regnaut d'Effour. The priest placed the Host on her tongue, turned, and started walking toward the altar. It was then that both men and a few of the communicants saw the Host fall from the woman's mouth and land upon the cloth that covered her hands. As the priest was then placing the ciborium inside the tabernacle, Thomas Caillot approached the altar and informed him of the accident. The priest immediately left the altar and approached the railing; but instead of finding the Host, he saw a spot of blood the same size as the Host, which had apparently dissolved into blood.

When the Mass was completed, the priest took the cloth into the sacristy and placed the stained area in a basin filled with clear water. After washing the spot and scrubbing it with his fingers numerous times he found that, far from becoming smaller and lighter, it had actually become larger and much darker. On removing the cloth from the basin he was surprised to find that the water had turned bloody. The priest and his assistants were not only astonished, but also frightened, and exclaimed, "This is the Precious Blood of our Lord Jesus Christ!" The priest then took a knife and, after washing it, cut from the cloth the piece bearing the bloody imprint of the Host. This square piece of cloth was reverently placed in the tabernacle.

Fifteen days later, an official of the Archdiocese of Autun, Jean Jarossier, journeyed to Blanot to initiate an investigation. With him was the Curé de Lucenay, a monsignor of Autun, and an apostolic notary. The interrogation of witnesses was conducted in the presence of Pierre Osnonout, the Curé of Blanot. The results of this investigation were sent by Archbishop Pierre Bertrand to Pope John XXII, who pronounced a favorable verdict and accorded indulgences to those who would celebrate Mass in the parish church of Blanot. Copies of the documents are still kept in the City Hall of Blanot and are described as being in an ancient style which is difficult to read.

The Hosts that remained in the ciborium after the distribution of Holy Communion on that Easter Sunday were never used, and were carefully reserved in the tabernacle. The reason for this is not known, although one might speculate that the priest wished to avoid a possible repetition of the prodigy. In 1706 these Hosts, preserved in good condition after 375 years, were taken in a five-hour procession around the parish of Blanot in observance of the anniversary of the miracle. Taking part in the ceremony were many prelates and a great many people of the parish and the surrounding areas. At the conclusion of the procession, the silver ciborium holding the Hosts was returned to the golden box in which it was kept. This was carefully placed in the main tabernacle of the church.

For many years there were commemorative processions and special observances, but these were discontinued at the start of the French Revolution when violent fanatics were desecrating Catholic churches and taking objects of value.

On December 27, 1793, a group of revolutionaries entered the church and boldly opened the tabernacle. The bloodstained cloth, now encased in a crystal tube, was actually handled by one of them, but fortunately was rejected as being of little value. After this desecration of the church, the relic was entrusted to the safekeeping of a pious parishioner, Dominique Cortet. While it was in his home it was venerated and given all respect, yet despite this care, the tube was cracked on both the top and bottom. One of the injuries was caused by M. Lucotte, the Curé of Blanot, who often kissed it and put it on the eyes of the faithful. The other end was accidentally cracked while it was hidden in the drawer of an armoire.

Following the Revolution, when peace was again restored, many persons were questioned about the authenticity of the cloth within the crystal tube. All agreed that it was the same one that had been kept in the church. After ecclesiastical officials were satisfied as to the relic's authenticity, it was solemnly returned to the church and placed in a box covered with velvet which, in turn, was placed within the tabernacle.

Sometime later a new crystal tube was designed for the relic. At either end are rings of gold and copper, with a cross surmounting the top. The tube, with the cloth clearly visible, is sealed and kept within a special ostensorium. This is adorned at its base with four enamel panels which depict events in the history of the relic.

Each year on Easter Monday, according to ancient custom, the relic is solemnly exposed in the church of Blanot.

The Eucharistic miracle of Blanot, France. The priest holds the ostensorium containing the piece of cloth which became red and bloodstained
when a consecrated Host accidentally fell onto it in the year 1331. The
parish church of Blanot is seen in the background.

A closer view of the ostensorium and bloodstained cloth, now enclosed in a crystal tube. The base of the ostensorium is decorated with four enamel paintings depicting events in the history of the relic.

LE JOUR DE PÂQUES MCCCXXXI
HUGUES DE BAUME VICAIRE DE BLANOT
CÉLÉBRANT LA MESSE
UNE PARCELLE D'HOSTIE TOMBA
ET SE TRANSFORMA EN GOUTTE DE SANG
SUR LA NAPPE DE COMMUNION.
L'OFFICIAL DE PIERRE BERTRAND
EVÈQUE D'AUTUN
FIT L'ENQUÊTE CANONIQUE.
LE PAPE JEAN XXII
ACCORDA DES INDULGENCES.

Plaque in the church of Blanot describing the miracle. It reads: "On Easter day of 1331, as Hugues de Baume, curate of Blanot, celebrated Mass, a particle of the Host fell and changed into a spot of blood on the Communion cloth. The official of Pierre Bertrand, Bishop of Autun, made the canonical investigation. Pope John XXII granted indulgences."

103

A contemporary artistic rendition of the Miracle of Blanot. This stained-glass window is in the parish church.

The interior of the parish church at Blanot.

Chapter 18

THE MIRACLE OF AMSTERDAM, THE NETHERLANDS

1345

The Eucharistic miracle of Amsterdam occurred on March 15, 1345, in a house on Kalverstreet where a man named Ysbrant Dommer, seriously ill and near death, was given Holy Viaticum by the parish priest. Shortly after the priest left the house, the patient became violently sick, expelling the contents of his stomach. The woman attendant, having collected this material in a basin, threw it into a large open fire in the hearth.

The next morning, when the woman went to the hearth to revive the fire, she was startled to see the Host, fresh and brilliant, lying among the coals that still supported a steady flame. She instinctively snatched the Host from the fire, carefully wrapped it in a clean linen cloth, and placed it in a chest for safekeeping.

The priest who was immediately summoned placed the Host in a pyx and washed the cloth in which it had been wrapped. He then carried the Host to the parish church of St. Nicholas (which is now the property of non-Catholics).

The following morning, the priest found the pyx empty, but the Host was discovered by the same woman when she opened the chest to remove some linens. Again the priest was summoned to return it to the church. Then, after yet another disappearance and discovery, the priest assembled other members of the clergy for consultation. All agreed that the occurrences were a direct proof of God's power, and apparently a sign that the miracle should be openly honored. The miraculous Host was then carried in solemn procession to the church.

An official inquiry was made by the civil magistrate and the city council, all of whom were satisfied with the truthfulness of the witnesses. They affirmed the occurrence as fact and also endorsed the miracle in official documents. The Church authorities, too, headed by the Bishop of Utrecht, held an extended inquiry before permitting the clergy to spread information about the event.

The house in which the miracle took place was soon turned into a chapel called *Nieuwe Zijds,* or Holy Place—not only because the miracle had occurred there, but also because the Host of the miracle was kept on its altar. The fireplace in which the miracle took place was maintained.

About 100 years later, in 1452, a great fire destroyed most of the town of Amsterdam and threatened the Holy Place. In an attempt to save the miraculous Host, locksmiths were called in to open the tabernacle—but their efforts proved unsuccessful when their tools broke off and the flames and heat forced them to retreat. When the fire was finally extinguished, another miracle was discovered: lying amid the smoldering ruins, untouched by the fire, was the vessel containing the miraculous Host, together with its silken cover.

The long list of special favors which had been received by the people previous to the fire was greatly augmented when the chapel was rebuilt. Enormous crowds flocked there and participated in the annual procession on the anniversary of the miracle.

At this point in the history of the miracle we should turn our attention to the Sisters of St. Begga, who left a small village near Amsterdam to establish a community near the site of the miracle. Later known as the Beguines, the community consisted of laywomen who lived in a community of sorts and took temporary vows of obedience and chastity, but not poverty, since they were permitted to own their own property and to dispose of it as they wished. They assembled for Mass and prayers and were allowed to come and go as they pleased, with many being engaged in educational and charitable endeavors. Their situation was unusual in that each lived in her own narrow house which was connected side by side with the others. These were arranged in a square with a courtyard in the center. In the space occupied by one of the houses was a chapel, which was enlarged through the years. The whole complex became known as the *Begijnhof.*

When the chapel house of the miracle was confiscated by the city authorities at the time of the Reformation, the miraculous Host was given into the care of the Beguines. The devotions and pious exercises that had become traditional continued to be observed. But in 1607 this last refuge was closed, although, in a small building adjoining the Beguines' chapel, private devotions were kept alive. Gradually conditions permitted the enlargement of this building at the *Begijnhof*; but it was not until 1845, the fifth centennial of the miracle, that a grand public demonstration took place. This has since been observed every year on the anniversary of the miracle.

In addition to these yearly observances, individual processions have taken place throughout the years since the time of the miracle, and continued even during the Reformation. They were called "silent processions," because the people would walk along the Holy Way in silence, as a private devotion. These processions of individuals still take place, but more people seem to participate on the vigil of the anniversary, especially through the night and in the early hours of the anniversary.

The little chapel house in which the miracle occurred was demolished in 1908 over the protests of both Catholics and Protestants. The little chapel is far from being forgotten, however, since its likeness has been captured in a stained glass window in the chapel of the *Begijnhof*.[1] Also, behind the high altar is a splendid stained-glass window depicting the miracle; and on either side, along the walls, are paintings depicting the medieval processions.

In commemoration of the miracle, the Blessed Sacrament is daily exposed for adoration in this chapel. Thus Amsterdam has become a place of pilgrimage for the whole of The Netherlands.

---

1. At the time of the Reformation there were in Amsterdam more than twenty monasteries, but only the *Begijnhof* has survived; its 164 side-by-side medieval houses are of great historical interest. Although fires over the years have destroyed some of the houses, these have been rebuilt; thus the collection of structures still forms a square of sorts, with the trees in the interior courtyard still providing a shady and quiet place for prayer.

Chapter 19

THE MIRACLE OF MACERATA, ITALY

1356

The Catholics of Macerata claim that their city can be called the City of the Most Blessed Sacrament—and this for two reasons: because of the Eucharistic miracle which occurred there, and because it was one of the first cities in the world to organize a confraternity in honor of the Most Holy Eucharist.

The miracle occurred in Macerata on the morning of April 25, 1356, while a priest was celebrating Holy Mass in the church of the Benedictine nuns. At the beginning of the Consecration, he entertained a momentary doubt about the reality of Christ's presence, when suddenly, at the breaking of the consecrated Host, fresh blood began to drip from the edges of the separated particles! The priest was then so overwhelmed with faith and devotion that his trembling hands caused the blood from the Host to fall beside the chalice, staining the corporal that was beneath it.

At the conclusion of Mass, the priest hurried to give news of the event to Bishop Nicolò of St. Martino, who ordered that the wet corporal be taken to the cathedral for a canonical examination. The miracle was likened to that which had occurred at Bolsena less than 100 years before, resulting in the introduction of the feast of Corpus Christi.

After being declared authentic by the canonical commission, the blood-stained corporal was reverently displayed for veneration.

While no official documents of the time can be found in the archives of Macerata, the illustrious historian Ignazio Compagnoni, in his fourth manuscript, relates the details of the miracle and clearly reports the commission's recognition of the relic's authenticity. The reports from the time of the miracle, and the subsequent pronouncements by many bishops and archbishops (in particular that of Bishop Cardinal Centini in 1622), have substantiated the authenticity of this relic. The spots of blood clearly visible on the cloth are regarded by all as being the Precious Blood of the Saviour.

Documents from 1647 indicate that a man named Orazio Longhi donated to the cathedral a precious reliquary of silver and crystal for the exposition of the relic. In 1649 Bishop Monsignor Silvestri organized a procession and a grand solemnity in honor of the holy corporal—festivities in which many of the faithful participated.

The relic was on constant exposition until 1807, when Napoleon began to threaten Italy and the Church. When Napoleon suppressed confraternities and prohibited traditional processions, the corporal was secreted in a closet behind an altar in the cathedral. It remained in safety during this time and also during another time of political unrest that disturbed Italy during the middle of the 19th century. The cloth was not forgotten during these years, however. It was authenticated on October 10, 1861 by Monsignor Zangari, and later on September 15, 1885 by Monsignor Galeati.

The precious cloth was finally removed from hiding in 1932. After it was properly authenticated again, it was arranged in its frame of crystal and placed on constant display in the Chapel of the Sacrament.

The size of the corporal has proved to be of interest to present-day viewers. Measuring 4 ft. 2-1/2 inches in length and 1 ft. 4 inches in width, it is much longer than corporals used today, which are about the size of a man's handkerchief. It is believed, however, that the cloth was folded in half during the Mass of the miracle, because its two blood stains are neatly combined when the cloth is folded.

A number of other folds are clearly visible on the linen. Five folds stretch horizontally and seven are marked vertically. Besides the bloodstains, traces of mildew and a few drops of wax are also noticeable.

It is said that chemical analysis of the relic cannot be undertaken because the centuries have homogenized every substance that is not textile; therefore, only a topographical observation can be made.

The authenticity of the linen has been established in three ways. First, the cloth (which is described as being very well executed and yellowed with age) has been determined by scholars to be from the

14th century. Second, the parchment attached to the corporal contains Gothic calligraphy, which has been authenticated by other knowledgeable persons as being from the time of the miracle. Third, while no official documents are preserved, there are a great many manuscripts by respected authors of the time who refer to its history and accept its authenticity.

The holy corporal can be seen in a new chapel in the Cathedral of Macerata, where it is particularly honored on the feast of Corpus Christi and during the octave of that feast.

The bloodstained corporal which is venerated in the Cathedral of Macerata. In the year 1356 a priest celebrating Mass entertained a momentary doubt regarding Christ's Real Presence; at the breaking of the Host, blood dripped from the edges of the Host, staining the corporal.

Chapter 20

THE MIRACLE OF BRUSSELS, BELGIUM

1370

The Eucharistic miracle of Brussels, Belgium occurred at a time when certain Christians and Jews were embroiled in bitter opposition. It appears that in 1369 a Jew named Jonathan resided in the little town of Enghien, some 15 miles from Brussels. Jonathan had a friend, Jean of Louvain (then residing in Brussels), who for some time had simulated a conversion to Christianity.

Jonathan repeatedly asked his friend to obtain for him some of the consecrated wafers used during Holy Mass. Jean was unwilling at first to comply, but Jonathan at last promised him 60 gold coins for his trouble. Greed eventually overcame Jean's scruples, and he immediately set about studying the churches in Brussels for one to which he could secretly gain entrance. He at last decided upon the Church of St. Catherine, which was little attended by the sacristan since the church was used mainly to enshrine the Blessed Sacrament for distribution to the sick.

During the night of October 4, 1369, Jean placed a ladder against the wall of the church, broke a window, and slipped inside. Then, opening the tabernacle, he found in a golden ciborium 15 small Hosts and one large Host that was used for Benediction. After leaving the church, he journeyed to Enghien and gave the Hosts to Jonathan, who rewarded him with a bag containing the promised coins.

The fate of the thief is uncertain, but it is reported that Jonathan was murdered in his own garden less than two weeks after the theft—to the horror of his young son, who witnessed the attack. After a time, Jonathan's widow moved to the metropolitan city of Brussels, taking the ciborium and the Hosts with her.

On April 4, 1370, Good Friday, the Jews assembled in their synagogue in Brussels. After laying the sacred Hosts out on a table, they inflicted upon them both verbal and physical abuse. At some point during the sacrilege, knives were drawn and the Hosts were stabbed.

Immediately, before the stunned eyes of the Jews, blood flowed from the stab wounds. Moreover, the attackers' weapons fell from their hands, trembling seized them, and they fell to the ground in terror.

In an effort to rid themselves of the bloody Hosts, the Jews pressed a Christian convert named Catherine into agreeing to take them to the Jews of Cologne. But feeling remorse and inexpressible agitation, she decided instead to tell the whole story to the curé of the church of Notre Dame de la Chapelle, Pierre Van den Eede. The curate of the Bishop of Cambrai à Brussels, Jean d'Yssche, was also told of the theft and together with a committee of churchmen reclaimed the Hosts from Catherine with great emotion.

After they were retrieved, they were taken to Notre Dame de la Chapelle. A few Hosts were left there, but the rest were taken in a magnificent procession of reparation in May of 1370 to the Cathedral of St. Michael. They were escorted by the clergy of the city, members of the mendicant orders, the duke and duchess of Brabant, and a great number of lords, nobles and citizens of the city, to the accompaniment of lights, incense, and sacred hymns, while the procession route was decorated to honor the Hosts. Amidst joy and universal emotion the Hosts were placed in one of the chapels of the choir until a more worthy chapel could be erected. Six of the Hosts had been completely destroyed on the day of the crime. Eventually three of the Hosts were placed behind a crystal in the center of a golden cross.

Following the investigations there were two different reports concerning the final disposition of the men who had perpetrated the sacrilege. One was that King Wenceslas, reigning in Brussels at the time, had the men arrested and tried; they admitted their deed, and were subsequently burned to death. The other report was that the Jewish community banished the accused from the province.

During the troubled years of 1579-1585, when the Calvinists were profaning churches and destroying relics and statues, the sacred Hosts that had been left in the church of Notre Dame de la Chapelle disappeared. Those that were in the golden cross in St. Michael's were at first hidden in the Hospital of the Twelve Apostles, but then were placed for safekeeping in a recess in a beam of wood in St. Michael's. When the Calvinists were looking for the Hosts, they paused under this very beam as they entered—unaware that the Hosts were right above their heads.

Another anxious time for the Church in Brussels came in 1794 during the French Revolution, when valuable brass railings and ornaments were seized and wall carpets and silver reliquaries were either destroyed or stolen. Also taken were paintings by Venius, Rubens and Van Dyck. A series of paintings representing events in the history of the miracle were saved during this time, and can be seen today in St. Michael's Cathedral.

It is important to the understanding and appreciation of this miracle that we examine the event as it is depicted in the cathedral's many stained-glass windows, paintings, sculpture and tapestries, which have attracted countless pilgrims and tourists. First we will give some information about the cathedral itself.

From the very beginning of its history this church had been named for St. Michael. But in the 12th century, with the veneration of St. Gudule at its peak, the name of the church was amended to include the name of this saint, whose relics had been venerated in St. Michael's since 1047. In February 1962, the name was once more changed, this time to St. Michael's Cathedral, in accord with its original patronage. But some books of history and architecture, as well as some travel brochures, list the name of the cathedral simply—and incorrectly—as the Cathedral of St. Gudule.

Here in the Cathedral of St. Michael rest the mortal remains of many notable personages both titled and crowned. Here also is a fine example of Gothic architecture from the 13th and 17th centuries, the early church having been ravaged, rebuilt and enlarged many times. Some areas of ancient origin have been retained, however: the baptismal area dating from the 9th century and the vestibule from the 12th century. The cathedral is known, of course, for its former enshrinement of the miraculous Hosts of 1370, for which a large chapel was built between 1534 and 1539.

One of the stained-glass windows in the cathedral depicts Jonathan's widow giving the Hosts to the Jews; another portrays the Hosts being brought in procession from the Church of Notre Dame de la Chapelle to the Cathedral of St. Michael. Still another window shows the Hosts being confided to John Hauchin, Archbishop of Mechlin, who was formerly the dean of St. Michael.

Three other windows represent other events in the history of the miracle.

Emperor Charles V endowed the Cathedral with other splendid stained-glass windows. In one of these he and his wife, Isabella of Portugal, are depicted in the act of worshiping God the Father, who shows them the golden cross containing three of the miraculous Hosts. The triumphal arch located here was also a gift of the Emperor to honor the miracle, as were four additional windows. These depict favorite saints, but in the upper portion of each window are seen different particulars concerning the miracle. Another window, installed in 1542 but later destroyed, was of the Emperor, his wife Isabella and their patron saints. In its place today there is a window executed in 1848 representing the triumph of the miracle. A stained glass window to the left of this one shows the Emperor with his wife and his children Philip, Mary and Joan, and their respective patron saints venerating the holy miracle.

Above one of the altars are images of St. Michael and St. Gudule and other saints who are honored in the cathedral, while under the altar are three sculptures in high relief showing events regarding the miracle. Of interest behind the altar and against the wall is a piece of the beam with its well-concealed recess in which the miraculous Hosts were hidden during the tumultuous 16th century.

Episodes in the history of the miracle are depicted in four Gobelin tapestries that are hung each year between the pillars in the choir during the months of July and August. This exhibition in July was doubtless started early in the history of the miracle, at the time when the feast of the miracle was celebrated with a grand procession every year on the Sunday after July 15; the observance took place annually for centuries. A tapestry on constant exhibition since 1770 shows a miraculous healing before the sacred Hosts.

All of these works of art and items of interest are outlined in a guide book of the cathedral published in 1975. Also in the same book is a very surprising notice:

> On December 30, 1968, the diocesan authorities of Malines-Brussels Archdiocese declared that the charges of theft and sacrilege of the Blessed Sacrament in 1369-1370 which were brought against the Jewish community of

Brussels were unfounded.

The visitors and the faithful will situate the iconography in the cathedral in its proper historical context and not misinterpret the worship of the Blessed Sacrament.

The reasons for this disclaimer were not given, but it would seem that some explanation is warranted for a devotion that has been observed since 1370 and which was commemorated for centuries with yearly observances. Moreover, it is undeniable that the miracle has been honored by the clergy and hierarchy, as well as by persons of title and position, since its very origin. Moreover, the history of the miracle has been recorded by many authors, including R. P. Lucq, O.P.; Navez; Estienne Ydens; Cafmeyer; and Griffet.

Regardless of the disclaimer, tourists and the faithful of Brussels still honor the miracle by visiting the chapel where the miraculous Hosts were kept. This chapel, whose construction was begun in 1534, is of substantial size and bears the dedication, "St. Sacrament des Miracles." Here in the chapel as well as in the main part of the cathedral, pilgrims, tourists and the faithful of Brussels admire the ninety-nine items of furniture, architecture and art, many of which depict the Eucharistic Miracle of Brussels.

Another noteworthy church in Brussels is the Chapelle de l'Expiation, which was built in 1436 on the site of the synagogue in which the miracle of Brussels occurred.

Right: Stolen consecrated Hosts are stabbed by a group of Jews in Brussels, Belgium in the year 1370. Before their stunned eyes, blood flowed out from the stab wounds. In the Cathedral of St. Michael (also called the Cathedral of St. Gudule), pilgrims can see the events of the miracle depicted in many stained-glass windows, sculptures, paintings and tapestries. (*This painting by de Crayer.*)

117

M. IEHAN DESROBE LE
S. Sacrement & le porte à En-
ghien, & le deliure à Ionathas.

Jean, a pretended Christian, steals a ciborium containing 16 consecrated
Hosts, then carries it to the city of Enghien and turns it over to his Jewish
friend, Jonathan, for payment of 60 gold coins.

I ONATHAS AVEC AVL-
TRES IVIFZ SE MOCQVE
du S. Sacrement, le traiɗant
tref-indignement,

Jonathan and other Jews mock the Hosts and subject them to shameful indignity.

LES IVIFZ ASSEMBLEZ
EN LEVR SYNAGOGVE A
Bruxelle, par le jour du vendredy
ſainᴅ, renouuellent leurs blaſphemes
& execratıons contre le S. Sacremĕt,
& l'ayant percé auec leurs dagues, le
ſang en eſt forty en grãde abondãce.

The Jews assemble in their synagogue in Brussels on Good Friday,
renewing their blasphemies and execrations against the Blessed Sacrament. They then draw their daggers and pierce the Hosts. To their great
horror and astonishment, blood flows forth from the Hosts in abundance,
their weapons fall from their hands, trembling seizes them, and they fall
to the ground in terror.

LE CONFESSEVR PAR
L'ADVIS DES AVLTRES
gens d'Eglife, à receu des mains
de Catharine le fainct Ci-
boire auec les facrées
hoftiez .

Above: On the advice of other people in the Church, a priest receives the
holy ciborium and the sacred Hosts from the hands of Catherine.
Following page: Engraving taken from a book on the miracle published in
1605.

121

Le Très Saint Sacrement de Miracle de Bruxelles.

O Salutaris Hoſtia, Quæ cœli pandis oſtium
Bella premunt hoſtilia, Da robur fer: auxilium.

Cette gravure et les suivantes sont tirées d'une
Histoire du Très Saint Sacrement de Miracle,
éditée l'an 1605.

Chapter 21

THE MIRACLE OF
MIDDLEBURG-LOUVAIN, BELGIUM

1374

Time has obscured the name of the noble lady who is first mentioned in the history of this miracle, but it is known that she was a wealthy native of Middleburg (located in the southwest section of the Netherlands). She was kind to her domestics and so solicitous for their spiritual advancement that she taught them herself, inspiring them by her zealous observance of the Church's traditional practices.

On the first Sunday of the holy season of Lent of 1374, in accord with her usual custom she encouraged her servants to prepare for this season of penance by going to Confession and receiving Holy Communion. Her words, however, were accepted by the servants only as a duty they had to perform. One of the servants, known simply as Jean of Cologne, felt obliged to participate with the others for fear of being disgraced, but he approached the Holy Sacrament without having first prepared himself by confessing his sins in the Sacrament of Penance.

Kneeling with the others at the Communion railing, he awaited the approach of the priest. But as soon as the Host was placed upon Jean's tongue, it turned to flesh, which he was unable to swallow! Frightened by the unexpected development, he attempted to hide his difficulty, but then made the mistake of biting into the flesh. At that moment three drops of blood fell from his lips, staining the cloth that was draped over the Communion railing.

Startled at the sight of the bloody flesh in Jean's mouth and the blood dripping from it, the priest reacted promptly by removing the Host and respectfully carrying it to the altar, where he placed it in a small golden vessel.

It is reported that Jean was punished for his sacrilegious Communion by being instantly blinded. Feeling overwhelming remorse for his sin, he knelt at the feet of the priest and confessed his sin before the entire congregation. His sincere sorrow resulted in the restoration of his sight. Thereafter, Jean is said to have led an exemplary life and to have maintained to his death a great reverence for the most holy Sacrament of the Altar.

Details of the miracle spread throughout the country and were dutifully reported to Frederic III, Archbishop of Cologne, formerly the Count of Sarwerden. Since the Netherlands then belonged to the German Empire, Middleburg came under the episcopal jurisdiction of Archbishop Frederic, who demanded that the miraculous Host be transported to the metropolitan city of Cologne and enshrined in the cathedral there.

The transfer of the Host from Middleburg to Cologne inspired great interest during this 700-mile journey. After the Host's safe deposit in the cathedral, an elaborate ostensorium was crafted for its exposition. Shaped like a cross, the end of each bar was embellished with golden circlets outlined with golden lace. Statues of the Blessed Mother and St. Joseph claimed positions beneath each arm, while further down the cross were miniature statues of St. Peter and St. Paul. In the central part of the cross was an oval glass through which the miraculous Host could be seen. The placement behind this oval was unusual in that the miraculous Host was positioned above a miniature golden chalice which apparently had a cover, since the Host rested at the level of the chalice's rim.

Prior Jean Bayrens, of the Augustinian Order in Cologne, obviously had great influence with the Archbishop, because he was able to obtain permission to remove the Host from the cathedral to the church of his monastery. As soon as the Augustinians were in possession of the Host, it was again venerated with special ceremonies.

In the year 1380 Prior Bayrens was transferred to the monastery of Louvain in Belgium. In an effort to extend devotion to the miracle, he asked permission of the Archbishop to bring a part of the Host to Louvain. At this time the Host, entire in all respects, still bore the impression of the teeth that marked its bloody origin. The Archbishop consented to this proposal, but it seemed to all that to divide the miraculous Host into two parts with an instrument would be disrespectful. For three days the monks prayed and fasted for a solution to this problem. In answer to their prayers, the Host was discovered to have divided into two parts without human intervention. One of the parts, together with the piece of bloodstained cloth, was given to the prior for transport to Louvain; the other portion of the Host remained in Cologne in the parish church of St. Alban.

In Louvain a new reliquary was crafted by a jeweler of the city. The half of the miraculous Host was enshrined in the same manner as it had been in Cologne—the Host situated atop a miniature chalice which was encased behind glass in a gold and silver cross-shaped reliquary. Kept within the church of the Augustinians, St. Jacques, it was peacefully honored for four centuries.

In honor of the miracle, the Confraternity of the Sacrament of the Miracle was organized in 1426 by the provincial of the Augustinians; the members of this society were to participate in the good deeds of the religious of the province. The Prior General of the Order in Rome approved certain concessions in 1429, and Pope Eugene IV awarded indulgences in 1431.

In 1665 the miraculous Host was solemnly transported to a new altar. For this occasion Pope Alexander VII accorded his blessings and indulgences. Medals were struck with the likeness of the Host in its beautiful and costly reliquary, and several large paintings depicting events in the history of the miracle were executed, some of which still decorate the Church of St. Jacques.

During the four centuries of its peaceful enthronement, the miraculous Host was venerated by civil authorities, many ecclesiastics and distinguished royalty. Its anniversaries and centennials were celebrated with the utmost pomp and fervor, and enriched with the blessings and indulgences of Pope Paul V and Pope Clement XIV. For its fourth centennial observance a new reliquary of gem-encrusted gold was crafted by a jeweler from Brussels.

With the death of Empress Marie-Thérèse in 1780 and the succession of Joseph II to the throne, the tranquility of the Church was seriously disturbed by the suppression of Catholic feasts, religious observances, and religious houses, and by the harrassment of priests and religious.

When the closure of the Augustinian monastery was imminent, the miraculous Host and the bloodstained cloth were entrusted to many pious persons, who found it necessary to transfer them from one safe place to another. At one point the relics were hidden in a tall oak chest, which still exists. Also preserved is a corporal which was used to wrap the relics when they were transferred to a safe location on January 18, 1793, at the height of the French Revolution.

During this time of danger the miraculous Host and blood-stained cloth were not neglected. Although priests were forbidden to wear clerical garb, they were occasionally able to offer Mass secretly in the presence of the holy relics.

After peace was restored, the miraculous Host and cloth were brought on September 27, 1803 to the chapel of the hospital which was under the care of the Augustinian nuns. This was necessary because the chapel of the Augustinian monastery had been seriously damaged by the revolutionaries. One month later, on October 20 of 1803, the miraculous relics were brought back to the Church of St. Jacques, where examinations were made to test their authenticity. It is in this church that the bloodstained cloth and this part of the miraculous Host are still kept.

During this time the cloth was loaned to the church of the Augustinians in Nimegue in The Netherlands. Upon its return it was again deposited in the Church of St. Jacques on January 13, 1808. That year, a special reliquary was made to enshrine it. The cloth is secured behind a small circle of glass which is framed in a circle of precious metal. This is enclosed in a reliquary consisting of a crystal tube closed at the bottom by a golden base and capped on top with a golden cross. The cloth can be clearly seen.

The part of the miraculous Host that is kept in Louvain is slightly brown and somewhat smaller than formerly, yet it is perfectly distinguishable as flesh. The Host and the miniature chalice which supports it are kept in a reliquary fashioned in 1803 and are situated behind a crystal in the center of a golden cross. When this reliquary was exposed on the main altar or carried in procession, a freshly consecrated Host was placed behind the small chalice with its fragment of the miraculous Host.

All the important papers regarding the history, travels and examinations of the miraculous relics are kept in the archives of the Church of St. Jacques. Although the Host and bloodstained cloth are still well kept in this church, the church itself is now closed to public functions because the ground on which it stands is sinking, rendering the structure unsafe.

Left: Case containing part of the Host which turned to flesh and then bled on the First Sunday of Lent, 1374, when placed in the mouth of a man who had not first cleansed his soul in the Sacrament of Penance. The Host has shrunk in size; it rests atop a miniature chalice in the center of the cross. On the band of silver around the case are the Latin words *Visibilis latuit caro facta hic hostia sacra.* This is kept in the Augustinian Church of St. Jacques in Louvain, and is placed in an elaborate ostensorium when on display.

Right: The ostensorium, crafted in the year 1803. In the center of the golden cross is the case that encloses the portion of the miraculous Host.

127

Left: Reliquary of the holy blood in the Church of St. Jacques, Louvain. This reliquary holds the bloodstained cloth upon which drops of blood fell from the miraculous Host.

Right: Reliquary in which the miraculous Eucharist was formerly enshrined.

Above: The miniature chalice containing the miraculous flesh.
Below: Fragment of the bloodstained Communion cloth.

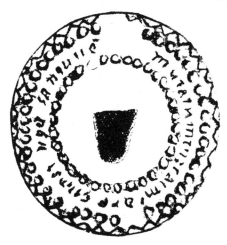

Chapter 22

THE MIRACLE OF SEEFELD, AUSTRIA

1384

In the diocese of Innsbruck, among the wooded mountains of the province of Tyrol in Western Austria, lie the village of Seefeld and the parish church of St. Oswald—a church which owes its popularity to a miracle that occurred there on Holy Thursday in the year 1384.

At that time Knight Oswald Milser was the guardian of Schlossberg Castle, located north of Seefeld. The castle was strategically situated to provide protection for an important pass and to serve as a border fortress. The knight, it seems, was filled with pride because of his position and authority; that which occurred because of his pride was recorded in the *Golden Chronicle of Hohenschwangau:*

> Oswald Milser came down with his followers to the parish church of Seefeld. He demanded—and a refusal could mean death—the large Host; the small one he regarded as too ordinary for him. He surrounded the frightened priest and the congregation with his armed men. At the end of the Mass, Milser, his sword drawn and his head covered, came to the left of the high altar, where he remained standing. The stunned priest handed him the Host, upon which the ground under the blasphemer suddenly gave way. He sank up to his knees. Deathly pale, he grasped the altar with both hands, the imprints of which can be seen to this day.

Other histories continue from here and relate how the knight, filled with terror, motioned imploringly for the priest to remove the Host from his mouth. As soon as the priest did so, the floor became firm once again. Immediately Oswald stepped out from the depression that remained, left the church, and hurried to the monastery of Stams, where he confessed his pride. He did penance and died a holy death two years later. In accordance with his wishes, he was buried near the entrance of the chapel of the Blessed Sacrament. The velvet mantle he had worn during the Holy Thursday Mass was made into a chasuble and given to the monastery of Stams.

Church records reveal that the Host taken from the knight's mouth was red, as though saturated with blood. Soon after the miracle, Knight Parseval von Weineck of Zirl donated a silver monstrance made in the Gothic style as a reliquary for the exposition of the miraculous Host, which is still preserved.

Because of the great crowds of pilgrims, a hostel was built for their accommodation soon after the miracle. Their numbers grew so rapidly that the church proved to be too small. In 1423 Duke Friedrich arranged for the erection of a larger church on the same site. The building was finished in 1472. Almost a century later, Emperor Maximilian I was so impressed with the Seefeld pilgrimages that he pledged to build an adjoining monastery. Begun in 1516, this monastery housed Augustinian monks until 1807. Since that time the monastery has served as a hotel, which proves to be a convenience for pilgrims.

Archduke Ferdinand II of Tyrol also demonstrated a special interest in the miracle. In 1574 he built inside the church the Chapel of the Holy Blood, in which the miraculous Host was enshrined for a time.

As for the scene of the miracle, the hollow through which the knight sank up to his knees is still kept and shown to visitors. In the interest of safety, the hollow is normally covered with a grate, which can be lifted for those who wish to examine it. The sunken area is located on the south side of the altar of the miracle.

Located in the sanctuary in its original position is the stone altar of the miracle. This is a goodly distance from the ornate high altar which was added later, when the church was enlarged. Directly above the stone altar is a new altar slab supported by pillars. The whole is arranged so that several inches of space separate the two slabs, allowing for a clear view of the altar of the miracle. Still seen on the side of the stone altar are the impressions of Oswald's hands, which sank into the stone at the time of the miracle. These impressions are also pointed out to visitors.

In addition to the hollow in the floor and the altar of the miracle, there is in the sanctuary the third remnant of the miracle—the monstrance with the miraculous Host. This is kept in a tabernacle situated in the south wall of the sanctuary near the high altar.

The church is embellished with many reminders of the miracle. A painted panel of 1502 adorns the south wall of the choir, while stained-glass windows capture the event. One of the reliefs in the tympanum above the main entrance is of the miracle, and a magnificent fresco on the ceiling of the Chapel of the Holy Blood depicts the priest and knight at the time of Communion, while hovering angels hold the reliquary monstrance. The church is also resplendent with other priceless examples of Gothic statuary, carvings and furnishings.

It is not known when the original Church of St. Oswald was built, but it is mentioned in a chronicle of 1320. The present church, completed in 1472, has the distinction of being the only remaining building constructed by the Innsbruck Builders Guild. It is regarded as the most striking example of North Tyrolian Gothic architecture.

In 1984 the Church of St. Oswald celebrated the 600th anniversary of the miracle that occurred within its privileged sanctuary.

Right: The sanctuary of St. Oswald's Church in Seefeld, Austria, where on Holy Thursday of 1384 the ground suddenly gave way under Knight Oswald Milser when he surrounded the priest and congregation with his armed men, then approached the high altar and pridefully insisted on receiving a *large* Host. The grate on the floor to the right of the altar covers the depressions made at the time of the Knight's unworthy reception of the Eucharist; the old stone altar, visible underneath the new altar, still bears the imprint of the Knight's hands which were made when he grasped hold of the altar as the ground sank beneath his feet. The present church, completed in 1472, is a larger building erected on the site of the original church.

Above: The Gothic monstrance in which the Host, which turned red at the time of the miracle, is usually kept. This is kept in a tabernacle in the south wall of the sanctuary near the high altar.

Left: The knight, accompanied by his armed men, receives the large Host and sinks into the floor up to his knees. In terror he grasps the stone altar with both hands. (*This painting in St. Oswald's Church was probably done by Jörg Kölderer in 1502*).

The interior of St. Oswald's Church.

The south wall of St. Oswald's Church and its main portal.

The Chapel of the Holy Blood in St. Oswald's Church and the painting
on its ceiling showing the proud Knight Oswald Milser in his velvet cape
receiving Holy Communion; hovering angels are depicted holding the
reliquary monstrance.

Marble stairway in St. Oswald's Church leading up to the Chapel of the Holy Blood.

Chapter 23

THE MIRACLE OF
DIJON, FRANCE

Before 1433

The exact year of this miracle is unknown, but it is reported that a great stream of blood issued from the Host when it was abused by a non-Christian. The Host was kept for a time in Rome, where it was accorded every mark of respect and was considered a great treasure.

The Host was removed from Rome on the authority of Pope Eugene IV, who offered it as a reward to Duke Philippe the Good of Burgundy, France, in recognition of his defense of the Pope at the Council of Basel. Canon Robert Anclou, a representative of the Pope, brought the Host to the duke in 1433, while Philippe was in Lille. As a proper place for the Host's enshrinement, Philippe chose the splendid Holy Chapel (la Sainte Chapelle) in Dijon, the capital of Burgundy. The duke's wife, Duchess Isabelle of Portugal, provided a magnificent ostensorium of gold and silver. This was embellished with precious stones, and bore in enamel the crests of Portugal and Burgundy. In this ostensorium the miraculous Host was exposed during special services which were repeated for over 300 years.

It is reported that King Louis XII, having been cured of a distressing malady by virtue of the Holy Host, sent his coronation crown to the church as a symbol of gratitude.

At the beginning of the French Revolution, the Holy Chapel was claimed by the revolutionaries, who despoiled the church of its ornaments and converted the building into a prison and workshop. Somehow the church's organ and the Holy Host were saved and brought to the parochial Church of Saint Michel for safekeeping. Because the Holy Host was kept there, it was proposed that the Church of Saint Michel be designated a cathedral.

This refuge, however, proved to be unsafe in the extreme. On

February 10, 1794, in the presence of a representative of the Revolution, the Holy Host was "burned to atoms."

The Church of Saint Michel was later converted into a "temple de la Raison," a Temple of Reason, where bulletins of the law were published.

As for the Holy Chapel, it was destroyed on August 23, 1802, after its use as a prison and workshop. It is said that no vestige of it remains.

Chapter 24

THE MIRACLE OF
AVIGNON, FRANCE

1433

After Louis VIII, King of France, was successful in exterminating the Albigensian heresy which, among other offenses, denied the Real Presence, he vowed to arrange a public demonstration in reparation for the sacrileges which the heretics had committed.

The city chosen for this public reparation was Avignon, and the date selected by the King was September 14, 1226, the feast of the Exaltation of the Holy Cross, the day he had set for his abdication. A procession of the Holy Eucharist was planned, which was to culminate in the new chapel which had been erected in honor of the Holy Cross.

Waiting to receive the procession at the new chapel was the King, dressed in sackcloth, with a coarse rope about his waist and a taper in his hand. With him was the Cardinal Legate and the whole court, along with a great crowd of the faithful. The procession was led by Bishop Corbie, who bore the Blessed Sacrament through the city. Such was the devotion of the King to the Holy Eucharist, and so moved with grace was the crowd who attended the service, that the Most Blessed Sacrament was exposed all night and remained exposed for many days, until the Bishop thought it best that the Eucharist should remain perpetually exposed—a custom which was continued by his successors with the approbation of the Holy Father.

The zeal of the people eventually gave rise to a pious confraternity known as the Grey Penitents. In the Chapel of the Holy Cross the members enjoyed the privilege of perpetual adoration for 200 years. At the end of this time there occurred a spectacular miracle.

In order to better appreciate the miracle, we should first consider the location of the city. Avignon is situated on the Rhone River, while the district around the city is watered by the Durance and a tributary of the Vancluse. More than once the city had suffered the effects of destroying floods.

In the year 1433, the rivers became swollen with heavy rains and overflowed their boundaries, completely inundating the city. On November 29, the waters threatened the chapel of the Grey Penitents. The rains were so great that the directors of the confraternity feared the Blessed Sacrament would be touched by the rising waters. To avoid this desecration, they decided to remove it to safety.

After securing a boat, some of the members rowed over flooded streets to the chapel. On opening the door they found, to their great astonishment, that the water which had entered the chapel had parted, much as the waters of the Red Sea had parted in the time of Moses. Before them the water stood on the right and on the left, toward the walls, to a height of four feet. A dry passageway was left open from the door to the altar. Two of the witnesses fell on their knees before the miracle, while the rest hastened to spread the news.

An extract from the chapel's records concerning the miracle reads as follows:

> Great was the miracle in this chapel when the water entered it in the year 1433. Very strong, on the morning of Monday, the 29th November, began the waters to rise. They pressed into the chapel as high as the high altar. Under the altar were placed all paper and parchment books, cloths, towels and reliquaries, none of which was the least damp, although on the following day, which was a Tuesday, the water had not ceased to rise. On the next day, Wednesday, the waters began to abate . . .

On December 1, the day when the waters began to recede, great crowds converged on the chapel to witness for themselves the fact that books, papers, cloths and all else that had been placed under the altar had remained perfectly dry.

The miracle gave rise to a tremendous increase of devotion to the Blessed Sacrament, and it was debated how to properly honor and commemorate the event. It was finally decided that November 30, the day on which the miracle was first recognized, should be observed as a special feast.

For many years on this anniversary the Grey Penitents removed their shoes and advanced on their knees from the door to the altar.

Unfortunately, in 1793, at the height of the French Revolution, the Chapel of the Holy Cross was destroyed. At the end of this frightful period, however, the chapel was rebuilt through the generosity of a noble family. After the chapel's completion the Archbishop of Avignon renewed the privilege it had enjoyed in former times, that of being a chapel of Perpetual Adoration. It is said that the privilege continues to the present day.

Chapter 25

THE MIRACLE OF
TURIN, ITALY

1453

At the time of the miracle of Turin, the faith of the people had grown feeble, and it is thought that God wanted to give a sign to arouse them from their apathy. The miracle that effected the desired change occurred on June 6, 1453.

Two soldiers, described as being men of low class who had no respect for sacred things, had recently been released from military service. They were traveling through the city of Exilles when one of them decided to pillage the church. The other apparently agreed. After gaining entrance, the men gathered together costly vestments, candleholders and other articles. Moving to the altar, they opened the tabernacle and removed an ostensorium containing a large consecrated Host. Then gathering everything together, they packed it all atop a mule and set off for the city of Turin, where they hoped to sell all they had stolen.

After entering the gate of Turin in the early evening, the mule stumbled and fell to the ground. Everything packed on his back was jolted free and scattered on the ground—including the ostensorium containing the consecrated Host. But the Host did not fall. Rather, it rose in the air, where it remained suspended amid splendid rays of light like a heavenly sunburst. This occurred in the marketplace called the Piazza of Grain, located in front of the Church of San Silvestro, which is now known as the Basilica of Corpus Domini—Church of the Body of the Lord.

People who lived in the vicinity rushed forward to examine the prodigy. Among these were ten laymen: Pietrino of Gorzano who belonged to a noble family of Turin; Pietrino Da Aieris; Gasparino Buri Miolerio; Martino Bellenda; the nobleman Giorgio Gastaudo; the respectable Michele Murri; Giovanni Franconino, a blacksmith; Bonifacio of Cassino; Antonio Manerio of

Milan; and Bartolomeo Canarino.

After examining the miracle, a priest named Bartolomeo Coccono quickly notified the Bishop of Turin, Ludovico of Romagnano. After vesting in proper regalia, and accompanied by many noblemen and members of the court, the Bishop went to the site of the miracle and fell to his knees in wonder before the suspended Host. After worshiping the Most Blessed Sacrament, he asked for a chalice. When the sacred vessel was given him he stood up and held it high. In view of everyone present, the Host slowly descended of its own accord until it rested within the chalice.

With the greatest devotion the sacred Host was conveyed to the Cathedral of St. John the Baptist, followed by many religious and numerous citizens, including the ten witnesses who had been among the first to see the miracle. Because of its brilliance everyone called the miracle the *Sun of Justice.*

In commemoration of the miracle a change was made in the responses following certain hymns sung during Benediction services in the Archdiocese of Turin. Instead of the usual versicle, *Panem de caelo praestitisti eis*—"He gave them Bread from Heaven," the priest would say *Hic est panis vivus*—"This is the living Bread." To this the people would respond: *Qui de caelo descendit*—"which from the sky descended." After Holy Mass, when the hymn *O Sacrum Convivium* was sung, the same two responses were recited. This practice was introduced by Bishop Ludovico of Romagnano, the one who had received the Host into the chalice at the time of the miracle. The practice was then extended to the Basilica of Corpus Domini by Mons. Rorengo di Rorà, and has been observed *immemorabili* in the parish church of Exilles, the church from which the Host was stolen.

The chalice in which the Host came to rest is kept in the metropolitan church. In shape it corresponds exactly to those used at the time of the miracle. Additionally, the coat of arms of the house of Rovere is found on the foot of the chalice, which indicates that it belonged to Canon Antoinetto Delle Rovere, who was the canon of the cathedral of Turin from 1449 to 1460.

The church at Exilles, from which the miraculous Host was originally stolen, suffered another loss closer to our own time when thieves entered the church on April 1, 1975. Apparently attracted by the value of the antique golden tabernacle, they actually detached it from the main altar and carried it off. This tabernacle, which many believe was the same one from which the ostensorium and the Host were stolen in 1453, was of stately appearance and intricate design. But the thieves were probably very disappointed to discover that it was actually composed not of gold, but of gilded wood.

And what of the Host of the miracle? On the order of the Holy See, conveyed to Turin during the canonical visit of Mons. Peruzzi in 1584, the Host was consumed, after having been perfectly preserved for 131 years. The reason given for this was ". . . not to oblige God to maintain an eternal miracle by keeping the Host always perfect and pure."

Because of the large collection of documents composed soon after the events of 1453, writings which are still extant, the miracle of Turin is a certainty. Documents of 1454, 1455 and 1456, the *Observations* recorded by Enea Silvio Piccolomini between 1460 and 1464, and the details written by the priest Giovanni Galesio a few years after the event, as well as the statements of the 10 laymen who were witnesses, all verify the event. For the details of the miracle given here we have relied for the most part on the writings of Father Galesio, a citizen of Turin whose writings, it is said, assumed the melody of verse.

In addition to the large number of manuscripts and documents dating from the time of the miracle, as well as those written in later centuries, various Popes have also recognized the miracle. Popes Pius II, Gregory XVI, Clement XIII, Benedict XIV, Pope St. Pius X, and Pius XI all granted indulgences and privileges. On the occasion of the fourth centennial celebration of the miracle, Pope Pius IX approved a special Office and Mass for the Archdiocese of Turin.

In 1953, for the fifth centennial observance of the miracle, special services were held in Exilles and also in Susa, one of the towns through which the thieves carried the Host. A magnificent procession in Turin re-enacted the journey taken by the thieves on their way to Turin. Taking part in this procession were cardinals, bishops and numerous priests and religious, as well as thousands of the faithful.

It is worth noting here that attached to the Cathedral of St. John the Baptist, where the miraculous Host was formerly enshrined, is the magnificent chapel in which is found another precious treasure: the Holy Shroud of Turin.

E. Reffo

Two soldiers pillage the Catholic church in Exilles. They took costly vestments, candleholders, etc., and removed from the tabernacle an ostensorium containing a large consecrated Host. They packed everything on a mule and set off for Turin to sell their acquisitions.

Above and following page: The miraculous elevation of the Host. In Turin, the mule stumbled and fell, scattering everything packed on its back—except the stolen Host, which rose in the air and remained suspended amid splendid rays of light like a heavenly sunburst. The Bishop was summoned; he came attired in proper vestments and fell to his knees in wonder, adoring the sacred Host. Then he held up a chalice. Slowly the Host descended until it rested in the vessel. Many contemporary documents attesting to this event are still extant, including the statements of ten eyewitnesses, and many popes have recognized the miracle of Turin.

E. Reffo

150

The Host is received in the Cathedral of St. John the Baptist after having been carried there by the Bishop and numerous other people in solemn procession.

The facade of the Basilica of Corpus Domini. It was in the square in front of this church that the miracle occurred; at that time it was called the Church of San Silvestro. Over the centuries many popes have granted indulgences and spiritual privileges to be gained in this basilica.

Chapter 26

THE MIRACLE OF
MORROVALLE, ITALY

1560

It was two o'clock in the morning on the Third Sunday after Easter, April 16, 1560, when the persistent ringing of the village fire bell awakened Padre Bonaventure, a member of the Order of Friars Minor. With a sense of dread, he hurriedly dressed and ran toward the patio of the monastery. From there he could see the Church of St. Francis. The light that flashed in the windows of the church meant only one thing—that a large fire was consuming it, and endangering the Blessed Sacrament.

Hearing the frantic ringing of the bell, the other priests and the people of the village rushed to help. A particularly valiant effort was made by two men, Antonio Lazzarini and Claudio Paganelli, but the intensity of the fire was too great, and they soon realized that all would be lost. The fire lasted seven hours. When it was over, the church had been reduced to a confusion of rubble and smoldering ashes.

From Ancona the provincial minister, Padre Girolamo, came to assess the damage, asking the assistance of Padre Battista and Friar Illuminato in inspecting the area around the destroyed high altar which lay on the ground.

While removing bits of burned wood and broken pieces of marble the three were astonished to discover, in a cavity amid ashes and small stones, a Host, pure white and perfectly intact. A closer inspection quickly revealed that the Host lay on a scorched corporal which, in turn, was arranged over a piece of linen that was badly burned.

At the sight of the perfectly preserved Host amid so much filth and destruction, the priests fell to their knees in adoration and prayed for mercy. All who saw the Host hailed the preservation as a miracle, especially since the tabernacle in which the Host was kept had been totally consumed by the fire, and the vessels in the tabernacle had all been destroyed. Further inspection of the area resulted in the recovery of the pyx in which the Host had been enclosed before the fire. The cover of this case is still preserved.

Since enthusiastic crowds of people from distant parts came to inspect the area, a commissioner of the Archdiocesan Curia of Fermo ordered that the place of the miracle be kept in a dignified and orderly manner.

The miraculous Host and the cover of the pyx were soon enclosed in a vase of crystal, which was then sealed. This was placed in a box of ivory, which was locked with three keys. Two keys were entrusted to the prior and one to the guardian of the monastery.

News of the miracle prompted Pope Pius IV to order a rigorous investigation. To supervise this duty he chose Ludovico, Bishop of Bertinoro, who was to be assisted by Cristoforo Bartoli, chancellor of the Church of Loreto. The details of the event were soon reported to the Pontiff, who in turn discussed the details with many distinguished ecclesiastics.

Five months after the miracle Pope Pius IV issued a papal bull dated September 17, 1560. In this document, after briefly citing the details given him, the Pope acknowledged Bishop Ludovico's integrity and prudence, and his considerable diligence in conducting the investigation of the miracle. Then he stated that he had consulted with many distinguished clergymen, who all agreed that there was no fraud or deceit in the report and that the event was above every natural explanation. It was their opinion and judgment that the event was *"indubitato miracolo"* (undoubtedly miraculous).

In his bull the Pontiff also announced that he was granting a plenary indulgence to all the faithful who would both confess their sins in a spirit of true penitence and visit the Church of St. Francis on the anniversary of the miracle. The Holy Father also granted permission for use of the Office of Corpus Domini on the anniversary of the miracle.

Thanks to the generosity of the people, who were intensely Christian, the Church of St. Francis was restored, becoming even more beautiful than it had been before the fire. The contributions of three families—the Lazzarini, Marchetti and Collaterali—financed the replacement of the altars. A plaque describing their generosity is still on display.

During the next 300 years the church experienced many transformations, and was visited every year by huge groups of people who wanted to avail themselves of the *Pardon,* the plenary indulgence granted by Pope Pius IV.

During the middle years of the 19th century, when Italy was divided among kingdoms, duchies and various nations, a great political unrest developed. There were wars between the various sections of Italy, and there was a great hostility between them and the Vatican. During this painful time, in the year 1860, anti-religious troops and vandals entered the Church of St. Francis, sent the friars away and stole various treasures and works of art. Some have speculated that the miraculous Host was stolen during this raid. Because of the valor of Padre Luigi and of his brother, the pharmacist Bartolomeo Baldassarrini, the painting entitled the Madonna of Grace was saved. This painting was of great age and value, and was greatly treasured by the people. It is now in the Church of St. Augustine.

After the desecration by the vandals, the Church of St. Francis fell into such a miserable condition that Mass and other religious services could no longer be held there. Because of this, the Vatican allowed the Pardon of Morrovalle to be transferred to the Church of St. Bartholomew, where it is still received. The Church of St. Francis has since been repaired in a grand fashion and is the admiration of pilgrims and tourists.

Although the miraculous Host has disappeared, the cover of the pyx in which it was enclosed before the fire is still preserved. This is kept in a crystal cylinder encased in a reliquary that is pedestalled and topped with a cross.

Above: Reliquary containing the cover of the pyx in which was kept the Host that was miraculously preserved from fire in Morrovalle in the year 1560. *Below:* The restored Church of St. Francis, also known as *Das Kloster* because of an adjoining convent. It was here that the fire occurred.

The Church of St. Bartholomew, where "The Pardon," a special plenary indulgence granted by Pope Pius IV and obtainable on the anniversary of the miracle, is now received. This church became the new place of receiving the indulgence when the Church of St. Francis was desecrated and pillaged by vandals in the 19th century.

Chapter 27

THE MIRACLE OF
ALCALÁ DE HENARES, SPAIN

1597

In the early part of 1597 the Jesuit church of Alcalá de Henares was visited by an unidentified man who confessed that he belonged to a Moorish group which had perpetrated a number of thefts in Catholic churches. Stricken in conscience, this man told the Jesuit priest, Juan Juarez, how he and his companions had stolen sacred vessels, which they had then sold for profit. The man also revealed the horrible sacrileges he and the others had inflicted upon the Hosts that were found in these vessels. He stated that he had with him a number of Hosts that had recently been taken from three different churches. Padre Juarez then received from the man 24 Hosts, all very white, and wrapped in a thick piece of paper.

Padre Juarez later confided the details of this recovery to Padre Gabriel Vazquez, who had first thought to use the Hosts in the next Holy Mass. But because in some places, such as Murcia and Segovia, some priests had been poisoned, they decided to keep the Hosts in a small silver box. Since they had no way of knowing whether the man's story was trustworthy, the priests did not know for certain if the Hosts had been consecrated. For this reason they were not put in a tabernacle, but in the church's pantry. Atop the box was placed a note which read: "Read this paper and do what is ordered in it." The instructions were that when the Hosts became spoiled they should be destroyed by water or fire, this being the method prescribed by the Church for the disposal of consecrated Hosts that are unusable for various reasons.

Eleven years later, in 1608, Toledo's provincial father, Dr. Luis de la Palmo, along with Padre Juarez, examined the Hosts and found that they had retained their whiteness and freshness. The provincial father then ordered that they be placed in a subterranean vault to see whether humidity would spoil them. The box in

158

which they were enclosed was properly labelled and placed in the vault beside a number of unconsecrated hosts, similarly boxed, and also labelled. In only a few months the unconsecrated hosts were found to have spoiled, while the original Hosts were still fresh and pure. This uncorrupted state was considered irrefutable proof that a supernatural power had protected them. A few months later, Padre Bartolome Perez suggested that the Hosts be placed in the tabernacle, where they belonged.

On hearing the opinion of illustrious doctors who confirmed that there was no scientific explanation for the non-spoilage of the Hosts, Don Pedro Garcia Carrero, a medical doctor and professor at the university, conducted a detailed public examination. During this examination five of the Hosts were broken. Their conservation and crispness convinced the professor that the preservation was truly miraculous, since the integrity of the Hosts defied the natural laws of science.

As soon as prominent theologians, religious and professors all likewise admitted without reserve that the soundness of the Hosts was a miracle, the rector, Don Francisco Robledillo, wrote to the Vicar General of Alcalá on July 16, 1619 asking for permission to declare the miracle publicly and to expose the Hosts for public adoration, as the people were eager to admire and worship the religious wonder.

The place chosen for the exposition of the Hosts was the chapel to one side of the altar of the Jesuit church. Here the Hosts were taken after a grand procession through the city's main streets, which were adorned for the occasion with hundreds of tapestries, flags and banners.

A memorable visit was made to the miraculous Hosts in 1620, when the monarch Don Felipe III came with his royal family and his entire court and gave to the Hosts a precious box made of mother-of-pearl and silver whose interior was covered with costly brocade. The Hosts remained in this box until an ostensorium was donated by Cardinal Spinola, Archbishop of Seville and Santiago.

The ostensorium measured two feet ten inches in height and was in the form of a four-sided lantern. Around a central post were positioned eight parts, each part containing three Hosts arranged vertically. The parts formed an octagon around the central post, and the whole was enclosed by four sides of glass. A small cupola at the top was surmounted by a small elegantly carved cross. It is said that for many years there hung from this cross a splendid ring given to the miraculous Hosts on September 18, 1810 during a visit by Joseph Bonaparte, who had been crowned King of Spain by his brother Napoleon.

The Hosts remained in the chapel of the Jesuit church until the year 1777, when King Carlos III dictated a royal order to Canon Ramón de los Herreros directing that the Sacred Hosts should be transferred to the Holy Magistral Church. In due time they were taken there in great solemnity. Also transferred were the images, jewels, ornaments, vases, lamps and everything else that depicted the miraculous Hosts or had been given to adorn their place of exposition.

In the Holy Magistral Church the Hosts were especially venerated on Ascension Thursday, a day designated as the feast of the miracle. Every year on that day the people of Alcalá de Henares dressed in their finest clothes to participate in the festivities, which were said to have been so elaborate that it was impossible to describe them properly.

In 1904 the Holy Magistral Church was declared a national monument, but in 1931, when political conditions were developing into what would become the Spanish Civil War, the government prohibited all outdoor religious demonstrations, forcing the celebrations to be conducted within the church. These, too, were curtailed and then discontinued in 1936 when the Spanish Civil War began.

Due to the increasing opposition of revolutionary forces, and the great restlessness of many Spanish people who had been influenced by the anti-Catholic fury of the revolutionaries, all holy objects were hidden in various places for safekeeping. The ostensorium containing the 24 miraculously preserved Hosts was hidden by a priest in a secret location in the church, known to only a few priests of the community.

Eventually, the church was seized and converted into a military fort. A cannon was placed in the tower, and machine guns were positioned in the windows. Later, both the city and the Holy Magistral Church were bombed. To complete the devastation, a flammable liquid was thrown inside the church and ignited.

Either before or during the destruction of the church, a priest who knew the hiding place of the Hosts entered the building to save them, but he was discovered and assassinated, as were very many other priests and nuns during the Spanish Civil War. While it is known that the Hosts were recovered from their hiding place in the church, their present safety and whereabouts are unknown. It is the prayer of the people that a miracle will be performed to restore to them the 24 miraculous Hosts, which they hope to enshrine above the main altar of the newly restored basilica.

Ostensorium containing 24 Hosts which were returned after having been stolen by Moors from 3 different Catholic churches in Spain in 1597. These Hosts remained miraculously fresh and incorrupt and were venerated for centuries, but were then hidden in a secret location in a church when the Spanish Civil War broke out with all its anti-Catholic fury. While it is known that the Hosts were recovered from the church before its destruction by the revolutionaries, their present safety and whereabouts are unknown. It is the prayer of the people that a miracle will restore the 24 miraculous Hosts for their adoration.

Chapter 28

THE MIRACLE OF FAVERNEY, FRANCE

1608

The Eucharistic miracle that occurred in Faverney, France involved not a Host turned to flesh, nor one that bled, but consisted of supernatural immunity from the law of gravity.

The abbey in whose church the miracle occurred had been founded by St. Gude in the eighth century. It was established under the rule of St. Benedict, and was named *Notre Dame de la Blanche,* Our Lady of the White, in honor of a small statue that is now situated in the chapel to the right of the choir. The abbey originally housed nuns, but monks replaced the nuns in 1132.

The religious life of the abbey in the early 1600's was not as fervent as it should have been. The community numbered only six monks and two novices. In order to maintain the people's faith, then weakened by the Protestant influence of the time, the monks held certain annual ceremonies, including adoration of the Blessed Sacrament in honor of Pentecost and the Monday following the feast. In preparation for the ceremonies, an altar of repose was arranged before a decorative grille near the entrance gate of the choir.

In 1608 the services on Pentecost Sunday were attended by a great number of people. At nightfall, when the doors to the church were shut and the monks were preparing to retire, two oil lamps were left burning before the Blessed Sacrament, which was left exposed on the altar in a simple monstrance.

The following day, Monday, May 26, when the sacristan, Don Garnier, opened the doors, he found the church filled with smoke, and flames rising on all sides of the altar. He rushed to the monastery to warn the monks, who immediately joined in his efforts to save the church. While the flames were being extinguished, a young novice named Hudelot, who was only 15 years old, noticed that the monstrance was suspended in the air—lightly inclined toward, but not touching, the grille at the back of the altar.

News of this prodigy spread quickly, and villagers and priests from surrounding areas soon filled the church. The Capuchin friars of Vesoul, too, hurried to witness the spectacle. Many knelt in awe before the suspended monstrance, while a great many of the skeptics approached to examine the miracle for themselves. Throughout the rest of the day and during the night no restrictions were made, and the curious were permitted to move freely about the area.

During the early morning hours of Tuesday, May 27, priests from surrounding neighborhoods took turns offering Holy Mass in unbroken sequence while the prodigy continued. At about 10 a.m., at the time of the Consecration of the Mass celebrated by Father Nicolas Aubry, Curé of Menoux, the congregation saw the monstrance shift its angle to a vertical position and slowly descend to the altar that had been brought in to replace the one destroyed in the fire. The suspension of the monstrance had lasted 33 hours.

As early as May 31, an inquiry was ordered by His Grace Archbishop Ferdinand de Rye. Fifty-four depositions were collected from monks, priests, peasants and villagers. Two months later, on July 30, 1608, after studying the depositions and the material collected during his investigation, the Archbishop decided in favor of the miracle.

We should study in some detail certain aspects of the miracle.

Burned in the fire were the altar—which, except for its legs, was reduced to a heap of ashes—and all the altar linens, as well as certain ornaments. One of the two chandeliers that decorated either side of the altar was found melted from the heat—yet despite this heat, the monstrance was preserved from harm. The two Hosts in this vessel remained intact, suffering only a slight scorching. Four articles inside a crystal tube attached to the monstrance were also spared injury; these included a relic of St. Agatha, a small piece of protective silk, a papal proclamation of indulgences, and an episcopal letter whose wax seal melted and ran over the parchment without, however, altering the text.

Concerning the suspension of the monstrance, 54 witnesses, including many priests, affirmed that while the vessel seemed to incline toward the grille, the little cross on top of it was not in contact with this grille—in fact, it remained a goodly distance from it.

The witnesses also affirmed that the monstrance had remained without support for 33 hours.

These witnesses, who gave sworn statements, also signed a document which is still preserved in the church. They also swore that the suspension of the vessel was not affected by the vibrations of the people who moved around the miracle—nor of the people constantly coming in and going out of the church, of those standing and whispering beside the burned altar, of those who touched the grille, nor of the activity of the monks in removing the effects of the fire and assembling a temporary altar in the same location.

A marble slab was installed beneath the place of the suspension to mark the location of the miracle. Chiseled on the slab are the words, *Lieu Du Miracle,* i.e., Place of the Miracle.

In December of the year of the miracle, 1608, one of the two Hosts that had been in the monstrance at the time of the miraculous suspension was solemnly transferred to the city of Dole, which was then the capital of the county.

During the time of the French Revolution the monstrance of the miracle was unfortunately destroyed, but the Host was preserved from harm by members of the municipal council of Faverney, who kept it hidden until the danger passed. Later, the monstrance was reproduced from paintings dating before the Revolution. Kept within the new monstrance is this same Host that had maintained a miraculous suspension for 33 hours, after surviving a fire of such heat that a nearby chandelier was reduced to melted ruins!

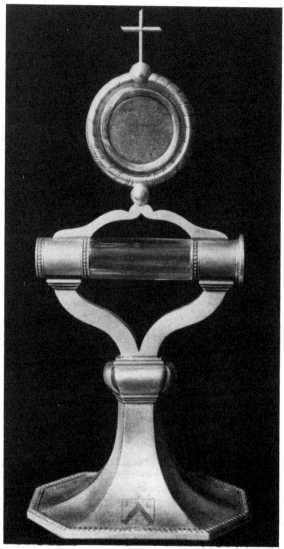

One of two Hosts which remained miraculously suspended in the air in Faverney, France on May 26 and 27 of 1608. The miraculous suspension of the Hosts in the monstrance began during a fire in the church and lasted 33 hours. The original monstrance was destroyed during the French Revolution; this one, including the crystal tube, was reproduced from pre-Revolutionary paintings. The four articles in the tube were also spared injury during the fire.

The Chapel of the Ostensorium in the Basilica of Faverney. The mural above the altar depicts the miraculous suspension.

A 17th-century engraving (see lower right-hand corner) in honor of the Host which was transferred to the city of Dole.

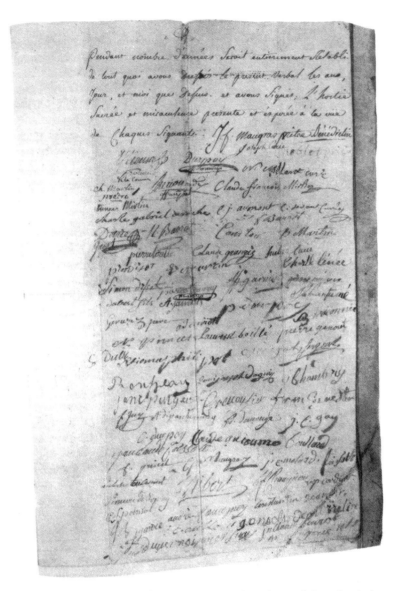

Document showing the signatures of those who witnessed the miracle in 1608.

Chapter 29

THE MIRACLE OF PATERNO, ITALY

1772

It was on January 18 of 1772 that the people of the Church of St. Peter first learned that the tabernacle of their church had been violated and that two containers holding consecrated Hosts were missing. Confused and outraged, the people searched the city for the missing Hosts and the culprit who had taken them. But after a few weeks their zeal diminished somewhat when no trace of either could be found.

Sometime later, outside the city near an estate belonging to the Duke of Grottolelle, neighbors were surprised and puzzled to see lights resembling stars appear at night in a field on the duke's estate. Night after night they sparkled, until at last it was concluded that they were of supernatural origin and indicated the place where the stolen Hosts were to be found. Accordingly, a number of pious persons gathered together and made a careful search of the area, but without results.

Then, on February 24, a great flame was seen darting around a heap of straw which lay in the field. On hearing of this latest phenomenon, an even larger group of people gathered to investigate. But after careful efforts most of the people, disappointed, abandoned the search. They were heading toward the city when they were called back by some of their companions who had lingered behind. Four members of the group returned: Tommaso Piccido, Giuseppe and Giovanni Orefice and Carlo Marotta.

Scarcely had they returned to the spot when all four found themselves seized, as it were, by some invisible and irresistible power that forced them to the ground. With great difficulty they stood up and were greeted by a bright ball of light issuing from the base of a nearby poplar tree. In the center of the blaze was a dove of dazzling whiteness. It rose a few feet above the ground and then flew back to the root of the tree, disappearing in a flood of light. Several people began at once to dig up the ground close to the poplar tree; at length one of the diggers came upon the Sacred Hosts, which had been buried only a few inches beneath the soil. One of the priests of the church gathered the Hosts into a clean linen cloth, and, amid great rejoicing and relief, the Blessed Sacrament was restored to the tabernacle.

The matter, however, did not end here. The next evening the lights again appeared in the field. This convinced the people that there were still other Hosts to be found. Another search was conducted, but without results. The following night a number of tiny flames appeared in the vicinity of a heap of straw. Then a glowing light seemed to rise at times from the earth and disappear again into the ground. Another search was conducted and, when a clod of earth was raised, a large number of sacred Hosts were found lying underneath.

In the company of many parishioners, the priest brought this second collection of Hosts to the church—but this time amid more pomp and celebration. Arriving at the church, the group offered heartfelt praise and thanksgiving for the heavenly signs that had given proof of the Lord's presence in the Blessed Sacrament.

The appearance of mysterious lights in the field should not be dismissed as a triviality or an invention. A similar phenomenon was witnessed by the people of Annaya, Lebanon in 1899 for 45 nights following the burial of St. Charbel Makhlouf, a Lebanese monk and hermit. Investigation of these lights resulted in the monk's disinterment and the discovery that his body was incorrupt. Not only was the body incorrupt, but for many years it also exuded a mysterious fluid that defied explanation by men of science. St. Charbel was canonized on October 9, 1977.

The Archdiocese of Naples possesses papers drawn by Cardinal Sersale, who was the Archbishop of the diocese when the miracle of Paterno occurred. These documents give the detailed statements of trustworthy persons who witnessed all the unusual events concerning the miraculous discovery of the Hosts and swore to their authenticity.

Chapter 30

THE MIRACLE OF BORDEAUX, FRANCE

1822

When order was restored following the French Revolution (1793-1798), there arose within the Church a great endeavor to repair the damage inflicted during those terrible years of upheaval, confusion and destruction. Thus a great period began for the Church in France, with the founding of many religious organizations that occupied themselves in various charitable endeavors.

The city of Bordeaux was blessed with three new religious communities. Father William Joseph Chaminade established a congregation for men called the Marianists; Mother de Laourous founded a congregation for the care of destitute women; and Father Peter de Noailles organized an association of women called the Holy Family of Bordeaux, whose members served the Church in various ways. This last congregation, whose members are sometimes called the Ladies of Loreto, was established in 1820, two years before the miracle. Its founder, Father de Noailles, was at that time a parish priest of the Church of St. Eulalie. The congregation of the Holy Family of Bordeaux increased rapidly, with many houses being established both in Bordeaux and in the surrounding countryside. It was in the chapel of one of these houses that the miracle of Bordeaux took place—specifically, the house at 22-24 rue Mazarin.

We will let the officiating priest relate the facts of the miracle as he carefully recorded them. The following is a translation of part of the document.

> I wish to declare that I am a priest now living near the parish of Saint Eulalie of Bordeaux. I have no intention but to confirm, in public, the favor that I wish to record concerning the event in the establishment of the Ladies of Loreto. I

171

was witness to this prodigy myself. I wish to attest and affirm before my Saviour, my God, the truth of the facts contained in the present declaration.

The priest Noailles, superior of the Institute of Loreto, could not himself give the Benediction to the community of Loreto and begged me to replace him for this service. I went to the house of these sisters, the third of this month, Sunday the feast of Septuagesima, at four o'clock in the afternoon. As soon as I arrived I was ready to give the Benediction. Naturally I exposed the Blessed Sacrament, but I was not finished blessing the Sacrament with the incense when I looked at the ostensorium. I realized that I had placed the holy Species there, but instead of the holy Species, I saw our Saviour, head, chest and arms, in the middle of the circle that served Him as a frame like a painting, but with this difference, that the painting looked alive.

His figure was very white and represented a young man about thirty years old, extraordinarily beautiful. He was dressed with a dark red scarf draped over His shoulder and chest. His head was inclined from time to time on the right side and the left side. Struck by this miracle and not believing my eyes, I thought it was an illusion, but the miracle continued. I could not stay in this uncertainty and I made a sign to the server who was holding the censer to approach me. I asked him if he saw something extraordinary. He answered that he had already perceived the miracle and that he could still see it. I told him to go and get the superior. There in the sacristy she was herself struck by this spectacle and absorbed with sentiments that inspired her. As for myself, I prostrated upon the floor. I only raised my eyes and was humbled in the presence of my Saviour. Tears of joy came to me because of the favor. The miracle continued during all the hymns of the Blessed Sacrament, the canticle and the orations. When the canticle was finished I approached the altar, I don't know how, because it seemed to me that I would not have the courage at this time. I took in my hands the ostensorium and gave the Benediction, contemplating all the time our Divine Saviour who was visible in my hands. I gave to the Ladies of Loreto the miraculous blessing which was, without a doubt, very efficacious to this new establishment. I placed the ostensorium on the altar, but when I opened it I did not see the Host in which our Saviour came to give the Benediction. All trembling and with tears in my eyes, I left the chapel.

As soon as I was outside the chapel all the persons of the house and the laypeople of the parish talked to me asking me if I had seen the prodigy and asked me many questions about the subject. I could only say these words: "You have seen our Saviour, which is a signal favor He has accorded us in order to make us remember that He is really with us and to ask you to love Him always, and more so than before, and to practice the virtues since He gave you such a great grace." I left and went home, but during the night I could only think about the miracle I had witnessed. Next day, Monday, I went to the parish of Saint Eulalie and I found the priest Noailles. I told him what had happened and other persons came, too, and spoke about the miracle. Even though I was thinking of talking about it at length, the altar boy and a few strangers who were in the chapel had already told him what they had seen . . .

Whatever happened I declare what I saw and what I almost touched with my own hands. Whatever will be the consequences of my testimony, I would be regarded as very ungrateful and the most guilty of all men if I refused to attest to the truth.

The document was signed, "Delort, priest," and was dated February 5, 1822.

In addition to this testimonial, the Mother Superior, who was kneeling in the sacristy, also gave an "Attestation." In the beginning of this declaration she acknowledged that although it was then the custom to lower the eyes before the Sacramental Jesus, she nevertheless felt inclined to look upon the Host. She continues:

I perceived that the Species was replaced by our Saviour Jesus Christ all illuminated. I could see His head to His chest. He was framed in the circle of the ostensorium, but He seemed to move from time to time and then His face seemed to want to come out of the circle on the side where I was. I saw light flashing from all sides and so quickly that each seemed, for a moment, to resemble long stems ending in a burst of a flower before it disappeared. Occupied with this during the hymn of the Blessed Sacrament, the orations and the canticle, I did not have the strength to sing because inside of me was a great fervor. I told myself I would be glad if it were really my God who wanted to show Himself, and I would be happy to see Him since I had often wished this favor. I was feeling it was only an illusion, but I could always see the Saviour under the same form. I was so occupied with this presence that I did not perceive the effect produced on the priest and the others. I went home without speaking to anyone, but there were people coming to me to tell me what they had seen. I then realized that I had not made a mistake and I bless our Saviour for the graces He had accorded our poor house. I attest all these things in the presence of Jesus, Mary and Joseph . . . Although we do not always see Him with the eyes of the body, He did give me the grace to see Him.

This document was signed "Mère Trinité, Supérieure de la Maison de Lorette, the 6th of February, 1822."

Other testimonials were given and signed by the altar boy and several of the witnesses, all of whom testified that they saw the head and chest of the Saviour with His arms moving while He smiled sweetly at the gathering. They declared that at times His left hand rested gently on the red scarf that was draped over His shoulder while the right hand was raised in blessing. The vision endured throughout the Benediction service, which lasted about 20 minutes.

On the basis of all the reports, the Archbishop of Bordeaux pronounced the Church's recognition. Pope Leo XII soon affirmed the event and signed a brief establishing the feast of the Holy Family within the church in commemoration of this event, and in recognition of the order in whose chapel the miracle had occurred. The Pope likewise arranged that the Sunday of Septuagesima, the day on which the miracle had taken place, should be observed as the Feast of the Holy Family—an unusual double observance which seems to have been allowed only to Bordeaux. In 1921 Pope Benedict XV extended the Mass and Divine Office of this feast to the entire Church. It is celebrated during the Christmas season.

Each year in the houses of the congregation of the Holy Family there are celebrations honoring this miracle, but only among the sisters, since few Catholics, we are told, know about the event. The simple monstrance used on the day of the miracle is always kept in a house of the order in Bordeaux.

Fr. Peter de Noailles, the founder of the congregation of the Holy Family and the parish priest at the time of the miracle, is a candidate for canonization.

The ostensorium in which Father Delort and a whole church full of people, both religious and lay, saw the head and chest of the Saviour as a young man about 30 years old, extraordinarily beautiful. He moved His arms and smiled sweetly at the gathering. This took place for a period of 20 minutes during Benediction of the Blessed Sacrament in the chapel of the "Ladies of Loreto" in Bordeaux, France in 1822.

A painting depicting the figure of Christ as He appeared in the
monstrance.

Mother Trinité, one of the witnesses of the miracle. She wrote and signed an attestation dated February 6, 1822; other testimonials were signed by the priest, the altar boy, and several other witnesses.

The chapel of Our Lady of All Graces at "the Solitude," Labrede, France, which was built to house the tabernacle of the Miracle.

Chapter 31

THE MIRACLE OF DUBNA, POLAND
(now Dubna, Russia)

1867

To fully appreciate the miracle of Dubna, one must consider the political and ecclesiastical conditions in Poland beginning in 1863, four years before the miracle.

Neighboring Russia was then exerting its influence on Poland, trying to eradicate the Polish nationality and language. The official language of Poland became Russian, with the use of Polish being strictly forbidden in public places and in classrooms. Poles were deprived of employment, all societies were suppressed, Polish place names were changed to Russian and private lands were confiscated.

For the Church in Poland, conditions were both unreasonable and difficult. Since Catholicism was acknowledged as the dominant religion, a forceful—and successful—effort was exerted to sever all allegiance to the Pope and to diminish his authority over the Church. Convents were suppressed, Church property was confiscated, and public devotions, processions, the erection of wayside shrines and the repair of places of worship were prohibited, while schismatic liturgical books and devotions were forcibly introduced into Catholic churches.

In 1865, all diplomatic relations ended between Russia and Pope Pius IX, who was favorably disposed and sympathetic toward the Poles. Instead of allowing the pope to direct the Church, a college of canons was formed at St. Petersburg to function as its chief governing body. The bishops, the deans and chapters opposed this measure, with the result that some high dignitaries of the Church were deported to Russia. Following their leaders' example, the rest of the clergy, too, courageously held their ground and refused to acknowledge the authority of the college of canons, much to the admiration and inspiration of the people.

Many frightened Catholics, however, succumbed to apostasy as schism within the Church became a reality.

In such oppressive times, it seems that the Saviour took pity on the embattled Poles. As if to renew their hope and give them a sign of His Fatherly protection, He appeared in a small Catholic church in Dubna, a small village of Poland. (Today, with the change in boundaries, Dubna is found in Russia, some 25 miles west of the city of Tula).

The people of the parish, being very devout, were secretly observing the Forty Hours Devotion on February 5 of 1867. While the monstrance was exposed atop the altar, the faithful who were closest to it remarked to one another that soft glowing rays were streaming from the Host. Then suddenly, the distinct form of Our Lord appeared in the midst of the Host!

The parish priest who was conducting the ceremonies carefully examined the miracle. Moreover, many men of the congregation approached the altar to examine the apparition for themselves—although through either fear or devotion they found themselves unable to ascend the altar steps. The apparition is said to have continued to the end of the devotions. It was seen by all present—both by Catholics who were attending out of reverence and by schismatics who had been attracted out of curiosity.

News of the occurrence spread throughout the neighborhood and the village, and since it had been witnessed by a few schismatics, it came to the attention of the authorities. The priest was subsequently called before the director of police to give a deposition. The information was then forwarded to the Governor of Schitomir, who threatened to imprison anyone who spoke of the miracle. The priest nevertheless gave a detailed accounting to his bishop, who requested silence on the subject for fear the government would order the closing of the church.

Although the news of this miracle spread quietly and secretly, it became well known throughout suffering Poland—to the great consolation and encouragement of the faithful as they awaited the restoration of their nation and the return of freedom to practice their holy Catholic Faith.

Chapter 32

THE TWO MIRACLES OF
STICH, WEST GERMANY

1970

Stich is the smallest of three hamlets that form a parish located in the Bavarian region of West Germany near the Swiss border. In 1970 all three hamlets were served by a priest from the shrine of Maria Rhein, which dates from Roman times. Because the parish priest was ill, a visiting priest from Switzerland assumed his duties and prepared to celebrate a Tridentine Mass in the chapel of Stich at 8:00 in the evening of Tuesday, June 9, 1970.

The Mass progressed in the traditional fashion until after the Consecration when the priest suddenly noticed, on the corporal next to the chalice, a small reddish spot that soon grew to the size of a coin. At the elevation of the chalice, the priest noticed another red spot on the corporal at the place where the chalice had rested. Suspecting a leak, he quickly passed his hand under the base of the chalice, but found it to be completely free of moisture.

After the completion of the Mass the priest thoroughly inspected the three cloths that covered the altar: the corporal, a small narrow cloth beneath it that served as a second corporal, and the long altar cloth that covered the whole altar. Since everything was completely clean, no cause could be found for the unexplained appearance of the spots. After the stained cloths were locked in a safe place, the priest journeyed to the rectory to report the incident to the ailing pastor.

On Thursday, June 11, the stained cloths were more closely examined by the pastor and the Swiss priest, both of whom were unable to find a natural explanation for the stains. After being photographed, the cloths were sent to a chemical laboratory for analysis.

The results of the tests were conveyed to the priests by Sister Marta Brunner of the Polyclinical Institute of the University of Zurich. In her letter to them, which was also signed by those who had conducted the tests, she declared that the cloths had been handed over to four different persons engaged in analysis, without their being told a single word about what had occurred on the altar. She wrote:

> I have complied with your strict order, merely asking the experts whether these were wine stains, blood stains or another substance. The results of the four analyses indicated that the stains were caused by human blood. In addition to this, the director of the clinical laboratory said that in his considered judgment the blood was most certainly that of a man in agony.

The persons engaged in the analysis were the Director of the Chemical Laboratory, the Chief of the Blood Control Laboratory, a student in medicine in his sixth term, and the Chief of the Laboratory for the Analysis of Hemorrhage and Coagulation.

Affixed to Sister Marta's letter were the stamps of the Clinical Institute for Radial Therapy and Nuclear Medicine, and the stamp of the Polyclinical Institute of Zurich University.

On July 14, 1970 at 8 o'clock in the evening, the Swiss priest was scheduled to celebrate another Holy Mass, according to the Tridentine missal, in the chapel of Stich. This date happens to have been the 400th anniversary of the issuance of Pope St. Pius V's bull *Quo Primum* in 1570. In that document the Pope ordered that Mass throughout the world be said according to the Roman missal; bishops were thus no longer free to issue their own missals. The missal of Pope Pius V has come to be known as the "Tridentine" missal, as it was issued as part of the reforms of the Council of Trent.

Before beginning Mass the priest made certain that the altar stone, the altar cloths, the corporal and the chalice were absolutely clean and in good condition. Nevertheless, shortly after the Consecration red spots again appeared on the corporal. Turning slightly aside, the priest signalled to the sacristan, who was in the sanctuary, to approach the altar. While the sacristan looked in bewilderment at the spots, the priest distributed Holy Communion. Noting the unusual behavior of the sacristan, members of the congregation suspected that something unusual had taken place and were noticeably restless during the remainder of the Mass. The priest satisfied the people's curiosity at the end of Mass by permitting them to approach the altar to inspect the stains for themselves.

This second incident was likewise reported to the pastor without delay. Because the cloths of June 9 had been entrusted to the Polyclinical Institute of the University of Zurich, the pastor decided to send the cloths of July 14 to the District Hospital of Cercee.[1] The same precautions were taken, and nothing was said about the origin of the stains. The scientists were simply asked to identify the fluid that caused them.

The results of the tests on the stains of July 14 were issued on August 3, 1970. The report, a copy of which was forwarded to the bishop, stated briefly that the stains consisted of human blood.

After the results of these tests had been received, depositions were taken from some of those who had seen the stains on the altar at the time of the July 14 miracle. On November 8, 1970, the sacristan of the chapel of Stich, Mr. Joseph Talscher, declared:

> On the evening of July 14, Father was celebrating Holy Mass in the chapel of Stich. Mindful of what had happened on June 9, we made certain that the cloths covering the altar were spotlessly clean . . . After taking Holy Communion, the priest made a sign to me and pointed to the altar. Then I saw the stains. After Mass we all took a closer look at the cloths and especially the large stain which was the size of a priest's host. We saw a cross very distinctly on it. We looked at each other in astonishment. There was little difference between the stains and those of June 9 when the same priest was saying Mass. I am prepared to repeat all this again on oath.

Mr. Johannes Talscher, the sacristan of the shrine of Maria Rhein, and brother of the sacristan of Stich, declared that he had attended Holy Mass on July 14 in the chapel of Stich. He added:

> I knew about the blood miracle of June 9 when the same priest was saying Mass, so I was hoping that it would happen a second time . . . At the end of Mass the Reverend Father told us to say three *Pater Nosters* in honor of the Most Precious Blood of Our Lord. Then, visibly moved, he told us that the phenomenon of June 9 had occurred again. We were allowed to come to the altar. I saw four spots. One was the size of a priest's host and a cross was visible on it. Another

was the size of a small host, and the other two were smaller. They were all brownish red. It is my firm and considered opinion that these mysterious blood stains have no natural explanation.

A nurse of the Municipal Hospital of Rosenheim, West Germany, who is also a religious sister, was present at the Mass of July 14 and gave further details in her deposition of November 10, 1970:

> We all went to the altar. First we saw three stains, one of which was the size of a large host like that which the priest takes. The other two were like those given to the faithful. Then my sister Maria let out a cry of surprise and pointed to a fourth stain on the gospel side of the altar. We all remarked excitedly, "Look, there is a cross on each of them!" The outlines of the stains were sharp. They did not disperse along the strands of the fabric as ordinary liquids do, but went right through the altar cloths, and it was "tacky." All those present were amazed and profoundly moved, as in a state of shock.

In still another deposition, jointly signed by several others who had been present at the July 14 Mass, it was declared that after viewing the stains it was found that they were still damp and of various sizes. "The same stains could still be seen on the small cloth beneath the corporal . . . Many of these stains had a cross in the middle. In addition to this, both the two altar cloths were soaked with the same stain."

The Bishop of Augsburg, Joseph Stimpfle, had been timely notified of both incidents. He appointed a commission of inquiry, and on October 9, 1970 the Swiss priest was asked to give all the particulars of both miracles. After study of the results of the scientific examinations and after interviews of the witnesses, the matter was referred to the Doctrinal Congregation in Rome.

The people of Stich feel privileged to have had two Eucharistic miracles occur in their humble chapel, and, as a result, have experienced a deeper reverence and love for the Holy Eucharist.

---

1. This is a phonetic rendition; the spelling has not been verified.

Chapter 33

MORE EUCHARISTIC MIRACLES

While interesting details are thankfully available about many Eucharistic miracles, there are a great number whose stories are more simply told. Many of these accounts have been bequeathed to us from the earliest Christian times in the writings and biographies of the saints and other holy persons.

There are, for instance, those miracles related by St. Cyprian, who was Bishop of Carthage for several years until his death in the middle of the third century. Sometime during the saint's bishopric there developed a great apostasy which inflicted every kind of torture on those who refused to deny the true faith in favor of idols. In fear of such sufferings many did deny the Faith, or were obliged to flee to safer territories.

One Catholic couple, forced to flee, found it necessary to entrust their child to the care of a servant who they thought was trustworthy. The servant, however, lost no time in taking the small girl before the apostate magistrates of the city. They forced her to eat a piece of bread that had been dipped in the blood of animals sacrificed to the idols. (This was a variation on the usual custom of giving a Christian a piece of the actual meat of an animal that had been sacrificed.)

After returning home, the mother, not knowing what the servant had done, took the child with her to Holy Mass, intending for her to take part, since at that time it was customary for children to consume a little of the Precious Blood. But the little girl, although too young to tell what the servant had done, experienced an uncontrollable restlessness as soon as she entered the church. St. Cyprian tells us that he himself witnessed the unnatural behavior of the child, who was crying and throwing herself from side to side. At the time of Communion, when the deacon approached her with the chalice, the child turned from him, closed her lips and refused to communicate. Nevertheless, a few drops fell onto her lips and entered her mouth, but she could not retain them. The child's unusual behavior in church led, it is said, to the discovery of the servant's guilt.

*   *   *   *   *

During the same persecution it seems to have been the practice to give the faithful a portion of the consecrated Host to keep in the home so that in the event of imminent capture, they would be able to strengthen themselves with the Body of Christ. St. Cyprian tells us that a woman who had received such a portion placed it in a coffer for safekeeping, but afterwards the woman lapsed into apostasy. When she finally opened the coffer, flames burst forth from the container. The saint related that the unexpected fire drove the woman away in great fear and remorse.

*   *   *   *   *

St. Cyprian also tells of a man who had fallen into apostasy and yet attempted to receive the Holy Eucharist, approaching a priest who did not know about the communicant's participation in idolatrous activities. According to the prevailing custom, the consecrated Host was given into the hands of the communicant. It is recorded that as soon as the Host touched his hands, it disappeared, and there remained before his astonished eyes only a few ashes.

St. Cyprian died during this persecution, but at his beheading he showed such courage and willingness to die for the Faith that many of the weak who had considered apostatizing drew great strength to proceed with renewed vigor in the practice of their religion.

*   *   *   *   *

St. John Chrysostom (347-407) had a disciple who induced his wife, an Arian heretic, to accompany him on one occasion to John Chrysostom's church. When the woman received the Host at the Mass, she held it in her hand until she reached home and then put it into her mouth to eat as a morsel of ordinary food. However, when she tried to bite it, she found it had become "a veritable petrifaction, hard as flint." Alarmed at this prodigy, she went without delay to the saint, showed him the stone with the marks of her teeth, and implored absolution. This miracle was related by Msgr.

Guerin, chamberlain of Pope Leo XIII, in his *Vies des Saints*.

* * * * *

A similar report of an unworthy reception was recorded by Sozomen, a fifth-century historian. He stated that at Constantinople a man attempted to convert his heretical wife. Under the weight of his persistence, she simulated a change of life and attended Holy Mass. At the time of Holy Communion, when she received the Host, she immediately realized that it had been changed into stone.

* * * * *

Numbered among the saints of the Church are the father, mother, sister and brother of St. Gregory of Nazianzus (d. 389). During the funeral eulogy for his sister, Gorgiona, St. Gregory related that for several years she had suffered from a palsy which physicians were unable to cure. Having the Blessed Sacrament reserved upon an altar in her home, as was permitted to some in the early days of Christianity, she turned to the Divine Physician one night and prayed earnestly for a cure. In imitation of the woman in the Gospel who touched the hem of Christ's garment and was healed, Gorgiona approached the altar, rested her head upon it and resolved not to leave until she was cured. After anointing herself with blessed oil, she wept bitterly before the Blessed Sacrament. St. Gregory tells us that Gorgiona experienced a complete restoration of health that very night.

* * * * *

St. Gregory of Tours (d. 595) relates a most unusual event in his book entitled *Of the Glories Of the Martyrs*. Despite its almost unbelievable elements, the facts are supported by the historian Evagrius, who wrote:

> In the days when Mennas occupied the episcopal chair of Constantinople . . . there was in that city an old custom, when a large number of the consecrated particles remained after Communion, of causing boys to come in from the schools in order to consume them. It happened once that amongst the boys who presented themselves was the son of a glass manufacturer who was a Jew. Now when his parents in-

quired of him the reason for his prolonged absence the child related what had happened, and how he, with the other boys, had been fed. The father, in a storm of fury, seized the boy and cast him into a fiery furnace in which he was accustomed to fuse the glass. His mother sought the child, and finding him not, she went throughout the town weeping and tearing her flesh with grief, and calling on her son by name. It came to pass that the boy heard the voice of his mother and answered her out of the furnace. Immediately she broke open the doors, went in, and there beheld her child standing in the midst of the fiery coals, unharmed. Now when he was questioned as to the manner by which he had remained without injury, he replied that a lady clothed in purple had very frequently appeared, bringing him water and quenching the coals around him; also, when he was hungry, she brought him food. When Justinian the Emperor heard of this he placed both mother and son, after they had passed through the waters of Baptism, under the care of the clergy; but the father, who continued to refuse to believe in the mysteries of the Christian faith, he commanded, as being the murderer of his child, to be crucified in the suburb of Syca.

St. Gregory of Tours adds:

The boy received the Holy Eucharist in the Church of St. Mary, in which stands the image of the Blessed Virgin in a conspicuous place, upon which the eyes of the boy fell, and being drawn powerfully he entered the church. The image which he had seen in the church, with the child in her arms, was that of her who appeared to him in the midst of the fire. The boy received the bread, and therein the glorious Body and Blood of Jesus Christ.

The experience of this young boy brings to mind the Canticle found in the Old Testament book of Daniel, chapter 3, in which three young men were also thrown into a fiery furnace for refusing to adore an idol. After praying that all creation should bless the Lord, they too were released unharmed.

*   *   *   *   *

St. Gregory the Great (d. 604), Pope and Doctor of the Church, was another who, fortunately, has left us many writings in which he illustrates his love for the Holy Eucharist and the power of the Holy Sacrifice of the Mass. In his 37th homily he relates:

Not long ago it happened that a man was taken prisoner and carried far away. Now after he had been a long time kept in prison without his wife knowing anything about it, she believed him to be dead, and caused every week, on certain days, the Holy Sacrifice of the Mass to be offered for him. After a long time had elapsed the man returned home, and related to his astonished wife that on certain days of the week the chains which bound him became loose; in this way he succeeded at length in making his escape. Now when his wife inquired on which days of the week this wonder took place, she discovered that the days on which his chains became loose were those upon which the Holy Sacrifice of the Mass was offered for him.

In the fourth book of his *Dialogues*, or conferences about the miraculous lives of the saints, St. Gregory the Great relates the following occurrence:

Agatho, Bishop of Palermo, journeyed from Sicily to Rome. Upon the way he fell into the danger of being shipwrecked. A frightful storm arose, which well-nigh sank the vessel in which he voyaged. No hope remained but in the merciful pity of Almighty God. Then all began to pray and to offer up petitions to Him that their lives might be spared. Whilst they were thus praying a certain sailor was occupied in steering a boat which was fastened to the ship, but which, through the violence of the storm, broke away from her holdfast and sank with the unfortunate man beneath the waves, and Bishop Agatho reckoned him as dead. In the meantime the ship in which the Bishop sailed arrived, after many dangers, at the island of Ostika. Here the Bishop offered the Sacrifice of the Mass for the unfortunate sailor; and as soon as the ship was repaired, continued his voyage to Rome. When he landed he found the sailor, whom he believed to be dead, standing on the shore. Full of joy, he inquired how he had escaped the great dangers of so many days. The sailor then related how his little boat seemed continually on the point of capsizing, but always rose unharmed again to the top of the waves. Day and night he succeeded in struggling with the waves; but being weakened with hunger and thirst he must inevitably have gone to the bottom had not help been sent to him. "At length suddenly," narrated he, "when I was quite prostrate, and as it were out of my mind, knowing not whether I was sleeping or waking, I saw a man standing before me, who offered me bread. Scarcely had I received it when my strength returned to me, and soon after I was picked up by a ship and brought hither." When the Bishop learned the day on which this event took place he discovered that it was the same on which he had offered Holy Mass for the unfortunate man on the island of Ostika.

There is also a traditional account of a Eucharistic miracle involving St. Gregory the Great himself. There are different versions of this story, but it is said that there was a miraculous manifestation of the flesh of Christ as St. Gregory was offering Mass in the Sessorian basilica in Rome. This is reported by St. Gregory's two ninth-century biographers, Paul and John the deacon.

* * * * *

The author of *The Imitation of Christ*, Thomas á Kempis (d. 1471) (whom some have claimed was merely the translator of the work), lived to the age of 92. Of the 63 years he lived as a monk, 58 of these were spent as an ordained priest. In his *Chronicle of Mount St. Agnes* he relates two miracles of the Holy Eucharist. Regarding the first of these he tells us:

> One of our brethren commenced to say Holy Mass at the altar of St. Agnes. For a long time he had been obliged to make use of two crutches in order to go there. After having said Mass he found himself, through the power of Jesus Christ and the intercession of St. Agnes, so much strengthened that he was enabled to leave his crutches behind, returning to us in choir with a joyful heart. One of the brethren asked him of what he had done and thought during Holy Mass; he replied, "I considered the words of the Evangelist St. Luke, who himself relates of Jesus, 'And all the people sought to touch Him, for there went virtue out of Him and healed them all.'" Therefore the Most Holy Sacrament, in union with the prayers of the saints, is able even now to heal the sick in soul and in body.

The previous miracle was witnessed by Thomas á Kempis; the

following was told to him by the priest to whom the gift of faith was granted.

> A brother of our house, whilst he was saying Mass at the altar of St. Agnes, was one day suddenly and severely tempted by the devil in his belief concerning the Most Holy Sacrament, although this heavenly mystery was a constant source of the greatest consolation to him. Full of sorrow and pain he turned himself weeping to our Lord, and behold he heard an interior voice, which said, "Believe thou as St. Agnes, St. Cecilia, St. Barbara, and other holy virgins have believed who suffered death for Christ, nor ever doubted the least of His words." As soon as he heard these words every doubt vanished and the temptation passed away. After this he replied to all who suffered from such devilish temptation, "Believe as did Agnes, and thou wilt never err in the faith."

* * * * *

Only a few details are given us about the unusual events surrounding the famous and venerable Dominican, Father Francis Lerma. This devout priest slowly lost his vision, until he was unable to offer the Holy Sacrifice. He bore his affliction with angelic patience, although he yearned for the privilege of performing this function of his priestly ministry. So much did he desire to offer Holy Mass that he prayed for the divine Healer to restore his sight for the length of time that would be required to celebrate the Mass. After praying earnestly for this intention he was inwardly prompted to open a missal. To his surprise he was able to read the words. With great joy he entered the sacristy, vested, and approached the altar. At the completion of the Holy Sacrifice he returned to the sacristy, where blindness once again darkened his vision. The same happened day after day: Father Lerma's vision was restored for the celebration of Mass, but as soon as he left the altar, blindness again returned.

* * * * *

No authority is cited for the following case, but it is told that a German girl in the year 1584 decided to oppose the law of the Church and communicated on Easter morning without having observed the usual fast. The same day, she was possessed by a devil and for many months was frightfully tormented. During this time she saw and heard nothing; she foamed at the mouth and gnashed her teeth; she experienced lengthy and serious convulsions and exhibited all sorts of abnormal behavior. She was sometimes dragged by the demon to a higher level of the house, and at other times to a lower area, and was occasionally found hanging on a tree.

At length her father presented the problem to the parish priest, who blessed the house, placed crucifixes in the girl's bedroom and hung relics around her neck. Prayers were offered publicly in religious houses and schools. But the girl resisted. She threw the crucifixes aside, tore the relics from around her neck and resumed her abnormal behavior with more intensity. Finally it was thought to bring her to the neighboring church of Hilfsburg, where a relic of the holy Archbishop St. Boniface, the Apostle of Germany, was enshrined. With difficulty they brought the girl into the church. She was no sooner before the altar where the Blessed Sacrament reposed than the demonic influence ended and the girl was restored to normalcy.

*   *   *   *   *

Of all the generals who served King Louis XIV of France (reigned 1643-1715), General Turenne was considered the bravest by the king and was the most respected by members of the court. Turenne, however, was a Calvinist, an error he refused to correct despite the wishes of the king and the efforts of the celebrated orator and bishop, Bossuet. Turenne's prejudices against the Church were many. He was especially opposed to the doctrine of the Real Presence of Christ in the Blessed Sacrament, which seemed to him to be incredible, although he allowed that such a doctrine must be beautiful and consoling to those blessed with faith. He was known to have said: "Were I to be convinced of the Real Presence of Jesus in the Sacrament, prostrate in the dust I would adore Him incessantly."

Despite Turenne's obstinacy, Bishop Bossuet continued to discuss the doctrine with him; the two met for this purpose in the Louvre, the palace which today is used as an art gallery. During one of these meetings, fire was discovered in one of the galleries. With the blaze threatening to destroy many works of art, Turenne hurried at once to the scene and proceeded to direct the men in their efforts. Every effort was exerted to control the fire, but all measures were in vain.

The bishop, seeing the immensity of the fire and the imminent danger, is said to have followed a divine impulse. With all haste he made for the chapel, removed the ciborium containing the Blessed Sacrament and carried it to the opposite end of the burning gallery. After walking through clouds of smoke he approached the flames and pronounced a benediction. At once the flames began to die down until they were at last extinguished. The workers were struck by the might and majesty of the miracle and fell to their knees, intoning the *Te Deum*. Turenne likewise was amazed and fell to his knees to adore the Blessed Sacrament, which he now acknowledged with newfound faith. From the time of this miracle in 1667 until his death, Turenne was known to have loved and practiced the true Faith and to have adored with all humility and devotion the Holy Redeemer present in the Sacrament of the altar.

* * * * *

Following the conclusion of the concordat between Napoleon and the Holy Father in the year 1802, the churches of France were allowed to re-open. The event coincided with the celebration of Corpus Christi, which occurred that year on the feast day of the patron saint of the little village of Creteil. A celebration was planned that would do honor to all three events.

While the church was being cleaned, the path of the Corpus Christi procession planned, an outdoor altar erected and decorated with clusters of flowers, a young girl of the village named Henrietta Crete was reminded of the incidents in Scripture when the sick were brought to Our Lord as He passed by. His pity for the suffering, she considered, was ever the same. She formulated a plan, which she shared with her companions.

There was at the time another young girl, Augustina Mourette, the daughter of a wine merchant, who had lost the use of her arms, legs and voice as the result of illness. At the time of the feast, she had endured 18 months of paralysis.

On the day of the celebration, Henrietta Crete and her companions, all dressed in white and wearing veils on their heads, visited the invalid; they dressed her in her feast day best, and carried her in an armchair to the outdoor altar. Placing her near the altar, they awaited the arrival of the procession. When the priest approached with the Blessed Sacrament, the girls knelt in a circle around the invalid and prayed with great devotion for their friend's cure.

Greatly impressed with their fervor, the priest raised the monstrance high and blessed the invalid while reciting the customary blessing of the sick. At the conclusion of the blessing the congregation saw the sick girl rise from her chair without assistance and kneel with ease in thankful adoration before the Divine Physician. Augustina Mourette had been spontaneously and completely healed.

*   *   *   *   *

In May of the year 1847 the celebrated musician and pianist Hermann Cohen, a Jew born in Hamburg, was in Paris for a series of concerts. The prince of Moskowa, a friend of the pianist, was at that time conducting the choir's May devotions in the church of St. Valere.

Hermann Cohen accepted an invitation from the prince to conduct the choir for one of the services, but he was distracted and irreverent during the sermon and often chatted with his neighbors. However, when the moment came for Benediction, his attitude was completely changed. He himself recounts:

> Although I was not at all moved to bow the knee with the multitude, I felt within myself an inexplicable commotion. My soul, accustomed to the distractions of the world, seemed to find itself again, so to speak, and was at the same time conscious that something had passed within which was until now quite unknown. Without giving it a thought I bowed my knees. At the instant that the benediction of the Blessed Sacrament was given I felt for the first time an indescribable but agreeable movement within me. On the following Friday I went again, and the same interior movement occurred, only much stronger than before, and I felt as if a weight pressed upon my back, requiring me to bend the knee once more. Against my will I obeyed the impulse, when suddenly the thought rushed overpoweringly into my soul: *Thou must become a Catholic!*
>
> A few days after this I happened to be one morning in the neighborhood of the same church of St. Valere. The bell rang for Holy Mass. I entered into the house of God, and remained an immovable spectator of the Most Holy Sacrifice. I heard one, two, three Holy Masses without thinking. I could not understand what kept me. Towards evening I was again led to the same church, against my will—the bell seemed to

call me. I found that the All-Holy was exposed, and as soon as I perceived it I was drawn irresistibly to the communion rail and fell upon my knees. I bowed myself this time without resistance at the moment of Benediction, and when I rose up I felt a strange sense of rest enter into my soul. I went back to my room and lay down upon my bed, but during the whole night my spirit, whether waking or sleeping, was ever busied with the Blessed Sacrament. I longed with impatience for the time when the Holy Mass should be said, and from thenceforward I heard daily many Masses at St. Valere with an interior joy which filled my whole being.

Until this time the pianist had looked upon Catholics and Catholic priests as people to be avoided, but now he felt an irresistible impulse to speak to a priest about his experiences. He was directed to Abbé Legrand, whose advice he meant to follow, but as Hermann admits, "... the devil was not yet overcome." His concerts brought him large sums of money, which permitted him to revert to his indulgence of worldly amusements.

After giving a concert in Elms on August 8, 1847, he went, in spite of his friends, to a church and attended Holy Mass. During this service he received the grace of supernatural contrition. Twenty days later he received the Sacrament of Baptism at the hands of Abbé Legrand. After receiving the Sacrament of Confirmation he never tired of saying, "I have found Him whom I love. He belongeth to me and I to Him. Never more will I let Him go."

Shortly thereafter Hermann tarried one evening in the chapel of the Carmelite sisters where the Blessed Sacrament was exposed. Impressed on learning that some of these holy women remained throughout the night in adoration before the Eucharist, he determined to organize a confraternity of men who would perform a similar devotion. The Men's Association for the Adoration of the Blessed Sacrament was soon founded and, on December 6 of 1848, the first nocturnal adoration was held. Since that time the confraternity is said to have spread throughout France.

Prompted by his love for the Blessed Sacrament, Hermann entered the Carmelite Order in 1849 and received the name of Augustine Mary of the Blessed Sacrament. Later he received the Sacrament of Holy Orders.

Thus the famed musician who had journeyed throughout

Europe, charming his audiences with the perfection of his talents, now journeyed to preach the glories of the Blessed Sacrament and the joys of those who embrace it with love and adore it with fervor.

Having been invited to preach in England, he founded in Kensington the beautiful church of St. Simon Stock and served as the first prior of its monastery.

* * * * *

The religious fervor of the people of Ireland and their zealous allegiance to the Faith is beyond question and is well documented in Irish history. Also prominent in Church history are three remarkable incidents that sustained the Irish during times of danger and trial. Each of the occurrences has been recorded in the writings of Wadding (d. 1657), a historian and theologian.

The first incident occurred during the period of Norman influence. Despite their many faults, the Normans brought with them an enthusiasm for building churches and religious houses. Members of religious orders who maintained these buildings soon established other places of worship throughout the isle, with small chapels being constructed even at fords and on bridges. Besides daily Mass in the morning, there was the *morrow Mass* (or vigil Mass) celebrated at six in the evening for the workers who had to be in the fields early the next morning. With the proliferation of houses of worship, it was said that anywhere a traveler went he could hear a Mass bell and attend Mass in a convenient location.

The miracle connected with the church at Clonmel illustrates the devotion of the people and some of the Norman nobles to daily attendance at Mass. The event is recounted in this way:

> Edmund Butler, Baron of Cahir, according to his custom, was one day hearing Mass in this church [the Franciscan Church at Clonmel] when word was brought that the Earl of Ormond and the Baron of Dunboyne, with their followers in great force, were invading his territory. Without the least sign of being disconcerted, he made up his mind to remain to the end of Mass. For he thought it unworthy for any human consideration to lose Mass, by which, through the power of prayer, the enemy might be more easily overcome than by military force. Moreover, one could suffer no great loss who neglected everything rather than leave the divine propitiatory

Sacrifice uncompleted. For when Mass was over, he, with a few relatives and fighting men, delivered an attack, recovered spoils and preys, upset the design of a powerful enemy, and put them to a disgraceful flight.

Later in Irish history, in the early 17th century, Protestants undertook a fierce persecution against the Church. Priests were imprisoned or killed, ordinations were forbidden, and every manner of threat and abuse was suffered by the faithful. During this time there were two other wonderful occurrences, which were dutifully recorded by Wadding, a contemporary of the events.

In the *Wadding Papers* we are told that the Protestant Lord Deputy of Ireland once invited the whole council to a dinner and for entertainment engaged a comedian to play the part of a fool.

. . . This Fleming being a subtle and crafty knave and understanding the council to be greatly delighted with such things as should be reproachful to the Catholics, among many other knaveries that he used, began to imitate them in celebrating the Blessed Sacrament, so that taking a mangel of bread, he said the words of consecration, and lifted it up as the Catholics are used to do. In like manner taking a jug of beer, as he was lifting it up, he fell down on the ground with the jog a-melted. The council seeing this was mightily terrified, saying with words (though otherwise in thoughts) that he was not dead, thinking to conceal the miracle how be it was manifestly known and afterwards publicly declared to the detestable confusion to all such heretics as did hear of it.

The third miracle took place in Waterford and demonstrated the grace accorded a vulnerable group of people who had placed their trust in the Blessed Sacrament.

James Daton, a Franciscan friar, saying Mass in the city of Waterford in a secular man's house, was besieged round about [by soldiers] thinking to apprehend him, which was at the very Elevation, and that being declared to him whereby he might flee, [he] requested them not to trouble him while he had his Master, the Blessed Sacrament, in hand, who was valianter than an army of such soldiers as they were. So that the soldiers entered, and could see nothing but the white walls, how be that the house was full of people, and the priest at the altar with the Blessed Sacrament between his hands. This happened the 18th February in the year 1609.

* * * * *

Italy, the country of so many Eucharistic miracles already mentioned in this volume, was granted yet another miracle, that which occurred in the province of Abruzzi, in the town of L'Aquila, where St. Bernardine of Siena died and where his remains are still enshrined.

L'Aquila had suffered from two previous earthquakes before that of February 2, 1703, which took place suddenly and devastatingly. Over 2,000 persons perished, many of whom were in church. The quake began at the time of Holy Communion and was so sudden and intense that the church collapsed almost immediately. After the ground settled and the search for survivors had taken place, the priest was found dead in the ruins, still holding the ciborium in his hands. Beneath and around the ciborium, amidst the splinters and debris, 200 Hosts were found. The preservation of these Hosts, all perfectly whole and without the slightest injury, was accorded as a miracle.

* * * * *

In more recent times there are the cures which have taken place at Lourdes after the Blessing of the Sick with the Blessed Sacrament. Among the most famous are the cures of two laborers: Gabriel Gargam (French) in 1901 and Jack Traynor (English) in 1923. Both had multiple serious injuries and were unable to walk. Gabriel Gargam's cure came at the Blessing of the Sick a few hours after a Holy Communion during which he had received overwhelming graces and a spiritual cure earlier that day. Jack Traynor's cure began as he bathed in Lourdes water and was completed after the priest made the Sign of the Cross over him with the Blessed Sacrament. This cure became famous in England and resulted in many conversions.

Following page: The conversion of the Calvinist General Turenne of France as Bishop Bossuet extinguishes a fire by giving a blessing with the Blessed Sacrament.

—PART TWO—

EUCHARISTIC PHENOMENA IN THE LIVES OF THE SAINTS

Chapter 34

THE EUCHARISTIC DEVOTION
OF THE SAINTS

Devotion to the Holy Eucharist has been expressed in one way or another by all the saints of the Church. This is a statement that cannot be contradicted. Since Our Lord instituted this holy Sacrament to unite Himself with us, to nourish our souls, and as a means of retaining His presence among us in tabernacles throughout the world, the saints have embraced this treasure with faith and love. Their veneration has been manifested in various ways, with some saints being better known for this expression than others. Such love and devotion have not always been recorded, but those statements that have been written by the saints or their confreres are eloquent expressions of their loving regard and appreciation for this heavenly gift.

St. Alphonsus de Liguori expressed his heartfelt appreciation for the Blessed Sacrament in this way:

> Our most loving Redeemer, on the last night of His life, knowing that the much-longed-for time had arrived on which He should die for the love of man, had not the heart to leave us alone in this valley of tears; but in order that He might not be separated from us even by death, He would leave us His whole self as food in the Sacrament of the Altar; giving us to understand by this that, having given us this gift of infinite worth, He could give us nothing further to prove to us His love.

This same thought is also expressed by St. Peter of Alcántara, who wrote in one of his meditations:

> No tongue is able to express the greatness of the love which Jesus bears to every soul. Hence that His absence

might not be an occasion of forgetting Him, He left to His
spouse the Church, before His departure from this world,
this most holy Sacrament in which He Himself remained,
wishing that between them there should be no other pledge
than Himself to keep alive the remembrance of Him.

St. Mary Magdalen de Pazzi expresses her faith and love for the
Sacrament by praying:

O Lord, You are as truly present under the sacramental
species as You are in Heaven at the right hand of the Father.
Because I have and possess this great wonder, I do not long
for, want, or desire any other.

St. Teresa of Avila had the following thought-provoking consideration:

I cannot doubt at all Your Real Presence in the Eucharist.
You have given me such a lively faith that when I hear others
say they wish they had been living when You were on earth,
I laugh to myself, for I know that I possess You as truly in
the Blessed Sacrament as people did then, and I wonder what
more anyone could possibly want.

St. Teresa of Avila gives us cause to consider the great wisdom
and kindness of the Saviour in veiling Himself under the appearance of bread. She prays:

How could I, a poor sinner, who have so often offended
You, dare to approach You, O Lord, if I beheld You in all
Your majesty? Under the appearance of bread, however, it is
easy to approach You, for if a king disguises himself, it
seems as if we do not have to talk to him with so much cir-
cumspection and ceremony. If You were not hidden, O Lord,
who would dare to approach You with such coldness, so unworthily, and with so many imperfections?

St. Bernard calls the Sacrament of the Altar "The Love of
loves," while St. Thomas Aquinas said that the Holy Eucharist is
"a Sacrament of love and a token of the greatest love that a God
could give us." St. Laurence Justinian tells us, "We have seen the
All-Wise made foolish by an excess of love"—to which the Curé

of Ars, St. Jean-Baptiste Marie Vianney, adds, "It is the destiny of every consecrated Host to melt with love in a human heart."

It is said of St. Francis of Assisi that "every fiber of his heart was kindled into love for the Sacrament of Christ's Body," and he constantly urged his brothers to bring others to know and love Christ living in the Blessed Sacrament. From this love sprang St. Francis' deep reverence for priests. He declared that if confronted with an angel and an unworthy priest, he would kiss the hand that had touched the Body of Christ before saluting the angel. One day someone pointed out a priest living in notorious sin. Francis instantly knelt before him, kissing his hands and saying, "These hands have touched my Lord, and out of love for Him I honor His vicar. For himself he may be bad; for me he is good." Even before his conversion St. Francis honored Our Lord in the Eucharist by sending costly and beautiful gifts to adorn poor churches. He felt nothing was good enough for the dwelling place of Christ.

Our Lord's words, "Take ye and eat, this is my body . . .," inspired St. John Chrysostom to remark, "It is as if He had said, 'Eat Me, that the highest union may take place.'" The saint further remarked, "To that Lord on whom the angels even dare not fix their eyes, to Him we unite ourselves, and we are made one body, one flesh." Of this union St. Cyril of Alexandria observed that "as two pieces of melted wax unite together, so a soul that communicates is so thoroughly united to Jesus that Jesus remains in it, and it in Jesus."

St. Francis de Sales adds:

> In no action does our Saviour show Himself more loving or more tender than in this one, in which, as it were, He annihilates Himself and reduces Himself to food in order to penetrate our souls and unite Himself to the hearts of His faithful ones.

These are but a few of the many thoughts recorded by the saints. It would seem that the Lord has often been so pleased with the faith, love and devotion expressed and demonstrated by His many chosen souls that He has not been able to restrain Himself from displaying a mutual affection by dispensing special graces and privileges and by performing Eucharistic Miracles of various kinds. We will now examine some of these wonders.

Chapter 35

EUCHARISTIC MIRACLES
AND THE SAINTS

History testifies to the fact that during the persecutions that occurred in the early days of the Church, many martyrs died attesting their allegiance to the Faith and their belief in the Holy Eucharist. The inscriptions and artwork that adorn their tombs in the catacombs clearly indicate this. It seems fitting that what may have been the Church's first Eucharistic miracle occurred during this time when Mass was celebrated secretly.

This first Eucharistic miracle involved a young Roman acolyte named St. Tarsicius, who lived during the third-century persecution by the Emperor Valerian. The leaders of the Church were so impressed with Tarsicius' fidelity and courage that they entrusted him with carrying the Blessed Sacrament to the Christians in prison who were awaiting martyrdom. Because adult men were often under suspicion of being priests, the custom was initiated of allowing young men not old enough to be priests to perform this service of consolation to the condemned. This was done with the utmost secrecy, since the discovery of their mission would result in imprisonment or death.

The history of the saint relates that unbelievers met him one day while he was carrying the Blessed Sacrament. For reasons not stated, Tarsicius had come under suspicion; it can be speculated that it was his reverential demeanor which aroused the pagans' interest. When they inquired about where he was going, he refused to speak. In anger, they beat him to death with clubs and stones. Afterward, when they turned over his body, they could find no trace of the Eucharist in his hands or in his clothing.

Devout Christians claimed the body of the young martyr and buried it in the cemetery of St. Callistus. It appears that for a time, however, his relics were kept in the tomb of Pope Zephyrinus—this fact being deduced from evidence of a devotion to Tarsicius which existed there. St. Tarsicius' relics are now rumored to be in the church of San Silvestro in Capite, Rome. The altar in the fresco-painted crypt of this church was built to receive the body of the saint, but his bones have not been found there.

The earliest and most positive information concerning this young martyr is found in a poem composed by Pope Damasus (366-384) in which the details of his martyrdom are given. In this poem, the pontiff compared Tarsicius to the protomartyr Stephen, who was also stoned to death for his faith and ministry to the Church. (*Acts* 7:57-60).

*   *   *   *   *

Another demonstration of faith was enacted by St. Louis (d. 1270), King Louis IX of France. His biographies relate that once, during the exposition of the Blessed Sacrament in the chapel in his residence, the saint was working in his study when a courtier excitedly burst in, exclaiming, "Sire, the Infant Jesus is appearing in the Host upon the altar!" The saint calmly continued his writing, quietly replying, "I could not believe more firmly in Christ's presence in the Eucharist if I were to behold a miracle."

*   *   *   *   *

A contemporary of St. Louis, St. Anthony of Padua (d. 1231), was involved in a most dramatic miracle of the Eucharist. It also involved, of all things, a mule.

The history of the saint relates that a man named Boniville, believed to have been an Albigensian heretic who rejected the validity of all the Sacraments, was one day in Toulouse questioning the saint about the Sacrament of the Altar. Boniville denied the real presence of Jesus Christ in the consecrated Host, while the saint steadfastly affirmed it. As a test, one or the other suggested that the choice be made by Boniville's mule. Both men agreed.

The mule was kept in its stall for three days, and deprived of food during all that time. At the end of the fast, a great crowd of both believers and unbelievers assembled to witness the proceedings. When the mule was brought before St. Anthony, he held a consecrated Host before the animal, while Boniville attempted to feed it oats and hay. The mule took no notice of the food, but fell to its knees before the Blessed Sacrament. The Catholics who witnessed the miracle expressed unbounded joy, while the unbelievers were thoroughly confused. Boniville is said to have been subsequently converted, together with a great number of the heretics.

*   *   *   *   *

Another miracle involving an animal is not so well known. It occurred in the 16th century in Ireland and involved Sir Richard Shee, an attorney. The traditional memory of Sir Richard of Kilkenney is that he was a great man, but an irreligious one. Some even believed that he participated in diabolical ceremonies. While his neighbors dutifully attended Mass on Sundays and holydays, Sir Richard chose the very time of the Holy Sacrifice to bring out his hounds for hunting, hoping the barking of his animals would distract those who were attempting to pray.

On one occasion, during a procession, a great many people were waiting in the streets for the Blessed Sacrament to be carried through their village. The lawyer rode toward the gathering with his hounds and contemptuously attempted to spur his horse through the worshipers, but the animal refused to proceed. It knelt down with the people and could not be compelled to rise until the Blessed Sacrament had passed. The man was so awe-stricken that he reformed his life and, as the local belief has it, built the Butts Cross to mark the place of his repentance.

*   *   *   *   *

Closer to our own time occurred a remarkable instance that demonstrated the faith and holiness of St. John Bosco (1815-1888) of Piedmont, Italy. The saint is known as a visionary, author, founder of two religious orders, a reader of hearts, a foreteller of future events, a miracle worker and, during his youth, an acrobat and magician. Always attracted to the ministry of aiding destitute boys, he opened various institutions for their care and education and has become known as the "Friend of Youth."

In one of these institutions, on the feast of the Nativity of the Blessed Mother (September 8), the boys who gathered in the church numbered almost 600. The sacristan had prepared a ciborium with enough hosts to be consecrated for the congregation, but a last-moment distraction prevented him from placing it on the altar. The ciborium reserved in the tabernacle contained only about 20 consecrated Hosts. After the Consecration, at the moment of the elevation of the Host, the sacristan realized his mistake, but could do nothing but await the saint's confusion, and later a well-deserved reprimand for his oversight. At Communion time, when St. John Bosco uncovered the ciborium that he had removed from the tabernacle and saw the small number of Hosts in it, his expression betrayed his disappointment over the fact that he would be unable to give Holy Communion to all the boys. Nevertheless, gazing heavenward, he quietly prayed for a moment and then walked toward the railing, where the communicants devoutly awaited him.

After he had distributed Communion to the first row of boys, another group took their places. One row succeeded another, and then another, yet the supply in the ciborium was not exhausted. When Don Bosco returned to the altar, all the boys had communicated and there remained within the ciborium a goodly quantity of Hosts. It is said that the sacristan was thoroughly bewildered.

St. John Bosco had the utmost confidence in the Blessed Sacrament and in Mary, Help of Christians, and often spoke of three "springs" to the supernatural life: Confession, devotion to the Blessed Mother, and the reception of Holy Communion.

* * * * *

St. Peter of Alcántara (d. 1562), the Franciscan friar who was known for his ecstasies, heavenly favors, levitations and love of the Blessed Sacrament, attracted crowds to his services wherever he went. The devotion which he had for the Blessed Sacrament was rewarded one Easter by a spectacular miracle.

In Pedrosa, where St. Peter of Alcántara stayed for a time, Easter was approaching and arrangements were being made for the festivity. The saint was scheduled to celebrate High Mass for the people from distant areas who usually gathered in Pedrosa for the feast. When news spread that the saint would celebrate the Mass, so great was the number of people who assembled that the church could not accommodate them. It therefore seemed necessary to erect an outdoor altar to satisfy all who wanted to attend the Mass offered by St. Peter of Alcántara.

During the Mass, while the Credo was being recited, a sudden and intense windstorm arose, threatening to destroy the altar and all that was on it. Although the people were alarmed, only a few left the scene, while the saint remained calm and continued the Mass.

The elements quickly became even more alarming, with lightning darting on all sides, thunder crashing, and a cloudburst rapidly approaching. The parish priest took it as a sign that evil spirits were intent on disrupting the celebration. Nevertheless, the saint prevented the priest from reciting prayers of exorcism, and quieted the people by calmly continuing the prayers. The fears of all were soon turned to amazement when it was discovered that while the rain had drenched the whole countryside, not a single drop had fallen on the altar or the congregation, nor had the wind extinguished a single candle. With the conclusion of the Mass, a song of thanksgiving arose from the multitude for this miracle which had given fresh proof of the sanctity of the humble Franciscan friar.

* * * * *

The intense devotion of St. Felix of Cantalice (d. 1587) and St. Isidore the Farmer (d. 1130) for the Holy Eucharist was confirmed by miracles involving an unusual ministry of angels.

St. Felix, who was known as Brother Deo Gratias because of the greeting he customarily pronounced, was also known for the many spiritual favors granted him for his great devotion to the Eucharist, including that of the gift of tears. As a child, the future saint tended herds of cattle, but when duty permitted he spent time on his knees reciting countless times the Our Father and the Hail Mary. His father placed him, at age 12, in the service of a rich citizen whom he served for 18 years in the capacity of cowherd and then field laborer. Through the kindness of his employer he was permitted to attend Holy Mass. Nevertheless, his responsibilities were not neglected, since angels were seen to work in the fields during his absence.

St. Felix eventually joined the Capuchin Order as a lay brother and later became the first saint of the Order.

Like St. Felix, St. Isidore the Farmer was also born into poor circumstances and likewise was placed at an early age by his father into the employ of a wealthy landowner. But unlike St. Felix, St. Isidore was a married man. However, after the death of their only child, St. Isidore and his wife agreed to live in holy continence while suffering the trials and hardships of their poverty.

Before reporting to the fields, Isidore attended Mass each morning. He is known to have shared with the poor his meager meals, which on many occasions miraculously redoubled in quantity until all were satisfied. His goodness and kindness toward all, however, did not prevent detractors from reporting him for tardiness and periods of inactivity during working hours. Isidore's employer, John de Vergas, in order to test the truth of their accusations and to gather sufficient evidence for Isidore's dismissal, hid himself one morning and discovered that while Isidore did indeed report late after lingering in church, his plowing was meanwhile accomplished by unseen hands who guided snow-white oxen across the fields.

After assuring themselves that angels did in fact perform Isidore's chores while he was rapt in prayer, John de Vergas and many other witnesses altered their opinion of him. In fact, noticing that the angels accomplished three times as much as Isidore, John de Vergas fell down at his servant's feet and asked pardon for his suspicions. To this Isidore replied, "Master, no time is ever lost by prayer, for those who pray are workers together with God."

St. Isidore became not only greatly revered by all, but was also placed thereafter in responsible positions. He is known to have worked miracles, including the multiplication of grain.

St. Anthony Mary Claret (d. 1870) relates that he was given the great grace of retaining the Blessed Sacrament in his breast. Thus he was day and night a living tabernacle of Jesus Christ.

The miracle which occurred when St. Anthony of Padua and an Albigensian heretic named Boniville agreed to let Boniville's mule decide whether Christ was really present in the Blessed Sacrament. St. Anthony held up the consecrated Host while the mule, which had not eaten for three days, fell to its knees, ignoring the adjacent oats and hay. It is said that Boniville and a great number of heretics were subsequently converted.

The wall miraculously opens up for St. Anthony of Padua. He was unable
to assist at Mass on this occasion, but when the monastery bell rang at the
moment of the elevation of the Host and chalice, he felt a sudden impulse
to fall to his knees. As he extended his arms and adored Our Lord present on the altar, all marvelled to see a hole appear in the wall, enabling
Anthony to contemplate the sacred Host in the hands of the priest.

Chapter 36

EUCHARISTIC FASTS

One of the most frequent of the miraculous phenomena which have occurred in the lives of the saints is the Eucharistic fast, in which the Eucharist was the principal, or only, food during prolonged fasts—or was the sole nourishment for years at a time. The following are some of the many saints who have maintained such fasts.

St. Gerasimus, a recluse of Palestine (d. 475), is said to have eaten nothing except the consecrated Host during the 40 days of Lent.

* * * * *

According to Alban Butler, perhaps the earliest mystic of whom it is recorded on reliable evidence that she lived for years upon the Blessed Sacrament alone is Blessed Alpais (d. 1211). As a peasant girl she worked with her father in the fields until she was stricken by a disease that may have been leprosy. Her biographer, a Cistercian monk who knew her personally and who wrote of her while she was yet living, recorded that she was cured of this ailment during a vision of the Blessed Mother. Later, as a result of another illness, she lost the use of her limbs and was confined to her bed, although she was perfectly healthy in all other respects.

Nothing in the way of food or drink except the Blessed Eucharist passed her lips for such a long time that she was brought to the attention of the Archbishop of Sens, who was also Legate of the Holy See. The Archbishop appointed a commission which examined and confirmed the truth of Alpais' fast.

So lengthy and complete was this fast, and so many were the miracles worked through her prayers, that a church was built adjoining the house of Blessed Alpais at Cudot, France. By means of a window she could assist at the religious services celebrated by a community of canons regular who ministered there. Her home became a place of pilgrimage where religious and nobles from all parts came to visit her. Even Queen Adela, wife of Louis VII of France, visited Cudot on three occasions. The devotion to the saint which had existed from the time of her death in 1211 was confirmed by Pope Pius IX in 1874.

* * * * *

St. Rita of Cascia (d. 1456) is known to have observed every year not just one Lent, but the equivalent of two others. During these fasts she took only a little coarse food whose flavor was altered with the roots of a bitter plant. So extreme were these fasts that the sisters marveled that her health was sustained on so little. To this she replied that the food which nourished her they could not see, this food being the sacred wounds of Jesus Christ and, of course, the Holy Eucharist.

* * * * *

The fast of St. Catherine of Siena (d. 1380) has been recorded for us by none other than one of her confessors, Bl. Raymond of Capua. In his biography of St. Catherine he informs us that following a vision of Our Lord, food was no longer necessary to the saint. Bl. Raymond writes:

> When she was obliged to take food, she was so incommoded that it would not remain in the stomach and it would be quite impossible to describe her grievous pains on such occasions.

At the start of her fast, the confessor who served her at the time commanded her to take food daily, but after a time the saint asked him:

> If therefore you see, by the numerous experiments of which you have been witness, that I am killing myself by taking nourishment, why do you not forbid me, as you would forbid me to fast, if the fast produced a similar result?

Bl. Raymond tells us that the confessor had nothing to reply to this reasoning and said to her, "Henceforth act according to the inspirations of the Holy Ghost, for I perceive that God is accomplishing marvelous things in you."

Sometime later, when her confessor inquired whether she did

not at least experience an appetite, the saint replied, "God satisfies me so in the Holy Eucharist that it is impossible for me to desire any species of corporal nourishment." On asking if she did not at least experience hunger on the days on which she did not communicate, the saint answered, "His sole presence satiates me, and I acknowledge that, to be happy, it even suffices for me to see a priest who has just said Mass."

When St. Catherine's fast became well-known many criticized her, and even religious persons were opposed to her. Some attributed the fast to ". . . a kind of vanity, that she did not fast really, but fed herself well in secret." Others said she wished to be noticed and that she was being deceived by the devil. Bl. Raymond writes:

> Catherine was willing to appease their murmurs, and determined that every day she would go once and take a seat at the common table and endeavor to eat. Although she used neither meat, nor wine, nor drink, nor eggs, and did not even touch bread, what she took—or rather, what she tried to take—caused her such sufferings that those that saw her, however hard-hearted they were, were moved to compassion: her stomach could digest nothing, and rejected whatever was taken into it; she afterwards suffered the most terrible pains and her whole body appeared to be swollen; she did not swallow the herbs which she chewed, she only drew from them their juice and rejected their substance. She then took pure water to cool her mouth; but every day she was forced to throw up what she had taken, and that with so much difficulty that it was necessary to assist her by every possible means.

To this Bl. Raymond adds, "As I was frequently witness of this suffering, I felt an extreme compassion for her, and I counselled her to let men talk, and spare herself such torture . . ."

*   *   *   *   *

St. Catherine Fieschi of Genoa (d. 1510) also observed two strict fasts each year, these being during Advent and Lent. During these times she took no food at all except "this heavenly manna" that was administered to her in the Mass. She observed these two fasts each year for more than 23 years. If during the fast she attempted to swallow any food or drink, her stomach immediately rejected it. Once when her confessor ordered her to take food, the reaction was the same, except that her efforts to obey resulted in an alarming illness.

* * * * *

St. Ita (or Ida) was one of the most popular saints in Ireland. Of noble descent, she was saintly from childhood and was the foundress of a great community of nuns at Hy Conaill, a few miles to the southwest of Limerick, where she died in the year 569.

We are told that she frequently went without food for three or four days at a time. Eventually, it is said, an angel appeared and counseled her to have more concern for her health. When she declined, the angel announced that in the future God would provide for her needs. From that time on she subsisted entirely on the Holy Eucharist.

A nun who sought lodging in her convent asked her one day,

> Why is it that God loves thee so much? Thou art fed by Him miraculously, thou healest all manner of diseases, thou prophesiest regarding the future, the angels converse with thee, and thou never ceasest to keep thy thoughts fixed upon the divine mysteries.

St. Ita gave her to understand that her practice of continual meditation, nurtured from her youth, was the source of all the rest.

* * * * *

The case of St. Nicholas of Flüe, Switzerland (d. 1487), is interesting and well documented. Nicholas was the son of peasants and as a child was prayerful and spiritually advanced. At the age of 21 he joined the army and participated in four major battles. Taking the advice of his parents, he married at the age of 25 and eventually became the father of 10 children. After 25 years of marriage, he obtained the consent of his wife to leave his family and live as a hermit. He settled in a valley only an hour's walk from his home. Known there as Brother Klaus, he lived in the area for 20 years, until the time of his death, without taking any bodily food or drink.

One year after St. Nicholas' death, Oswald Isner, the curé at

Kerns, disclosed that when the saint had first begun his life of total abstinence and had reached the 11th day,

> ...he sent for me, and asked me privately if he should take food or continue to abstain. He wished to live wholly without food that he might sever himself from the world. I felt his members and found only skin and bone; all the flesh dried up entirely, the cheeks were hollow, and the lips wonderfully thin. I told him to persevere as long as he could without endangering life. For if God had sustained him for 11 days, He could sustain him 11 years. Nicholas followed my advice; and from that moment to the day of his death, a period of 20 and a half years, he took no sort of food or drink. As he was more familiar with me than with any other person, I often spoke to him on the subject. He told me he received the Sacrament once a month and felt that the Body and Blood of Christ communicated vital forces which served him for meat and drink, otherwise he could not sustain life without nourishment.

To test the authenticity of the saint's complete fast, the bishop of Ascalon took up residence in an adjoining cell to observe him. After several days, the bishop ordered Nicholas to eat a little bread and to drink a little wine. But the saint's agony after obeying the order was so great that the bishop pressed him no longer, and declared that Nicholas' obedience proved that he was a child of grace.

The Archduke Sigismond of Austria sent the royal physician, Burcard von Horneck, to examine the case. Even Emperor Frederick III sent delegates to investigate the matter. Both tests proved the fast to be genuine.

* * * * *

Another well-documented case is that of St. Lidwina (Lydwine) of Schiedam, Holland (d. 1433). Born to poor parents, Lidwina, while still a child, was deeply devoted to the Mother of God. During the winter of 1395, while ice skating, one of her companions caused her to fall on the ice with such force that a rib was broken. This fall initiated the illness that was to plague Lidwina the rest of her life. Gangrene developed in the wound and spread throughout her body, introducing many other complications. Lidwina was always in extreme pain.

In addition to her natural sufferings, Lidwina was privileged to bear the stigmata, the wounds of Our Lord. She was favored with visions, ecstasies and the gift of prophecy; she could describe events occurring at a distance, and she frequently beheld angels. Celebrated preachers and holy persons visited the stigmatist's bedside and many sickly persons were healed there.

Although Lidwina yearned to receive the Eucharist, for many years her confessor permitted its reception only twice a year. However, this situation changed when, by means of a bleeding Host, the parish priest was made to realize his error. Afterward he allowed Lidwina to receive Holy Communion whenever she desired it. For the last 19 years of her life, according to the sworn depositions of witnesses, she depended entirely upon the Holy Eucharist for nourishment. Whenever Lidwina's reception of the Eucharist was delayed her strength failed, but after receiving the Sacrament her strength was restored and she experienced great joy and consolation.

Following the death of the saint, both Joannes Brugmann and Thomas á Kempis wrote biographies describing St. Lidwina's sufferings and mystical favors.

* * * * *

St. Joseph of Cupertino (d. 1663), known for his levitations, was another who observed an unusual fast. It is reported that he practiced mortification and fasting to such a degree that every year he kept seven Lents of 40 days each, accepting only a little food on Thursdays and Sundays. For a period of five years the saint lived without eating, and for 15 years without drinking. During these long abstinences he was sustained only by his reception of the Eucharist. It was often noticed that before communicating he appeared pale and haggard, weary and spiritless, but when he left the altar he walked briskly and was full of vigor and animation.

* * * * *

The various mystical favors experienced by Venerable Ursula Benincasa (d. 1580) were such that Pope Gregory XIII wondered about their genuineness, and placed St. Philip Neri in charge of an investigation.

As a member of the Immaculate Conception Order in Naples,

Ursula Benincasa was known for her ardent love of the Blessed Sacrament. After she received Holy Communion her love was made apparent by the almost violent palpitations of her heart, movements which were easily discerned by the movement of her clothing. Her extreme bodily sufferings were made endurable by her reception of the Eucharist, and although she was unable to retain food she experienced no difficulty in receiving Holy Communion.

As one of the tests of Ursula's mystical gifts, St. Philip forbade her to receive the Eucharist. For months she obeyed, although grieved beyond measure. After a time she experienced such weakness that her physician declared she could not survive. The community implored St. Philip to allow her the Eucharist as a means of recovery. As soon as the priest arrived with the Blessed Sacrament, Ursula's strength began to return, and after receiving the Host she was completely recovered. This and other miracles convinced St. Philip Neri of Venerable Ursula's sanctity, and she was thereafter permitted to receive the Holy Eucharist freely.

As an extraordinary privilege, the Archbishop of Naples permitted her to retain the Holy Eucharist in her cell every Thursday for her special adoration. On these occasions Ursula would remain undisturbed, and would be deeply grieved when it was time for the Blessed Sacrament to be removed.

*   *   *   *   *

The great mystic and contemplative, Blessed Angela of Foligno (d. 1309), was born into a wealthy family, and later married and became the mother of several children. By her own account her life was self-indulgent, pleasure-seeking and sinful. But after a conversion, said to be as sudden as that of St. Paul's, she entered the Franciscan Third Order. Following the death of her husband and the deaths of all her children, she sold all her possessions and gathered around her a large family of tertiaries (members of the Third Order). What is known of her visions and spiritual experiences was recorded by her confessor. Many of these favors and visions were granted her at Mass and after receiving the Eucharist. It is known that she subsisted on the Eucharist alone for a period of 12 years.

*   *   *   *   *

When St. Columba of Rieti (d. 1501) was still very young, her parents attempted to pledge her in marriage to a wealthy young man. In desperation the saint cut off her hair, renounced marriage and fled to the church of St. Dominic. As a Dominican tertiary, she responded to the advice of her confessor and journeyed to Perugia. The townspeople there, because of her reputation for holiness, built a convent for her, and soon many young women petitioned for entrance. She served as their superior although she was only 19 years old.

Since girlhood Columba had practiced great penances and had subsisted for long periods on the Eucharist alone. When she was about 20 years of age, she began to live entirely on the Blessed Sacrament. Her desire to communicate was so ardent that she often expressed the opinion that she could not live without the Holy Eucharist, and it is true that whenever she was deprived of the Blessed Sacrament she fell into great weaknesses.

St. Columba's fast attracted the attention of Pope Innocent VIII, who then resided in Perugia. He is known to have instituted a strict inquiry, which satisfied those who conducted it. When asked by her confessor how it was possible to live by the Eucharist alone, she replied:

> When I receive the Bread of Life, Father, I feel so fully satisfied, spiritually and bodily, that all desire for earthly food leaves me, and I hope of the goodness of God that before the conclusion of this year He will give you such light upon this subject as will remove all your difficulties.

A short time later, while in ecstasy on Christmas Eve, St. Columba prayed for her confessor and was heard to say, "Today he will receive the explanation." The following morning, Christmas, a day on which priests then customarily offered three Holy Masses in succession, her confessor was afforded a spiritual peace and a sensible joy of God's presence which increased in intensity until, at the Third Mass, he realized he had lost all desire for earthly food. For the rest of the day he found it impossible to eat.

When told of her confessor's experience the saint told him, "I am happy that you have tasted my nourishment, and that now you have learned how it comes to pass that I am satisfied with the Bread of Angels alone."

*   *   *   *   *

St. Mary Frances of the Five Wounds (d. 1791), a Franciscan
tertiary, was imprinted with the invisible stigmata, and on Fridays,
especially the Fridays of Lent, she experienced the pains of the
Passion of Christ. Priests, religious and pious lay persons visited
her for guidance. She, too, is known to have lived for lengthy
periods on the Eucharist alone.

*   *   *   *   *

St. Juliana of Cornillon (d. 1260), who was left an orphan at the
age of five, was placed in the care of the Cistercian nuns. At 14
she was admitted to the order, where she quickly advanced in virtue and love of the Eucharist. At 16 St. Juliana was favored with
visions, and soon thereafter began prolonged fasts. These fasts
aroused concern and curiosity among the sisters, but their plead-
ings that she should eat for the health of her body were met with a
sweet refusal. As she stated repeatedly, food was distasteful to her
and the Holy Eucharist was the only delight of her soul.

*   *   *   *   *

The Lily of Quito, as St. Mary Anne de Paredes (d. 1645) was
affectionately called, was born in 1618 in Quito (now Ecuador,
but then part of Peru). The daughter of illustrious parents, Mary
Anne was holy from childhood. She showed early signs of an extraordinary attraction for prayer and mortification, which was ex-
ceeded only by her love for God and the Blessed Mother. At age
ten she pronounced the vows of poverty, chastity and obedience,
but her desire to enter a religious order was never realized. Instead, she remained in her father's home and led an intense life of
prayer.

The fast which the saint kept was so strict that she took scarcely
an ounce of dry bread every eight to ten days. The food that
miraculously sustained her life was the Holy Eucharist, which she
received every day. The details of this fast were recorded and
affirmed by many witnesses.

St. Mary Anne worked many miracles, could read the secrets of
hearts and saw distant events as if they were passing before her.
She cured diseases with a Sign of the Cross or a sprinkle of holy
water and, on at least one occasion, raised a dead person to life.

She was beatified in 1853 and canonized in 1950.

* * * * *

St. Rose of Lima (d. 1617) was often so weak from fasts and penances that she was obliged to rest periodically while walking to the church for Holy Mass. After the reception of the Eucharist, like many of the previously mentioned saints, she would be restored to health, so much so that her brisk pace on the way home made it difficult for her mother to keep up with her. On Rose's arrival at home she would become so absorbed in contemplation that she took no notice of food, even though she had kept a strict fast the day before. And whenever Rose was permitted to receive Holy Communion for several days at a time, the Holy Eucharist substituted for ordinary food.

* * * * *

Among the non-canonized, there was the German mystic and visionary Anne Catherine Emmerich (d. 1824), who lived on water and the Holy Eucharist for the last 12 years of her life. And in the 20th century, Alexandrina da Costa (d. 1955) of Balasar, Portugal, and Therese Neumann of Konnersreuth, West Germany (d. 1962) experienced long total fasts, except for the Holy Eucharist. Alexandrina's fast lasted 3 years. She spent most of her life as an invalid, after having been crippled in a jump from a window to escape a rapist. She suffered the Passion of Christ on Fridays in expiation for sins. Alexandrina's writings were approved in Rome in 1979.

The stigmatist Therese Neumann took no food or water, except the Holy Eucharist, from 1926 until her death in 1962. The Host would remain within her for about a day, but toward the end of each 24-hour period she would feel her life ebbing away until she received the Bread of Life. Officials of the Diocese of Regensburg have been collecting much information on Therese Neumann's life and virtues, and the opening of her cause for beatification is expected at any time.

Chapter 37

RAPTURES AND ECSTASIES

Ecstasy is an extraordinary state in which God raises a person to supernatural contemplation of such intensity that the activity of the senses is suspended. Sometimes the soul even seems to leave the body and fly towards Heaven. St. Paul described his experience in this way:

> I know a man in Christ who, fourteen years ago—whether in the body I do not know, or out of the body I do not know, God knows—such a one was caught up to the third heaven. And I know such a man—whether in the body or out of the body I do not know, God knows—that he was caught up into paradise and heard secret words which it is not granted to man to utter. (*2 Cor.* 12:2-4).

What is the difference between a rapture and an ecstasy? While theologians and others differentiate between the two and describe the distinctive characteristics of each, St. Teresa of Avila, a Doctor of the Church and an acknowledged authority on such matters, tells us that basically the words "rapture" and "ecstasy" refer to the same experience. The saint writes of this matter in Chapter 20 of her autobiography (*The Life of Teresa of Jesus*):

> I should like, with the help of God, to be able to describe the difference between union and rapture, or elevation, or what they call flight of the spirit, or transport—it is all one. I mean that these different names all refer to the same thing, which is also called ecstasy.

With this in mind, the words "rapture" and "ecstasy" will be used interchangeably in the following accounts of saints who experienced this supernatural state while they prayed before the Holy Eucharist.

Some ecstasies are of short duration, as those in the life of St. Catherine of Genoa (d. 1510). If this saint fell into a rapture during Holy Mass, she would always become fully aware of the present at the moment of Communion. She used to say, "O Lord, I believe that were I dead I should revive in order to receive Thee."

*   *   *   *   *

A much longer ecstasy was experienced by St. Francis Xavier (d. 1552), during the time when he was a missionary in India. He was scheduled one day to transact some business with the Viceroy. When St. Francis' young assistant, Andrew, was sent to remind him of the time, he found the saint sitting on a low stool before the tabernacle, his face tilted upward and his hands folded across his chest. Hesitating to disturb him, Andrew finally whispered his message, but St. Francis did not respond. Two hours later he was found in the same position, but this time Andrew was successful in rousing him. When St. Francis learned how long he had been in ecstasy, he at once prepared for his appointment. But hardly had he left his dwelling when, walking down the street, he once again fell into a rapture. He stood motionless in the street until nightfall, when he emerged from his ecstasy and returned to his home. "My son," he said to Andrew, "we must visit the Viceroy another day. This day God has willed for Himself alone."

*   *   *   *   *

St. Ignatius of Loyola (d. 1556), the founder of the Jesuit Order, is said to have required at least an hour to prepare for the celebration of Holy Mass. While at the altar he often fell into raptures which consumed a much longer period of time, and periodically he found it impossible to offer his daily Mass due to his loving adoration and deep contemplation of the Eucharist.

*   *   *   *   *

St. Francis Borgia (d. 1572), who joined the Jesuit Order after the death of his wife, experienced such an ecstatic union of his soul with the Redeemer that frequently he would begin Mass in the morning and conclude it at Vespers (the evening hour of the Divine Office). Because of the length of his Masses, he seldom offered Mass in public.

*   *   *   *   *

St. Teresa of Avila (d. 1582), we are told, often fell into ecstasy after receiving Holy Communion, and often at the place of its reception—thus it became the custom of the sisters to guide her back to her place in chapel. Once at Toledo, at the conclusion of the Mass, she was found by the portress leaning against a wall, motionless and enraptured. Although the portress tried vigorously to arouse St. Teresa, she remained in ecstasy "like a statue" until God's appointed time for its conclusion.

The saint herself tells of one of these incidents in Chapter 39 of her autobiography:

> I assisted at Mass and communicated. I do not know how I
> did so. I thought I had been there only a very short time and
> I was astounded when the clock struck and I found that I had
> been in that state of rapture and bliss for two hours . . .

*   *   *   *   *

While celebrating his first Mass, St. Philip Neri (d. 1595) was so overwhelmed with consolation and joy that he was scarcely able to pour the wine and water into the chalice because of the excessive trembling of his hands, which continued until the end of the Holy Sacrifice. His ecstasies, especially at the elevation and Communion, were so intense that he frequently found it necessary to lean against the altar to avoid collapsing. So frequent were his raptures during Holy Mass that the Sacrifice occupied two hours or more. For this reason he was obliged to offer Mass in a private chapel.

It was St. Philip's practice from time to time after receiving the Eucharist to cover his face with a linen cloth so that he might pray and enjoy the presence of his Heavenly Guest without being distracted and without having his enraptured expression observed by his companions. During St. Philip's illnesses, it often proved beneficial for him to receive the Holy Eucharist, which served as a healing agent.

During the last five years of his life, whenever St. Philip offered Holy Mass in his private chapel, the server would leave the chapel at the *Agnus Dei* ("Lamb of God . . .") shortly before Communion, lock the doors, and hang up a sign that read: "Silence, the Father is saying Mass." When the server returned in two or more hours, the saint would be so absorbed in God that he seemed to be at the point of death.

During the early part of St. Philip's life it was not the custom for priests to offer a daily Mass, nor for the laity to confess and communicate often. As part of his apostolate in the city of Rome the saint preached a reform in this matter and encouraged Confession and purity of conscience. As a result, the number of Communions multiplied and Confession was restored as an integral part of a Catholic's spiritual life.

* * * * *

While recovering from a severe illness early in her religious life, St. Margaret Mary Alacoque (d. 1690) asked permission of her superior to stay in adoration before the tabernacle one Holy Thursday night, the night which commemorates the institution of the Blessed Sacrament. Her superior was of the opinion that St. Margaret Mary's strength would not be equal to her desire, but the saint assured the superior that strength would be given her. After permission was reluctantly given, Margaret remained before the Blessed Sacrament from half past eight in the evening until the next morning, kneeling motionless and enraptured until the sisters assembled for Prime, when she joined them without the least sign of fatigue.

* * * * *

It is reported of Blessed Anna Maria Taigi (d. 1837) that the ecstasies she experienced after Communion were impossible to number. As soon as she received the Blessed Eucharist her ecstasy would commence—as easily as vocal prayer came to others. During one of these experiences she heard the voice of Jesus telling her, "O My daughter, I am the flower of the field; I am fair, and I am all thine, as I am for all who take up their cross and follow in My footsteps . . . He who desireth to win Heaven must lead a life of penance, and he who suffereth shall not be deceived, for he walketh in a way of great security."

* * * * *

After being rejected by many monasteries because of his youth and feeble health, St. Benedict Joseph Labre (d. 1783) began to wander about visiting famous places of worship in Italy, particularly the House of Loreto and the churches of Rome. Because of his unkempt appearance and his lack of provision and shelter, he became known as both the beggar saint and the "Poor man of the Forty Hours Adoration."

His demeanor before the Blessed Sacrament during the Forty Hours devotion was most edifying. During the process of his canonization it was said that, with his eyes fixed on the Blessed Sacrament, he would remain so motionless in his contemplation that he resembled a statue or an adoring angel.

In each of the churches that he visited during the course of his pilgrimages, he was seen to kneel immovably before the tabernacle from daybreak until the church was closed in the evening hours. His devotion was not only well known by his confessor, but it was also observed by other worshipers, members of the Confraternity of the Adoration of the Blessed Sacrament and various religious in charge of the churches, many of whom testified to his sanctity.

Reflecting on his own unworthiness, the saint had the pious custom of offering to Our Lord, in substitution for what he considered his own lack of love, all the loving aspirations which the Blessed Mother, the Apostles and all the saints had made on receiving the Holy Eucharist.

At the death of St. Benedict Joseph Labre the cry, "The saint is dead!" was heard throughout the streets of Rome. The saint was buried beneath the miraculous portrait of Our Lady which he greatly admired, in his favorite church, St. Maria dei Monti.

* * * * *

The founder of the Order of the Congregation of the Most Holy Redeemer (Redemptorists), St. Alphonsus Liguori (d. 1787), was often rapt in ecstasy before the Blessed Sacrament and was frequently heard to exclaim, "O my God, my Love, O everlasting Love, I love Thee!" It is said that no other saint visited Jesus in the Eucharist as often as did St. Alphonsus. He encouraged frequent visits to the Blessed Sacrament and even wrote a treatise called *Visits to the Most Holy Sacrament of the Altar*, which has been translated into numerous languages, to the welfare of countless souls. When he became unable to offer the Holy Sacrifice of the Mass because of his advanced years, he would ask to be carried into church, where he heard five or six Masses and spent from five to six hours in prayer before the Blessed Sacrament. The saint was often heard to remark:

> One thing is certain, that next to Holy Communion no act
> of worship is so pleasing to God, and none is so useful, as the
> daily visit to our Lord Jesus Christ in the Blessed Sacrament
> dwelling upon our altars. Know that in one quarter of an
> hour which you spend before Jesus in the Blessed Sacrament
> you attain more than in all the good works of the rest of the
> day.

* * * * *

St. Peter of Alcántara (d. 1562) experienced visions of the Blessed Mother during his childhood and was known for his devotion to the cross of Christ. After his ordination as a Franciscan priest he served for a time as a confessor of St. Teresa of Avila. From the time of his first Holy Mass, he was often found in ecstasy before the tabernacle. When approaching the divine mysteries, the saint lost all consciousness of things about him and prayed as though only he and Jesus existed. On account of his frequent ecstasies, wherever he traveled he was given a cell next to the chapel so that he might be near the high altar and pray there whenever he pleased.

A spectacular miracle of the Eucharist which occurred during a Mass offered by the saint is detailed in another section of this volume.

The holiness of St. Peter of Alcántara is well illustrated in Chapter 38 of the *Autobiography of St. Teresa of Avila*, in which St. Teresa relates that:

> . . . from none of the visions that I have seen have I ever
> gathered that any soul has escaped Purgatory save the souls
> of this Father [she does not identify this friar of her order],
> of the Dominican Father [P. Ibañez] and the saintly Fray
> Peter of Alcántara.

After his death St. Peter of Alcántara appeared to St. Teresa of Avila a number of times. Referring to the great austerities he had practiced, he exclaimed, "O blessed penance, which has secured for me so glorious a reward!"

* * * * *

St. Charbel Makhlouf (d. 1898), Maronite rite Catholic mystic of Lebanon, would usually offer Mass about noon so as to spend the morning in preparation and the evening in thanksgiving. On one occasion when St. Charbel was praying before the tabernacle, a violent storm arose, in which the altar was struck with lightning, and the saint's habit was even singed. He prayed on, completely oblivious to what was going on around him.

St. Charbel suffered a paralytic stroke while offering Holy Mass; this occurred at the moment of the Major Elevation. After an agony of eight days, he passed to his eternal reward. St. Charbel's body remained incorrupt, and even perspired (giving off a liquid which was a combination of perspiration and blood) until the day of his beatification in 1965.

Padre Pio (d. 1968), the Capuchin friar of Pietrelcina, Italy, who was the first priest ever to be stigmatized with the wounds of Our Lord's crucifixion, had many mystical gifts including the ability to read hearts, the gift of prophecy and the gift of bilocation. His raptures during Holy Mass were also well documented.

Rising from his bed at 3:00 in the morning, the holy friar spent hours in prayer before approaching the altar. During Holy Mass he entered an enraptured state in which he witnessed the Passion of Our Lord and experienced some of His pain. He once confided to a colleague, "All that Jesus has suffered in His Passion, inadequately I also suffer, as far as is possible for a human being . . ."

Because of his mystical state the holy friar was unaware of the passage of time and frequently had to be encouraged to proceed to the next part of the Mass. Some of his Masses have been known to last 4 hours or more.

Padre Pio's many devotees around the world are awaiting his beatification.

S. FRANCISCUS BORGIAS

St. Francis Borgia in rapture before the Blessed Sacrament. He experienced such ecstatic union with his Redeemer that though he would
begin offering Mass in the morning, he would conclude it only at
Vespers, in the evening.

S. PHILIPPUS NERIUS.

St. Philip Neri in ecstasy while offering Mass. His ecstasies, especially at the Elevation and Communion, were often so intense that he had to lean against the altar to avoid collapsing. Masses offered by St. Philip lasted two hours or more.

Chapter 38

MIRACULOUS RECEPTIONS
OF HOLY COMMUNION

One of the earliest reports of a mystical reception of the Eucharist is that of St. Clement, Bishop of Ancyra, who suffered a long imprisonment and torture for the Faith during the fourth-century persecution of Diocletian. After being persecuted elsewhere, he was imprisoned in Rome, where he so impressed his fellow prisoners with his patience, his inspired words and his compliance with the will of God, that many asked for Baptism at his hands. Instructions in the Faith and Baptisms took place during the late hours of the night so as not to arouse the fury of the guards.

During one of these nights the assembled group saw the cell become illuminated by an extraordinary light. Through this light stepped a handsome young man clothed in shining garments. Walking toward the bishop, the heavenly being gave him a chalice and a large Host, and then disappeared. St. Clement divided the Host among the astonished witnesses and shared the contents of the chalice. History relates that the following day all went joyfully to their execution except St. Clement, who suffered still more before he was eventually beheaded.

*　*　*　*　*

St. Pascal Baylon (d. 1592) experienced many unusual receptions of the Eucharist. As a Franciscan lay brother, Pascal served his community in a number of lowly positions. He performed many miracles—so many in fact, that during the consistory that heard the case for his canonization, the number of miracles recounted prompted a cardinal to cry out, "The like has never been seen!"

As an adolescent, Pascal was entrusted with the care of his father's sheep. While on the mountainside, he would often fall on his knees in adoration on hearing the bell that signaled the consecration of the Mass. During these times when his occupation prevented his attendance at services in the church, an angel often appeared before him bearing the Host for his reception.

The saint was distinguished by his ardent love of the Eucharist. When he was able, he would spend hours on his knees before the tabernacle. Often the fervor of his prayers raised him from the ground. During his lifetime he was known by all as the saint of the Blessed Sacrament—thus it was with good reason that Pope Leo XIII proclaimed St. Pascal Baylon the patron of all Eucharistic societies and congresses.

*   *   *   *   *

During a brief period in the life of St. Bonaventure (d. 1274), the saint's humility sometimes prevented him from receiving the Holy Eucharist—this despite his great desire to communicate. But his fears were completely overcome one day, as is recorded in the acts of his canonization:

> Several days had passed, nor durst he yet presume to present himself at the heavenly banquet. But whilst he was hearing Mass and meditating on the Passion of Jesus Christ, Our Saviour, to crown his humility and love, put into his mouth by the ministry of an angel part of the consecrated Host, taken from the hand of the priest.

"From this time," Butler informs us, "his Communions were without scruple and were sources of great joy and grace."

*   *   *   *   *

In his biography of St. Columba of Rieti (d. 1501), Sebastian of Perousa writes that the saint's confessor one day celebrated Holy Mass in a distant church. Unable to journey there to communicate, Columba entreated the Virgin Mary to satisfy her ardent desire to unite herself to Christ. In a few moments an angel came to her, "holding between his fingers the sacred body of Christ," which he gave to her. St. Columba's confessor, missing the Host, was greatly distressed until the saint reassured him, "Grieve not, for an angel brought the missing fragment of the Host to me and it now reposes in my heart."

*   *   *   *   *

The servant of God, Catherine of Jesus (d. 1594), experienced great longings to receive the Holy Eucharist, and these holy desires were satisfied in most extraordinary ways.

Before Catherine's entrance into religious life, her parish priest, knowing of her sanctity, consented one day to satisfy her longing for Holy Communion and proceeded to enter the church. To his amazement the church, which had been vacant and locked, was now lit with candles, and on the altar the tabernacle was open for his convenience. The priest accepted this as a sign of the pleasure God received from Catherine's devotion to the Most Blessed Sacrament.

On another occasion Catherine journeyed to a Carmelite church but found the doors locked. Wishing to receive the Eucharist, she fervently prayed that somehow her longing would be satisfied. At once a priest, accompanied by many people, approached, and without a word he unlocked the church doors. On entering, Catherine saw at the altar two ministers, who held the Communion cloth on either end, and three vested religious, who beckoned for her to approach and receive the Sacrament. After communicating, she fell into a profound ecstasy. It was then revealed to her that the religious were actually angels sent by God to answer her prayer.

The servant of God became a Discalced Carmelite nun and is now awaiting beatification.

*   *   *   *   *

Closer to our own time, in 1917, in one of the first visions seen by the children of Fatima, an angel appeared to them holding a chalice and a Host. One of the children, Lucia (now a Discalced Carmelite nun), relates the incident in her memoirs, *Fatima in Lucia's Own Words.*

Together with her cousins, Jacinta and Francisco, Lucia had taken her father's flock of sheep to pasture in an olive grove called Pregueira. After eating lunch, the three children decided to pray in the hollow among the rocks on the opposite side of the hill. On reaching the place, they knelt down to recite a prayer previously taught them by an angel: "My God, I believe, I adore, I hope and I love Thee. I ask pardon for those who do not believe, do not adore, do not hope and do not love Thee." Lucia continues:

> I don't know how many times we had repeated this prayer
> when an extraordinary light shone upon us. We sprang up to

see what was happening, and beheld the Angel. He was holding a chalice in his left hand, with the Host suspended above
it, from which some drops of Blood fell into the chalice.
Leaving the chalice suspended in the air, the angel knelt
down beside us and made us repeat three times: "Most Holy
Trinity, Father, Son and Holy Spirit, I offer Thee the most
precious Body, Blood, Soul and Divinity of Jesus Christ,
present in all the tabernacles of the world, in reparation for
the outrages, sacrileges and indifference by which He Himself is offended. And, through the infinite merits of His most
Sacred Heart, and the Immaculate Heart of Mary, I beg of
Thee the conversion of poor sinners."

Then rising, he took the chalice and the Host in his hands.
He gave the Sacred Host to me, and shared the Blood from
the chalice between Jacinta and Francisco, saying as he did
so: "Take and drink the Body and Blood of Jesus Christ, horribly outraged by ungrateful men! Make reparation for their
crimes and console your God."

Once again he prostrated on the ground and repeated with
us three times more the same prayer, "Most Holy Trinity . . ." and then disappeared.

We remained a long time in this position, repeating the
same words over and over again. When at last we stood up
we noticed that it was already dark, and therefore time to
return home.

* * * * *

Not only have angels functioned as ministers of the Holy
Eucharist, but in at least one incident an angel was assisted by a
saint. This occurred to St. Stanislaus Kostka (d. 1568) during the
time he was preparing for his admission into the Society of Jesus.

A violent and dangerous sickness overtook Stanislaus while he
was on a journey, and he was forced to stay for a time in the home
of a Lutheran couple, who would not permit the Eucharist to be
brought into their house. Since the physician had abandoned all
hope for his recovery, St. Stanislaus was in extreme affliction, not
from fear of death, but because he was being denied the reception
of the Sacraments. He appealed to St. Barbara, whose confraternity he had joined, as had many of the students of the Jesuit college. St. Barbara was known as the patroness who would insure the
reception of the Sacrament of Penance and Holy Communion at
the hour of death. For this reason she is depicted in art carrying a

chalice and a Host, as well as the palm of martyrdom.

After Stanislaus had prayed to St. Barbara, the saint appeared to him, accompanied by an angel. In answer to his prayers St. Barbara brought him the Holy Eucharist. After communicating, St. Stanislaus slowly recovered his health. Nevertheless, he died at an early age, sometime later, as the result of another ailment.

It is said of St. Stanislaus that he communicated as often as the practice of the time permitted, and that he would fast the day before the reception. He was often found in ecstasy during Holy Mass and after receiving the sacred Host.

*   *   *   *   *

Blessed Anna Maria Taigi (d. 1837) was a wife, a mother of seven children and a member of the Third Order of the Most Holy Trinity. In spite of her quarrelsome husband, a sickly mother and the many distractions and inconveniences of her overcrowded home, Anna Maria was often in ecstasy. She also worked miracles of healing, read hearts and counseled many who came to her seeking advancement in the spiritual life.

As a daily communicant, Anna Maria was one day attending Holy Mass in the church of St. Charles when, during the *Agnus Dei*, the Host left the hands of the priest. To the astonishment of all who were present, it was conveyed by unseen hands to Anna Maria's lips.

*   *   *   *   *

Blessed Joanna (or Jane) of the Cross (d. 1673) founded a religious order of cloistered nuns and is known to have provided food for them in a miraculous fashion during a time of great need. She once revealed that when the church bell rang for Holy Mass "during which I am to receive the Most Holy, a storm of joy arises in my heart. My whole body trembles . . ."

Blessed Joanna relates:

> Once a Capuchin, with the Body of Jesus in his hand, delayed in communicating me; then, whilst I fixed my gaze upon the All-Holy, it appeared to me that the priest was raised in the air, that he became illuminated, and that Christ appeared to escape from his hands without having refreshed me. Then all the powers of my soul arose in an uproar, look-

ing for my Saviour, until the Heavenly Food was given me, to
the unspeakable rest of my soul.

On another occasion the Host seemed to leave the hands of the
priest and pierce Joanna's heart as if it were an arrow; she fell to
the ground as though mortally wounded. She remained in this condition for several days, feeling in her heart, hands and feet the
pains Jesus endured in His crucifixion. These pains were relieved
during another reception of the Eucharist, when the Host entered
her soul to convey a sweetness that strengthened her. She then
heard these words of Our Lord: "See now thou bearest Jesus the
Crucified within thee; seek Him no longer on Calvary, but rather
in thy heart."

*   *   *   *   *

The privilege of receiving the Holy Eucharist from the hands of
Jesus Himself was experienced by a number of saints, including St.
Laurence of Brindisi (d. 1619), a Capuchin, whose unusual talents
and rare virtue were called upon by Pope Clement VIII for several
unusual missions. One of these was his chaplaincy to the Imperial
army of Prague.

With the Turks still menacing nearby Christian countries, the
Imperial army of 18,000 men assembled to do battle with the
Turks, who numbered 80,000. Vastly outnumbered, the Christians
appealed to St. Laurence for advice and encouragement. After
delivering a rousing discourse, the saint, despite his mature years,
mounted a horse and with the cross held high in his hands led the
troops against the infidels. The crushing defeat of the Turks was
attributed by all to the prayers and inspiration of the saint. It is
told that on his return from the campaign he joined his brethren at
Gorizia, where Our Lord appeared to them and gave them all
Holy Communion with His own hand.

St. Laurence of Brindisi had the grace never to allow his secular
activities to influence his advancement in virtue, and his sanctity
was such that he often fell into ecstasy while offering Holy Mass.

*   *   *   *   *

Les Petits Bollandistes disclose that St. Honoré (sixth century)
journeyed to the abbey of St. Acheolus to assist in the celebration
of Holy Mass in the chapel of the Holy Virgin. During the Mass,

Jesus Himself appeared and gave him Holy Communion. In memory of this event, an image of the hand of Christ is emblazoned on the abbey's coat of arms.

*   *   *   *   *

Several unusual receptions of the Eucharist are related in the life of St. Catherine of Siena, the Dominican mystic. One such Communion took place on the Feast of the Conversion of St. Paul.

Being weak from spiritual tribulations, St. Catherine entered the church of St. Dominic, but instead of joining her sisters within the church she stood in a corner near the door, close to an unused altar. One of the sisters, catching a glimpse of her, went over and led her to the rest of the community for the reception of Holy Communion. When Catherine's turn came, the priest passed her by without giving her a Host. When the same happened at two more Masses, the saint accepted it as a sign of her unworthiness and bowed to the will of God.

Unknown to those within the church, the prior of the monastery, Fra Bartolomeo Montucci, had given orders to the priests to withhold Communion from the saint. It was his intention to avoid any extraordinary manifestation of Catherine's mystical experiences that would distract the huge crowds expected to attend the services. After the second Mass, however, when the saint had resigned herself to the denial of the Blessed Sacrament, a bright light surrounded the altar and in the midst of it appeared a vision of the Holy Trinity: the Father and Son seated on thrones with the Holy Spirit above them in the form of a dove. A hand of fire holding a Host emerged from the vision. The Host was placed upon the tongue of St. Catherine, now rapt in ecstasy.

Catherine's confessor, Blessed Raymond of Capua, wrote a biography of the saint in which he tells us:

> Several individuals, worthy of credit, assured me that when they assisted at the Mass at which Catherine received Holy Communion, they saw distinctly the sacred Host escaping from the hands of the priest and flying to her mouth; they told me that this prodigy happened even when I gave her the sacred Host; I own that I never remarked it very clearly, only I always perceived a certain trembling in the consecrated Host, when I presented it to her lips. It entered her mouth

like a little stone thrown from a distance with force . . . Friar
Bartholomew of St. Dominic, professor of Sacred Scripture
and now Prior Provincial of my order for the Roman province, told me also, that when he gave Catherine the Holy
Communion he felt the sacred Host escaping, notwithstand-
ing his efforts to hold it.

Blessed Raymond of Capua tells us of another occasion when he
celebrated Holy Mass without Catherine being present. At the
proper time after the Consecration he broke the Host, but instead
of separating in half, it divided into three parts, two large and one
small. This small part, "whilst I was attentively regarding it, appeared to me to fall on the corporal, by the side of the chalice over
which I made the fracture. I saw it clearly descend toward the
altar, but I could not distinguish it on the corporal." After search-
ing in vain, Raymond continued with the Mass. Afterward he
carefully covered the altar and asked the sacristan to guard the
surrounding area.

Hurrying to find Catherine, Blessed Raymond related the incident of the missing particle and voiced his suspicion that perhaps
Catherine had mystically received it. Catherine reassured him with
the words, "Father, have no further anxiety respecting the particle
of the sacred Host. Truly I tell you, as my confessor and spiritual
father, that the Heavenly Bridegroom brought it to me Himself and
I have received it out of His divine hand."

*   *   *   *   *

Three miraculous Communions are mentioned in the biographies of St. Mary Magdalen de Pazzi (d. 1607). The earliest occurred on Holy Thursday in the year 1585 when the saint was 19
years of age and a novice in the Carmelite Order. She was then
already experiencing ecstasies and participating in Our Lord's
sufferings. During one of her ecstasies, while she was following the
events of the Passion, she was seen to assume the position of a
communicant; with great devotion she opened and closed her
mouth, and then bowed her head. When she emerged from the
ecstasy she confided to the sisters what had taken place, namely,
that she had received Holy Communion from the hands of the
Saviour Himself.

That same year, during Mass on the feast of St. Albert of the

Carmelite Order (August 7), while reciting the *Domine non sum dignus* ("Lord I am not worthy . . ."), St. Mary Magdalen de Pazzi opened her mouth and, while in ecstasy, participated in a long discussion with Our Lord. Afterward she revealed that she had once again received Holy Communion at the hands of the Redeemer.

The third occasion occurred on Holy Thursday of the year 1592, when the saint again received Holy Communion miraculously. This occurred while she was participating in the Passion of the Saviour.

*   *   *   *   *

Before the birth of St. Mary Frances of the Five Wounds (d. 1791), her sanctity was predicted by a holy priest, Francis Jerome, who told her expectant mother, "Have a care of the little daughter whom thou shalt bear, for she will become a great saint."

At her Baptism the future saint received the name Anna Maria Rose. Before she was two, many marveled at her interest in religious matters and her desire to receive the Holy Eucharist. At the age of four, she spent long hours in prayer, having been led by God to practice mental prayer and mortification. After her First Holy Communion—and before and after subsequent Communions—her face was seen to beam with a holy joy and to assume a heightened color.

When she was old enough to help in her family's weaving shop, her demanding and ill-tempered father protested that her frequent contemplations while at the loom delayed her work. A short time later, her spiritual director and her mother attested that a beautiful boy sat by her side and conversed with her about heavenly matters, and also gave her as much help as was needed to satisfy the demands of her father. The saint readily admitted that her helpful companion was her guardian angel.

Upon entering the Third Order of St. Francis, which was under the guidance of the Alcantarians, she pronounced the three vows of poverty, chastity and obedience, and accepted the name Mary Frances of the Five Wounds, yet she remained living in her father's house. From that time on she suffered a great deal, but she was consoled by Our Lord, who frequently appeared to her during ecstasies.

One day when Dom Cervellino was celebrating Holy Mass, holding the Host between his fingers as he recited the *Agnus Dei,* the Host suddenly disappeared from his hands. Looking around to see where it had fallen, he noticed within a few moments that St. Mary Frances looked as though she had received it upon her tongue. Upon his request, she permitted him to see it. This was witnessed by the servers, and by Brother Forelli, Dom Pessiri and Mary Felice, who confirmed the facts under oath.

On another occasion while in a profound ecstasy, St. Mary Frances found it impossible to rise and advance toward the Communion rail. After she had prayed earnestly that Our Lord would come to her, a Host was seen to leave the ciborium and enter her mouth. So great was this saint's love for the Eucharist that whenever the Divine Mystery was spoken of, or whenever she received Our Lord in Holy Communion or even adored Him present in the tabernacle, she fell into ecstasy.

After a lengthy and painful illness St. Mary Frances of the Five Wounds died in 1791, shortly after receiving the Holy Eucharist.

*   *   *   *   *

It is worthy of note that the stigmatist Therese Neumann (d. 1962) is said to have received Holy Communion in a miraculous manner on numerous occasions. The Host would appear on Therese's tongue without having been placed there by the priest, and would then disappear without any swallowing motion on her part. This phenomenon was witnessed by various priests and prelates. Often at Communion time Therese Neumann, in ecstasy, would see Our Lord Himself approach to give her Communion. Priests witnessed Therese in ecstasy on various occasions as she received Holy Communion from Our Lord.

St. Clement, Bishop of Ancyra (4th century), receives Holy Communion from Our Lord while in prison awaiting martyrdom. St. Clement shared the Host and the contents of the chalice with the other Christians in his cell.

Artistic representation of St. Barbara and the angels who brought Holy Communion to St. Stanislaus Kostka as he lay deathly ill in the home of a Lutheran couple who would not permit the Eucharist to be brought into their house.

St. Catherine of Siena receives Holy Communion from Our Lord Himself. St. Catherine also received Communion from angels, experienced deep ecstasies after receiving the Eucharist, and could distinguish a consecrated Host from an unconsecrated one.

St. Mary Magdalen de Pazzi receiving Holy Communion from Our Lord. Three miraculous Communions are recorded of this saint's life, two of them occurring while she was following the events of the Passion in ecstasy.

St. Mary Frances of the Five Wounds and her guardian angel, who helped her with her work so she would not fall behind because of her frequent contemplations. Before age two St. Mary Frances conceived a desire to receive the Eucharist. On at least two occasions in her life, the Host was miraculously transported to her for her reception.

The three children of Fatima receive Holy Communion from the Angel of Portugal in 1917. Holding the Host and the chalice, the Angel said, "Take and drink the Body and Blood of Jesus Christ, horribly insulted by ungrateful men. Make reparation for their crimes and console your God." The children could see drops of Blood falling from the Host into the chalice. The Angel gave the Host to Lucia, and presented the chalice to Francisco and Jacinta, who had not yet received their First Communion. The Angel then prostrated himself in adoration, after which he faded from their sight. *(These statues can be seen in Fatima.)*

Chapter 39

VOICES AND VISIONS

Many saints have had the privilege of hearing the voice of Jesus speaking from consecrated Hosts. One of these was St. Paul of the Cross (d. 1775), founder of the Passionist Order.

As a young man, St. Paul of the Cross enlisted in a crusade against the Turks in the hope of dying for the Faith. However, a voice from the tabernacle instructed him that he was to serve Christ by founding a religious order in His honor. It is recorded that the saint's heart often beat with a supernatural palpitation due to the intensity of his love for his Saviour. These beatings of the heart were especially strong on Fridays and at times were so intense that heat actually escaped from the region of his heart.

* * * * *

St. Clare of Assisi (d. 1253) heard the voice of Jesus during a dramatic and turbulent time in Italian history—the period when the ambitious German emperor, Frederick II, was bent on conquering Sicily and Italy, including Rome and the Papal States. His efforts, and the activities of his army, caused radical antagonism between his empire and the papacy and produced great confusion in the Church in Italy.

During the year 1244, Frederick's army ravaged the valley of Spoleto, which was part of the patrimony of the Holy See. His soldiers then advanced toward Assisi, but first they approached the convent of San Damiano, which lay in their path. When the Saracens had scaled the walls and entered the cloister, the sisters in the convent rushed to the bedside of their ailing foundress St. Clare, who assured them that Our Lord would save them.

With the assistance of her nuns St. Clare went to the door of the monastery. Before her, in a silver box encased in ivory, was carried the Body of the Holy of Holies. Prostrating herself before Him she prayed aloud, "Does it please Thee, O my God, to deliver

249

into the hands of these beasts the defenseless children whom I have nourished with Thy love? I beseech Thee to protect these whom I am now not able to protect." A voice like that of a small child sounded from the Host, reassuring Clare with the words, "I will have thee always in My care." When the soldiers saw the Blessed Sacrament a sudden panic confused them all, resulting in their immediate retreat. It is with reference to this incident that St. Clare is usually represented in art carrying a monstrance or a ciborium. Clare ordered the nuns never to speak of all this during her lifetime.

Emperor Frederick II, the cause of all the trouble, was apparently reconciled to the Church, since his tomb can be found in the cathedral of Palermo. The emperor's son Manfred wrote to his half brother that "on his deathbed our father, full of contrition, submitted himself as a good Catholic to his mother the sancrosant Church of Rome."

Like St. Francis of Assisi, St. Clare was most earnest in providing beautiful articles to adorn churches. A fellow sister, Sister Francesca, said that Clare had made some hundred corporals of the finest materials for various churches. This same sister reported that on one occasion she had seen a beautiful child in a Host which was being brought to Clare; on another occasion she saw that same child resting on Clare's heart and covering her with luminous wings.

* * * * *

The Eucharistic miracle of St. Clare was instrumental in aiding another house of her order during a similar threatening circumstance. This occurred in Ireland to a small community of Poor Clare nuns in a convent called Bethlehem. The event was recorded by Mother Bonaventure Browne who, though away from her convent at the time, was given a detailed account of the incident immediately on her return.

Mother Bonaventure was told that Catholics in the little hamlet on the shore of Lake Lough Ree were notified that a band of heretics known as the Black and Tans were intent on destroying the little Bethlehem convent. Mother Bonaventure writes:

> As these doleful tidings came to the poor little flock of Christ, which lived therein, they were surprised with great

fear and horror, not knowing where to seek for help, nor from whom to hope for delivery, but only from God, by the merits of St. Clare, their most holy mother, having strong confidence that Christ, Our Lord, would accomplish His promise to her when He drove the heretics from her convent; therefore they set up in the choir a picture of St. Clare on which the miracle was painted, to be still praying before it in the presence of the Most Blessed Sacrament of the altar . . . It can hardly be expressed with what fervor and devotion those sacred virgins prayed to God to deliver them from that peril, for which respect almost all their time both day and night was spent in prayer . . .

Although escape from the convent had seemed impossible, as events developed the nuns were aided by friends who took them safely away to a shelter prepared for them on the opposite side of the lake. When the heretics arrived at the convent, they sacked it and profaned it by making sport of the altar and its ornaments. But they were promptly punished when a small troop of Irish soldiers met them and, reinforced by Catholics from neighboring villages, killed all 120 intruders. All attributed the nuns' safety to their devotion to the Eucharist.

* * * * *

Because of her great love for the Blessed Sacrament, St. Teresa of Avila felt a certain joy when she received a Host somewhat larger than the usual size, reasoning that the Saviour would linger longer after reception. St. John of the Cross, wanting to correct this opinion, once gave her not a whole Host, but one divided between her and one of the sisters. After receiving this half of a Host, St. Teresa heard Our Lord say, "Fear not, My daughter, that anyone can separate thee from Me." The saint afterwards remarked, "Therewith He gave me to understand that the size of the Host was a matter of small consequence."

* * * * *

A spiritual child of St. Teresa of Avila, the servant of God, Catherine of Jesus (d. 1594) was also a member of the Discalced Carmelite Order. Instead of hearing the voice of Jesus, as did the holy foundress, Catherine heard the voices of ministering angels.

Catherine was one night kneeling in prayer before the altar and growing sorrowful that so many churches were without worshipers when she began to hear a sweet melody sung by heavenly voices: "Benediction and glory and wisdom and thanksgiving, honor and power and strength to our God forever and ever. Amen." (*Apoc.* 7:12). At the same time the church was filled with an amazing light. Catherine was given to understand that in this manner the angels make reparation for the negligences of those who do not adequately adore or appreciate the Blessed Sacrament.

Catherine's joy compelled her to sing with the voices, "Holy, Holy, Holy . . ." As though it were a sign that her voice was pleasing to the Lord, Catherine found herself surrounded by celestial brightness.

*   *   *   *   *

Not only has Our Lord seen fit to speak to some of His saints from the Eucharist, but it has also pleased Him to favor certain of His saints by appearing to them within the consecrated Host. In this way He has rewarded their devotion, strengthened them in trials and crowned their virtue.

One recipient of such favors was St. Philip Neri (d. 1595), who is the founder of the Congregation of the Oratory. St. Philip often employed a gentle jest to veil the miracles that constantly surrounded him.

There were times, however, when his spiritual experiences could not be dismissed or disguised. One such instance occurred as he celebrated Mass on Christmas Eve.

After the Consecration, St. Philip saw the Host transform itself into the Child Jesus. The saint's rapture was noticed by others in the church; to those who questioned him about this, he confided that the beauty of the vision surpassed earthly description. On other occasions, St. Philip was privileged to behold within the Sacred Host a multitude of angels and the glory of Paradise.

*   *   *   *   *

The Child Jesus appeared in a spectacular manner to St. Lawrence of Brindisi, a native of Naples who belonged to the Capuchin Order. Known as a man of prayer, he was often in ecstasy while celebrating Holy Mass. His chief biographer recorded:

One day the Blessed Lawrence, during the Sacrifice of the Mass, immediately after the Consecration, saw the Saviour Himself, visibly, in the sacred Host. He was under the form of a little child who caressed Lawrence and smiled on him lovingly. Brother Adam de Rovigo, who was officiating, says he also saw the Infant Jesus, and fell as if dead in a faint at the foot of the altar. On coming to himself he knelt in adoration before the divine Infant.

* * * * *

A similar event was experienced by St. Waltheof (d. 1159) one Christmas day as he was celebrating Mass. St. Waltheof was a member of the Cistercian Order and the second abbot of Melrose Abbey in Scotland. Immediately after the Consecration of the Host, the saint was ravished in contemplation and saw in his hands, instead of the Host, the radiant form of the Child Jesus. After adoring the Infant, he placed the Host on the altar, but then saw only the sacramental species. He related this vision to his confessor, Everard, who told several others. St. Waltheof's biographer, Jordan, a monk of Furness, recorded that he heard the details of the vision from the mouth of the saint's confessor and also from several Cistercian monks, both at Melrose and at Holm Cultram.

* * * * *

On a Christmas day some 200 years later, St. Catherine of Siena knelt in silence before a crib and was privileged to behold the Virgin Mother, who placed the Infant Jesus in her arms. After caressing Him and whispering words of love, she returned Him to His Mother. Later, during Holy Mass, she saw the Infant emerge from the Host. From His bosom grew a vine laden with grapes, which black-and-white dogs reverently consumed. This she interpreted as predicting the reform of the Church through the efforts of the Dominican Order, to which she belonged, and whose habits are composed of both white and black parts. (In Latin, the word for "Dominicans," *Dominicani,* contains a pun; *Domini canes* means "Dogs of the Lord.")

* * * * *

Not only did our Saviour favor some of His saints with a vision of Himself as an Infant, but for others the consecrated Host took the form of Our Lord as a grown man. Such visions were accorded to St. Teresa of Avila, who tells us in her autobiography that sometimes she saw Jesus within the Host at different phases of His Passion and sometimes in His resurrected form. "Almost invariably the Lord showed Himself to me in His resurrected body, and it was thus, too, that I saw Him in the Host."

* * * * *

St. Columba of Rieti (d. 1501) experienced frequent visions and ecstasies which were witnessed by her mother and her confessor. Many of these were carefully recorded by her biographer, Sebastian of Perousa, including one that occurred during the celebration of Holy Mass. Sebastian related that at the elevation of the chalice Columba saw a vision of Jesus nailed to the cross, pale and dead. His side had been pierced with the lance, and His head was bloodied from the crown of thorns. St. Columba fell in a faint and, on recovering, said to her confessor, "Pray for me, my Father, that God will spare me these sad visions, or I shall die of grief."

* * * * *

The same privilege of seeing Jesus within the consecrated Host was repeatedly afforded St. John of San Facundo (d. 1479), a priest of the Augustinian canons. Our Lord seems to have rewarded his successes in reconciling enemies and healing dissensions, and above all his devotion to the Holy Sacrifice, by permitting St. John to see with his bodily eyes the human form of Our Lord at the moment of consecration. The *Acta Sanctorum* records that "John of St. Facundo, in Spain, had often the advantage of seeing with his eyes the visible Saviour in the eulogie or consecrated bread, and this visible manifestation of Christ took from him all difficulty of understanding this sacred mystery."

* * * * *

Blessed Anna Maria Taigi, the housewife, mother and mystic who is now counted among the beati of the Church, was one day in church when our Lord appeared to her in the Eucharist. She saw within the Host a beautiful lily in full bloom; and upon this flower, as though it were a throne, appeared the Saviour in supernatural beauty. While admiring this vision she heard a voice saying, "I am the flower of the field, the lily of the valley. I am thine alone."

*   *   *   *   *

St. Margaret Mary Alacoque, the visionary of the devotion to the Sacred Heart, was once kneeling in deepest contemplation before the Most Holy Sacrament when Jesus appeared to her and bestowed upon her the rare privilege of permitting her to recline softly upon His Heart. Our Lord then revealed to her His deep love for men and the hidden mysteries of His Divine Heart.

St. Clare with the Blessed Sacrament confounding the infidel troops. On this occasion the voice of God, like that of a small child, sounded from the Host, assuring Clare that He would always take care of her nuns.

St. Cajetan receives the Divine Child in his arms. While praying before
the altar on Christmas eve of 1517, Our Lady and the Child Jesus appeared to him, accompanied by St. Joseph and St. Jerome.

Chapter 40

TEARS, FIRE AND LIGHT

The gift of tears, in which a holy person weeps for his sins or the sufferings of Our Lord, is an unusual and little-understood manifestation experienced by a number of saints, including St. Joan of Valois (d. 1505), daughter of Louis XI, King of France. She was deformed, and according to a biographer, "she was remarkably plain in her appearance." This, however, gave no indication to the casual observer of the great beauty of her soul. Because of pressure from her father, Joan consented to marry the Duke of Orleans, but was soon rejected by him and obliged to submit to a divorce. She retired to Bourges and there founded the Order of the Annunciation of the Blessed Virgin. It is said that whenever she received Holy Communion she dissolved into abundant tears, and all who observed her were greatly edified. The saint experienced many apparitions of Our Lord and the Blessed Mother and suffered much from her deformities and illnesses.

* * * * *

St. Laurence Justinian (d. 1455) was another recipient of the gift of tears. As a member of the Canons Regular of St. George, St. Laurence eventually became a superior, a general of the order, the bishop of his diocese and the first patriarch of Venice. In spite of these offices, it is said that he always desired to remain a simple priest. It is known that he shed copious tears while offering the Holy Sacrifice and was often in rapture during the service.

* * * * *

St. Clare (d. 1253) also shed tears before the Blessed Sacrament. Her contemporary, Celano, states that

> when Clare came to Holy Communion she wept hot tears of love, and was filled with the utmost awe and reverence

towards the Lord of Heaven and earth who thus abased Himself. She cried so much that it seemed as though her heart were being poured out. For her the thought of the consecrated Host was as awe-inspiring as that of God the Creator of all things. Even in illness she was always perfectly recollected in Christ, and always thanked Him for all her sufferings, and for this the blessed Christ often visited and comforted her, and gave her great joy in Himself.

* * * * *

St. Felix of Cantalice (d. 1587) was a humble lay brother of the Order of Capuchins who is known to have shed tears of compunction on many occasions while serving Holy Mass. With great difficulty he would repeat the *Confiteor*, and being unable to suppress his tears, he found it most difficult to say the *Domine, non sum dignus* ("Lord, I am not worthy"). Because of this inability to recite the prayer properly, he asked a distinguished preacher of his order if it was necessary for him to attempt the words. On finding that it was not necessary, his heart was comforted. After Holy Communion he continued his thanksgiving with great recollection until it was time for him to venture from the monastery to collect alms.

Although St. Felix concealed many of the graces he received, his brethren were, nevertheless, witnesses to his nightly adorations before the Blessed Sacrament. After making certain no one was in church, the saint would station himself before the altar, where he fell into deep contemplation. With arms extended in the form of a cross he was heard to pray aloud, "Lord, I commend to Thee this people, and I commend to Thee these well-doers . . . Compassion for sinners." Felix then wept bitterly until the grace of God fell upon him and he abandoned his grief for pleasant tranquility.

On one occasion when St. Felix was over 70 years of age, it happened one night during his usual adoration that he approached the high altar and stood still. Brother Lupus, who had secreted himself in the church, heard the saint address a statue of the Blessed Mother with a request that she place the Child Jesus in his arms. To the astonishment of Brother Lupus, the statue was replaced with a vision of the Blessed Mother, who did, indeed, place the Child Jesus in the saint's arms. Pressing the Babe against his heart with the greatest tenderness, Felix shed abundant tears for some time, until the vision disappeared.

* * * * *

Another who shed tears before the Sacrament of the Altar was St. Francis Solano (d. 1610), a native of Andalusia, Spain who was pious and contemplative in his youth. He communicated frequently and devoutly and was able, because of his edifying example, to draw other youths to a similar devotion. At the age of 20 he entered the Franciscan Order, where he so impressed his superiors that soon after his ordination he was given the assignment of novice master. When King Philip II of Spain asked for missionaries for South America to evangelize the native Indians, St. Francis Solano volunteered and set out with a party of priests in 1589. After a trying trip in which his ship was wrecked in a storm, he found his way to Lima, Peru, where his principal labors took place. Because of his gift of tongues he was able to preach to wild tribes in their own dialect. It is said that during his missionary endeavors more than 9,000 persons asked for Baptism. The wildest animals were subject to him, and birds sang at his invitation—as they had for St. Francis of Assisi, the founder of his order.

Like many saints, St. Francis Solano was unable to offer the Holy Sacrifice without shedding abundant tears. For this reason, and because of his other mystical favors, the members of his order took turns in being privileged to serve his Masses. Moreover, the President of the Royal Council of the Indies and the Vice-King de Velasco frequently served the saint's Masses so that they could have the happiness of being strengthened by his great devotion to the Eucharist.

* * * * *

Considering himself unworthy to touch his God, St. Francis of Posadas (d. 1713) wept without ceasing during his celebration of Holy Mass. At the elevation of the Host his whole body is said to have trembled, and he could not restrain his sighs.

Yet another mystical manifestation was witnessed in the life of this saint, that of a mysterious glow. After some of his ecstasies and levitations, many witnesses saw that he was encompassed with a great light, his skin looked transparent as crystal and his cheeks were fiery red. It was also noted that twice during Pentecost, such a brilliant light issued from his body that the whole altar was illuminated. On at least one occasion rays of light issued from his mouth and enlightened the missal he held in his hand.

*   *   *   *   *

A similar phenomenon was noted in the life of St. Alphonsus Liguori (d. 1787). One morning the saint was occupied with spiritual reading before the Blessed Sacrament when members of his order entered the semi-darkened church. They were amazed to discover that a ray of light, originating from the saint's brow, illuminated the book he held in his hand.

*   *   *   *   *

St. Ignatius Loyola (d. 1556), the founder of the Jesuit Order, was still another saint who had the gift of tears. After one of his Masses, a stranger who had attended, but who did not know of the saint's reputation for holiness, felt compassion for him. He approached Father Strada, who had served St. Ignatius' Mass, and said to him, "He who has just said Mass must indeed consider himself to be a great sinner. Let us hope that God has forgiven him. He has wept enough." It is said that during some of the saint's Masses his love for the Eucharist was so intense that the beating of his heart was clearly audible.

In addition to St. Ignatius' ecstatic Masses and his gift of tears, yet another manifestation was noted during one of his Masses. Attending this particular Mass was Father Nicholas Lannoy, who saw a flame of fire hovering above St. Ignatius' head during the *Memento* of the Mass. Father Nicholas was in the act of rushing forward to extinguish it when he suddenly stopped, catching sight of the saint's face which clearly indicated that he was lost in contemplation and was unharmed by the blaze.

*   *   *   *   *

An unusual manifestation of fire was also noted in the life of St. Philip Neri (d. 1595), the founder of the Congregation of the Oratory. Called the second Apostle of Rome, St. Philip Neri is acknowledged by the Church as having had so much love for God that this love could not abide within the normal limits of his heart. This abundant love caused such a dilation of his heart that two ribs broke in order to accommodate it. In addition, his heart was so afire with love that it produced a heat which caused his body to glow. Even more amazing is the phenomenon which occurred during ecstatic prayer, or during the celebration of Holy Mass, or in the performance of certain pious exercises: sparks of fire seemed to emanate from his eyes and face. As astounding as this seems, it was mentioned in the Bull of Canonization: "That interior fire ofttimes overflowed upon his outer body, when he directed his attention to divine things, so that his face and eyes sent forth sparks of fire."

So warm was St. Philip's body with this excessive heat of love that night and day, even in winter, it was necessary for him to open the windows in an attempt to maintain a normal temperature. In addition, this glow of love often caused him to faint so that, without the least sign of illness, he was obliged to remain in bed for whole days at a time.

* * * * *

The mystical glow like that which surrounded St. Philip Neri was also noted in the lives of other saints. One Christmas Eve when Blessed Joanna of the Cross was praying in church, an irresistible longing to receive the Eucharist came over her. Unable to contain her ardent desire, she sent a request to her confessor to satisfy this longing. After communicating, her cheeks became aflame with a heavenly glow, whereas before communicating she is said to have been as pale as a corpse.

* * * * *

The "beggar saint of Rome," Benedict Joseph Labre (d. 1783), exhibited a similar phenomenon while in the presence of the Blessed Sacrament. It is claimed that the saint's interior fire of love for the Sacrament shone exteriorly on his face, illuminating it with a glow that astonished all who saw it. When not engaged in prayer his face is said to have been colorless, but when he prayed before the tabernacle he became insensible to all about him, and his face glowed with a rosy hue which remained for the five or six hours he customarily spent in uninterrupted prayer.

* * * * *

St. John Joseph of the Cross (d. 1734) had frequent ecstasies during which he, like all ecstatics, was insensible to all around him, neither seeing, hearing nor feeling. He was quite unaware that his head was often encircled with a supernatural light or that his face glowed with a celestial brightness.

* * * * *

St. John of the Cross (d. 1591), who with St. Teresa of Avila restored the unmitigated rule to the Carmelite Order and founded the Discalced branch of this order, was occasionally irradiated with light. It is claimed that after one of his Masses a student saw him aglow and was so impressed that he eventually entered the religious life.

At the convent of Caravaca, when a new prioress was to be elected, St. John offered Holy Mass and prayed that the newly elected would be blessed with the wisdom and grace to fullfil the office to the satisfaction and pleasure of God. During this Mass a heavenly light engulfed the saint. Two of the nuns thought it proceeded from the tabernacle, but when the saint turned around, the rays were seen to originate from his face. Another sister observed the same as she stood by a different grille.

* * * * *

St. Mary Magdalen de Pazzi (d. 1607) was known for her deep love of the Blessed Sacrament and her frequent ecstasies. During her novitiate she fell dangerously ill and was taken to the infirmary, where she fell into an ecstasy. During the hour she was in this state her face became intensely luminous.

* * * * *

One day when St. Peter of Alcántara (d. 1562) was still a youth, he remained unusually long in church after attending Holy Mass. When midday passed and he had not returned home, his mother sent a servant to search for him. The saint was found in the choir of the church, kneeling behind the organ, his face glowing with a celestial brightness. His contemplation was so deep that the servant had great difficulty in arousing him.

* * * * *

Father A. Tanquerey, in his classic treatise on ascetical and mystical theology entitled *The Spiritual Life* (no. 1519), informs us that ecstasies are often accompanied by a luminous phenomenon—either a halo about the head or a glow which may envelop the whole body. He summarizes the teachings on the subject as written by Pope Benedict XIV, who outlined the various ways in which the phenomenon must be investigated to determine its authenticity. The saints in this chapter, by virtue of their canonization, have evidently met the criteria set forth by Pope Benedict XIV and successfully passed the tests required by other pontiffs.

A flame appears above the head of St. Ignatius Loyola at the *Memento* of the Mass. Another priest, Fr. Nicholas Lannoy, rushed forward to extinguish it until he caught sight of Ignatius' face and realized he was lost in contemplation and was not harmed by the fire.

Chapter 41

LEVITATION

Levitation is the mystical phenomenon of one's body being lifted in the air with no apparent physical assistance. Alban Butler tells us that levitation is recorded in some form or other in the lives of over 200 saints and holy persons. It is interpreted as a special mark of God's favor whereby it is made evident to the physical senses that prayer is a raising of the heart and mind to God.

In Chapter 20 of her *Autobiography*, St. Teresa of Avila tells of her experiences with this phenomenon and about the fear it produced in her.

> One sees one's body being lifted up from the ground and although the spirit draws it after itself, and if no resistance is offered does so very gently, one does not lose consciousness—at least, I myself have had sufficient to enable me to realize that I was being lifted up. The majesty of Him who can do this is manifested in such a way that the hair stands on end, and there is produced a great fear of offending so great a God, but a fear overpowered by the deepest love, newly enkindled, for one who, as we see, has so deep a love for so loathsome a worm that He seems not to be satisfied by literally drawing the soul to Himself but will also have the body.

The saint tells us that on one occasion she resisted the phenomenon by lying on the ground and having her nuns actually hold her down. This was done during a sermon on a patronal festival when the saint wished to avoid alarming some ladies who were attending the Mass.

Although levitations seem to come gently to some saints, St. Teresa tells us that at times

> . . . it seemed that I was being lifted up by a force beneath
> my feet so powerful that I know nothing to which I can com-
> pare it, for it came with a much greater vehemence than any
> other spiritual experience . . .

While many saints have experienced this mystical phenomenon
under various circumstances, the following are some of those to
whom it occurred either before or during Mass or while at prayer
before the Blessed Sacrament.

For instance, during the celebration of Holy Mass, St. Francis
Solano (d. 1610) was often seen floating several feet above the
ground.

*   *   *   *   *

With regard to the levitations of St. Alphonsus Liguori (d.
1787), the saint's biographer P. Tannoia described an event he
witnessed when Alphonsus was close to 90 years of age:

> . . . One morning, in October 1784, being at Pagani, I said
> Holy Mass whilst St. Alphonsus prayed before the Blessed
> Sacrament. After a while I heard a slight rustling with his
> feet, and being convinced that something extraordinary was
> taking place I glanced sideways, and saw the saint raised in
> the air above his seat, although it had been with the greatest
> difficulty that his servant had succeeded in bringing him into
> the church and placing him in his chair. After Holy Mass I
> went into the choir in order to say my thanksgiving, and I
> saw again the same floating in the air, which happened
> quietly and easily as though a light feather was being moved.

*   *   *   *   *

St. Angela Merici (d. 1540), foundress of the Ursulines, was
once attending Holy Mass when she was suddenly and publicly
entranced. Her body was lifted from the ground in the sight of the
whole congregation and remained in this position for a considerable length of time.

*   *   *   *   *

Probus, a contemporary biographer of St. Arey, Bishop of Gap
(d. 604), is said to have often visited the church where the saint
passed many nighttime hours before the tabernacle. Probus relates
that the saint was often found ravished in spirit and lifted high into

the air by the ministry of angels. At such times, the whole church was ablaze with heavenly light.

*   *   *   *   *

When St. Peter Celestine (d. 1274) journeyed to Rome to obtain approval for the religious order he had founded, the assistants of the pope, having already heard of St. Peter's frequent levitations during Holy Mass, asked him to celebrate Mass for the pope. Instead of the splendid vestments offered him, Peter begged to be allowed to retain his simple hermit's clothing. When he began the Mass he was lifted in the air, and remained suspended until Mass was completed. After seeing this marvel, the pope confirmed the new order without delay.

*   *   *   *   *

Pope St. Celestine V, after his abdication, was imprisoned by his successor, Pope Boniface VIII, for reasons explained in their biographies. While in custody he was closely watched. One day, when he was celebrating Holy Mass, his guards were astounded to see him surrounded with light and suspended in the air.

*   *   *   *   *

St. Francis of Posadas (d. 1713), who is mentioned elsewhere in this volume as having had the gift of tears, was often surrounded by a glow during his ecstasies and was frequently lifted above the ground by unseen forces. At the conclusion of his levitations he would say, "I cannot tell whether I left the earth or the earth withdrew from me." On one occasion, while pronouncing the words of consecration, he fell into a rapture and remained suspended in the air until the conclusion of the Mass. After this, as mentioned previously, the congregation saw to their amazement that he was surrounded by a great light.

*   *   *   *   *

St. John Joseph of the Cross (d. 1734), during his ecstasies, was often lifted supernaturally into the air and remained suspended until the conclusion of his rapture. When his monastery was being built he would often assist in carrying the bricks, mortar or timber to the workmen. On one occasion when the workmen missed him, they went in search of him and found him in the chapel in deep contemplation and lifted off the ground—so high, in fact, that his head actually touched the ceiling.

*   *   *   *   *

The saint who perhaps experienced more levitations than any other saint is St. Joseph of Cupertino (d. 1663), who was born in a stable in 1603. In his youth he was apprenticed to a cobbler, but feeling an attraction to the Order of Conventuals, he applied for assistance to his paternal uncle, who was a religious of that order. This priest, however, regarded his nephew as unfit for the exalted dignity of the priesthood because of his lack of education, and therefore was unwilling to help him. Overcoming many obstacles, St. Joseph was eventually accepted into the Order and demon-strated many virtues, although he had great difficulty with his studies. In examining him for ordination, the bishop asked him to explain the meaning of the passage, "Blessed is the womb that bore Thee"—which, providentially, was the only one St. Joseph understood, having learned it by long study. So well did he in-terpret this passage that the bishop assumed the others would be equally well prepared, and ordained them all without further ex-amination.

St. Joseph of Cupertino is known to have performed severe pen-ances and to have fasted a good part of each year. It is also well known that he levitated almost daily at Holy Mass. Of his many levitations we will mention only a few.

One Holy Thursday, while praying with other religious before an altar of repose which was erected above the high altar and lit with many lamps, the saint rose in the air and advanced toward the vessel in which the Blessed Sacrament was kept, without touching any of the many decorations close to him. He remained there in adoration, returning to his original place only when his superior called to him.

During a visit to Naples, St. Joseph was once praying in the Church of St. Gregory of Armenia, which was the church of the nuns of St. Ligorio. He suddenly rose in the air and flew to the altar, where he remained for some time, bending over the flowers and candles with arms spread in the form of a cross. The startled nuns were fearful that he would catch fire, but he returned unharmed to the middle of the church, where he praised the Blessed Virgin.

On entering a church during one of his travels, St. Joseph's companion asked him if he thought the Blessed Sacrament was reserved there, since the sanctuary lamp was not burning. Immediately the saint flew towards the tabernacle, embracing it and adored the Blessed Sacrament, which he knew to be present.

One Christmas Eve Joseph invited some shepherds to join him in celebrating the birth of the Child Jesus. During the service he flew through the air from the middle of the church to the high altar, a distance of almost 40 feet. He remained there about a quarter of an hour, without disturbing any of the many lighted candles or burning his clothes. The shepherds are said to have "marveled exceedingly."

At Nardo, where he stayed for a time, St. Joseph was seen lifted up in ecstasy in the Church of St. Francis—to the terror of those present. Another time, when the Litany of the Blessed Mother was being recited, he flew to the altar of the Immaculate Conception and returned through the air to his original place.

In 1645 the Spanish ambassador to the papal court, the High Admiral of Castile, passed through Assisi with his wife with the intention of meeting St. Joseph of Cupertino. While in church, the saint looked upon a statue of the Immaculate Conception on the altar and flew over the heads of those present to the foot of the statue. After remaining there some time in prayer, he flew back and returned to his cell. The incident amazed the Admiral, his wife and their numerous retinue.

Because of the 70 ecstatic flights or levitations that are recorded in the acts of his beatification, St. Joseph of Cupertino is quite appropriately regarded as the patron of those who travel by air.

Many are the saints who have experienced the unusual phenomenon of levitation, but the ones mentioned here are only some of those who experienced this manifestation before the Blessed Sacrament.

St. Teresa of Avila in levitation. On one occasion this happened when she was on her knees and about to communicate.

Above: St. Joseph of Cupertino levitating during Mass. Seventy ecstatic flights or levitations are recorded in the acts of his beatification.
Right: St. Alphonsus Liguori levitating in ecstasy despite extreme old age and weakness.

Chapter 42

THE HISTORY OF
EUCHARISTIC DEVOTION

From the earliest Christian times the Eucharistic "bread" and "wine" have been venerated as the actual Body and Blood of Jesus Christ. As proof of this early veneration we have only to study the frescoes in the catacombs which were constructed beneath the city of Rome between the 1st and 3rd centuries. Here we find numerous symbols representing the Holy Eucharist. The most persistent of these are baskets of bread in conjunction with fish, recalling Jesus' miraculous multiplication of the loaves and fish, an event which led up to His feeding of souls with His own flesh and blood. In the catacomb of Callistus is a painting of a large fish beside a woven basket, and on top of the basket are pictured round loaves of bread; the front part of the basket has a square opening in which is seen a glass containing red wine. In the catacombs of St. Priscilla, archeologists have found sculptured loaves (about the size of a fist) indented on the top with a cross, the mark of salvation—which brings to mind the words of Jesus in the Gospel: "If any man eats of this bread, he shall live for ever; and the bread that I will give is my flesh for the life of the world." (*John* 6:52).

It has been the firm and constant Christian belief, from the time of the Last Supper to the present, that the Eucharist is a permanent Sacrament, the elements reserved in the tabernacle continuing to be the Body and Blood of Christ even after the Mass is completed. Recall the martyrdom of St. Tarsicius, who was carrying the Eucharist to Christians imprisoned in Rome; he died at the hands of a heathen rabble rather "than surrender the Sacred Body to the raging dogs." As the centuries passed, the reserved Eucharist was venerated with increasingly striking ceremonies of honor and adoration in accord with the teaching of Christ, passed down from the Apostles and handed on by the Magisterium of the

Church, that the Eucharistic elements are truly the Body and Blood of Jesus Christ.

The Elevation of the Host during Mass

Called by some historians "the epoch-making liturgical development," the elevation of the Host in its present sense is first mentioned about the year 1200—although all the ancient liturgical writings, including the Apostolic Constitutions, had an elevation of the Blessed Sacrament just before Holy Communion so that the people could see the consecrated Host. The elevation immediately following the Consecration was adopted as a defense against the erroneous teachings of Peter Comestor and Peter the Chanter, who held that the bread was not changed into the Body of Christ at its Consecration, but only after the words of Consecration had been spoken over the wine also, at which point (in their opinion) both bread and wine were changed into the Body and Blood of Christ. To show that on the contrary, the bread was changed into the Body of Christ as soon as the words, "This is My Body," were pronounced, the consecrated Host was held up for the adoration of the people without waiting for the words of consecration to be spoken over the chalice.

It quickly became recognized as a meritorious act to gaze upon the elevated Body of the Lord, and the practice was in such high favor that various means were used to increase the visibility of the Host. In some Spanish churches, black cloths were hung behind the altar, and in other places lighted torches were held behind the priest by a deacon or server. Strict injunctions were often given to servers that on no account should the view of the Host be obstructed by incense smoke from the thurible.

According to Thurston, during the Middle Ages the viewing of the Host at the elevation was judged by many people to be the most vital part of attendance at Mass—so much so, in fact, that if they had not seen the Blessed Sacrament some thought they had not properly heard Mass and therefore waited for another.

The earliest written record of the elevation is found about the year 1200, in the synodal statutes of Eudes de Sully, Bishop of Paris, who ordered the practice in response to the erroneous opinion of the two theologians. Pope Gregory X (1271-1276) ordered the elevation of the Host to be included in the Mass throughout the West. The elevation of the Host is likewise mentioned in the Ordo

Romanus XIV (1311), the papal ceremonial of Pope Clement V. And on May 18, 1907, Pope St. Pius X granted an indulgence. to the faithful who would look upon the elevated Host with piety, faith and love while praying, "My Lord and my God."

The Feast of Corpus Christi

The introduction of this feast can be traced back to a vision of St. Juliana, who was born at Retinnes near Liège, Belgium in 1193. Orphaned at the age of five, Juliana was placed in the Augustinian convent at Mont-Cornillon, where she was veiled at the age of fourteen. She made rapid progress in virtue and was known for her love of the Blessed Virgin, the sacred Passion and especially the Blessed Sacrament. At the age of sixteen she began to experience visions, and in one of these she saw the full moon, whose brightness was disfigured by a single dark spot. She described the vision to her superior, Sr. Sapientia, but an interpretation of its meaning could not be determined. Finally, after many days of prayer, Juliana heard a heavenly voice render the meaning:

> That which disturbs thee is that a feast is wanting to My Church Militant, which I desire to establish. It is the feast of the Most High and Most Holy Sacrament of the Altar. At present the celebration of this mystery is only observed on Maundy Thursday, but on that day My sufferings and death are the principal objects of consideration; therefore, I desire another day to be set apart in which it shall be celebrated by the whole of Christendom . . .

Three reasons were then given for this request: First, that faith in this Sacrament would be confirmed by this feast when future attacks against its validity would be introduced; second, that the faithful would be strengthened on their way to virtue by a sincere and profound adoration of the Blessed Sacrament; third, that because of this feast and the loving attention given to it, reparation would be made for the irreverence and impiety shown to the Blessed Sacrament.

For 22 years Juliana said nothing of this vision to the clergy, but at last she made it known to Robert de Thorete, then the Bishop of Liege, and to the Dominican Hugh, who later became cardinal legate in the Netherlands, and to James Pantaleon, who was then the Archdeacon of Liège. Later, James Pantaleon became a bishop, and soon thereafter was elected as Pope Urban IV.

Since bishops were then permitted to establish feasts for their dioceses, Bishop de Thorete called a synod in 1246 in which these learned and holy men took part. Fully 16 years elapsed, however, between Juliana's sharing of the message of her vision and the opening of this synod. After discussing the possibility of establishing the feast, the men decided that it was not contrary to the teaching of the Church. It was further decided that the feast would be instituted as a means of thanking Almighty God for giving us the great Sacrament of the Altar. The new celebration was then ordered to be held the following year. A monk named John was to write the office for the occasion. (The original decree and parts of this office are preserved in Binterim.)

Bishop de Thorete did not live to see the execution of his order. He died later the same year, on October 16, 1246, but the feast was nonetheless observed for the first time by the canons of St. Martin at Liège.

James Pantaleon, one of the first who had deemed the vision of Juliana genuine, became Pope Urban IV on August 29, 1261. He was urged by Henry of Guelders, the new Bishop of Liège, to extend the celebration to the entire world. The Pope, always an admirer of the feast, published the bull *Transiturus* on September 8, 1264. In it he ordered the feast of Corpus Christi to be celebrated annually on the Thursday after Trinity Sunday, at the same time granting many indulgences to the faithful who would attend Holy Mass and the Office. This Office, composed at the request of the Pope by the Angelic Doctor, St. Thomas Aquinas, is considered to be one of the most beautiful in the Roman Breviary.

The celebration of the feast was ordered again by the Pope's successor, Clement IV. It was not until the days of Pope John XXII (1316-1334) that the feast was celebrated with processions and the carrying of the Blessed Sacrament in a monstrance. For participation in these processions Pope Martin V and Eugene IV granted other indulgences.

The feast of Corpus Christi is observed in the United States on the Sunday following Trinity Sunday.

Today in Catholic areas of Europe, notably Austria and southern Germany, the feast of Corpus Christi is a national holiday, celebrated with magnificent processions through the city streets. In

Freiburg im Breisgau in the Black Forest, for example, it has long been customary for the bishop, all the priests of the city (some 200), hundreds of altar boys, and all the Catholics of the city to take part in a magnificent four to five hour procession with the Blessed Sacrament. There is Mass at all the parishes at 7:00 a.m., and then the procession begins around 10:00 a.m. at the Cathedral, moves through the city, stopping for Benediction at four different altars set up outside, finally returning to the Cathedral. Twenty-five or thirty bands—from the police, fire department, Red Cross, army, air force, athletic clubs and many other institutions, all in uniform—play beautiful hymns as they proceed through the city. The faithful, too, sing hymns, and the music moves along in waves as the songs are picked up by each succeeding section of the procession.

The entire length of the procession path is lined with birch tree branches inserted into holes in the earth; this is done at the expense of the city of Frieburg. In front of each of the four altars, for a length of about 200 feet, a pathway of flower petals in intricate patterns is laid out. People from all the parishes in the city cooperate in making these floral carpets, staying up from midnight to 5:00 a.m. Women, girls and old people spend hours pulling flowers apart, placing the petals in piles according to color. Men and boys then take the petals and place them by color on the streets, following patterns which have been drawn on long strips of paper. Many additional people are employed in keeping the flower petals damp. In recent years, however, because of the danger of disruption by wind and storm, colored stones have been used instead of flower petals.

Along the streets, people decorate their windows with the yellow and white Catholic flag, banners, fabric hangings, crucifixes and other religious objects. At the conclusion of the procession, all the bells in the city are rung continuously for 15 minutes. The entire celebration is seen as a profession of faith, a public acknowledgment that one is a Catholic, as well as an act of homage to the Blessed Sacrament.

Benediction of the Blessed Sacrament

Ordinarily an afternoon or evening devotion, Benediction consists in the singing of certain hymns before the Blessed Sacrament as it is exposed on the altar within a monstrance of precious metal.

The most solemn part of the service takes place when the priest, wearing the ankle-length cope, takes the monstrance in his hands and with it makes the Sign of the Cross, blessing the adorers.

While there is a great deal of diversity in the ceremony in various countries with regard to details—such as the recitation of litanies, hymns to Our Lady, the singing of canticles or the times of incensing—certain elements are constant. The use of incense and wax candles, the singing of the *Tantum Ergo* and the blessing given with the Blessed Sacrament are obligatory everywhere.

A less formal version of this service is now seldom observed wherein the priest, wearing a surplice and stole, simply opens the tabernacle door. Prayers and devotions are then said or sung. The priest blesses those present with the veiled ciborium before the Blessed Sacrament is put back into the tabernacle and the tabernacle door is again secured.

During the early part of the 13th century, when the elevation of the Host at Mass was introduced and the feast of Corpus Christi was established, a custom began among confraternities and guilds of singing canticles in church before a statue of the Blessed Mother. These canticles were called *Laude*, and the members of the confraternities, which were organized for the sole purpose of singing these canticles, were called *Laudesi*. It was such a company of Laudesi that brought together the seven holy founders who established the Order of Servites, or Servants of Mary, in the first half of the 13th century.

The idea of an evening service of a popular character sung before the statue of Our Lady spread throughout Europe. In particular, the *Salve Regina* was adopted for use in these services. We find traces everywhere of its being sung, sometimes by choirs of boys, as a separate evening service. In France this service was commonly known as *Salut*, in the Low Countries as the *Lof*, and in England and Germany simply as the *Salve*.

Our present Benediction service seems to have resulted from the general acceptance of this evening singing of canticles before the statue of Our Lady. It was later enhanced in the 16th and 17th centuries by the exposition of the Blessed Sacrament, which was added to lend additional solemnity to the service. The blessing with the Blessed Sacrament at the conclusion of the service seems to have been added because at that time it was customary to make the Sign of the Cross whenever the Blessed Sacrament was replaced in the tabernacle, such as after processions or after the Blessed Sacrament had been carried to the sick.

One of the hymns most often used for Benediction is the *O Salutaris Hostia*, which consists of the last two verses of the hymn *Verbum Supernum*, composed by St. Thomas Aquinas for the hour of Lauds for the office of Corpus Christi. It is customarily sung as soon as the Blessed Sacrament is taken out of the tabernacle. The *Tantum Ergo*, which has many musical variations, consists of the last two verses of the hymn *Pange Lingua*, a hymn composed by the same saint for Vespers of the feast of Corpus Christi. This hymn and the blessing with the Host are the only essential and prescribed parts of the service. Another hymn that is sometimes used is *Sacris Solemniis*, which is more popularly known as *Panis Angelicus*, "Bread of Angels." The title, *Panis Angelicus*, comes from the first two words of the sixth stanza. This hymn was written for Matins of the feast of Corpus Christi. The author is again St. Thomas Aquinas.

Exposition of the Blessed Sacrament

The ceremony in which the Blessed Sacrament is removed from the tabernacle and placed in a monstrance for exposition to the faithful was formally introduced in the 14th century under the newly established feast of Corpus Christi. Reports dating to the 13th century reveal that scholastic theologians of the time debated whether looking upon the consecrated Host was permissible to those in the state of mortal sin. It was commonly decided that, far from being an offense against God, such an act was praiseworthy and likely to obtain the grace of true contrition for the sinner.

In the 14th century the practice of exposition was already established, especially in Germany, and in Dantzig the Blessed Sacrament was reserved during the day in a transparent monstrance. A decree passed at Breslau in 1416 speaks of permission "for the body of Jesus Christ, on some few days of the week, to be visibly exposed and shown to public view." In 1452, however, a decree enacted at Cologne under Cardinal Nicholas de Cusa altogether forbade the reserving or carrying of the Blessed Sacrament in monstrances, except during the octave of Corpus Christi. During the 15th century numerous synodal decrees prohibited the continuous and informal exposition as wanting in proper reverence. An unnamed bishop declared that he had perceived that "by this frequent exposition, the indevotion of the multitude only becomes greater, and reverence is lessened."

Despite these restrictions, it is clear that the custom of exposition of the Blessed Sacrament was retained—with a curious compromise. It became the practice throughout a great part of central Europe for the Blessed Sacrament to be reserved in *Sakramentshäuschen*, or "Sacrament Houses." Often of great height and imposing appearance, Sacrament Houses were usually beautifully carved of stone and were situated in a conspicuous part of the church near the sanctuary. There the Host was kept in a monstrance behind a locked metal door of lattice work, in such a way that it could still be dimly seen by those who prayed before it. In Vadstena, Sweden, in the motherhouse of the Brigittines, there is a record of the erection of such a Sacrament House in 1454.

Another custom prevalent in Germany and the Netherlands before the close of the 15th century was the practice of exposing the Blessed Sacrament during the time of Mass. This, however, was checked by the official episcopal ceremonial, which directed that the exposed Blessed Sacrament should be removed from the altar when High Mass was to be celebrated. The present Canon 941.2 states that "exposition of the Most Holy Sacrament is not to be held in the same part of the church or oratory during the celebration of Mass."

In the time of St. Philip Neri (d. 1595) and St. Charles Borromeo (d. 1584), many varieties of services involving exposition of the Blessed Sacrament began to prevail.

Exposition of the Blessed Sacrament is observed in two forms, public and private. In the public ceremony, the Host in its monstrance is placed on the altar or in a niche above the tabernacle proper. In private exposition, the ciborium is placed in front of the open tabernacle.

Canon 941 states: "In churches or oratories where it is permitted to reserve the Most Holy Eucharist, there can be expositions either with the ciborium or with a monstrance, observing the norms prescribed in the liturgical books." Canon 942 recommends that "in these same churches and oratories an annual solemn exposition of the Most Holy Sacrament be held during a suitable period of time, even if not continuous, so that the local community may meditate and may adore the Eucharistic Mystery more profoundly; but this kind of exposition is to be held only if a suitable gathering of the faithful is foreseen and the established norms are observed."

For private exposition any good and reasonable cause is sufficient.

Forty Hours Devotion

The Forty Hours Devotion, or *Quarant' Ore*, an extended period of adoration of the exposed Blessed Sacrament, corresponds to the 40 hours of loneliness and darkness spent by Jesus in the tomb. Italy is given as the place of its origin, but its originator is uncertain, with St. Philip Neri, St. Antonio Maria Zaccharia, Brother Buono of Cremona, St. Ignatius Loyola and members of the Theatine Order being mentioned—as well as other saints, religious and holy persons. The year of its introduction is also variously given, but it is certain that the practice in its present form originated in the early 16th century and that the devotion spread rapidly, with pontifical approval being quickly obtained.

Adding to the confusion is St. Charles Borromeo, who speaks as if a practice of praying for 40 hours was introduced even earlier. Indeed, it seems to have been observed in the 13th and 14th centuries, with the 40 hours being solemnized each year only from Good Friday to Easter Sunday. It is unclear, however, whether the Blessed Sacrament was exposed during these periods of prayer.

The practice as it developed in the 16th century involved exposition of the Blessed Sacrament and prayers for 40 hours, a devotion which could be performed at any time of the year. It is now a universal custom, regulated by the bishop of each diocese, to arrange the hours of adoration in a succession of churches throughout the year in such a way as to have continuous devotion, that is, the conclusion of the devotion in one church being taken up by adoration in another. The ideal situation is for the exposition of the Blessed Sacrament to be maintained by night as well as by day, but when this is not feasible, the devotion can be interrupted during the night.

In 1539 a request that indulgences be granted for participants in this devotion was presented to Pope Paul III. Two years later the pontiff replied, granting indulgences. Father Herbert Thurston believes that this is the earliest pronouncement of the Holy See upon the subject. The parchment reads in part:

Our beloved son the Vicar General of the Archbishop of Milan, at the prayer of the inhabitants of said city, in order to appease the anger of God provoked by the offences of Christians, and in order to bring to nought the efforts and machinations of the Turks who are pressing forward to the destruction of Christendom, amongst other pious practices, has established a round of prayers and supplications to be offered both by day and night by all the faithful of Christ, before our Lord's Most Sacred Body, in all the churches of the said city, in such a manner that these prayers and supplications are made by the faithful themselves relieving each other in relays for forty hours continuously in each church in succession, according to the order determined by the Vicar . . . We, approving in our Lord so pious an institution, and confirming the same by Our authority . . .

Not only did the pontiff approve the devotion, but he also granted numerous indulgences for those who would take part in the observance. Pope Clement VIII, on November 25, 1592, likewise endorsed the devotion, while Pope Clement XII, more than a century later, issued a very minute code of instructions for the proper observance of the *Quarant' Ore* devotion.

While there is uncertainty as to the originator and the exact date of its beginning, there is absolutely no uncertainty regarding the introduction of the devotion in the United States. This was the work of St. John Neumann (1811-1860), the first naturalized United States citizen of his gender to be canonized. The saint was likewise the first Redemptorist to be professed in America, and at 41 he was appointed the fourth bishop of Philadelphia by Pope Pius IX.

Papers kept in the St. John Neumann Center in Philadelphia reveal that the saint himself arranged the schedule for the devotion to be observed in a succession of churches in his diocese. Owing to its success in Philadelphia, other bishops throughout the United States gradually followed the saint's lead, and the devotion became general throughout the country.

Perpetual Adoration

Perpetual Adoration is the uninterrupted exposition of the Blessed Sacrament both day and night for lengthy periods of time during which pious persons take turns as adorers.

Probably the earliest and longest instance of perpetual adoration on record is the continuous adoration of the Blessed Sacrament in the Cathedral of Lugo, Spain for more than 1,000 years in expiation of the fourth-century Priscillian heresy. This thousand-year-long adoration was referred to in an official letter written by Cardinal Vaughan in 1895 to the Cardinal Primate of Spain.

An instance in which Perpetual Adoration continued for half that time took place when King Louis VIII of France on September 14, 1226, recommended that the veiled Sacrament should be exposed for prayers in the Chapel of the Holy Cross as an act of thanksgiving for his recent victory over the Albigensians. As mentioned previously, in the chapter on the miracle of Avignon, the throng of adorers was so great that Bishop Pierre de Corbie thought it appropriate to continue the adoration by night as well as by day—a privilege that was subsequently ratified by the Holy See. After a period of over 500 years, the Perpetual Adoration of the Blessed Sacrament was interrupted in 1793, but it was resumed in 1829.

The general practice of Perpetual Adoration developed after the establishment of the Forty Hours devotion. After Perpetual Adoration was observed in several churches in Rome, it was gradually extended throughout the world.

This devotion is the special object of many pious associations and religious congregations. Worthy of particular mention are the orders founded by St. Peter Julian Eymard (1811-1869) after receiving an interior illumination that there was no religious congregation whose major purpose was the glorification of the Most Blessed Sacrament. St. Peter Julian eventually founded a congregation of male religious, an order of contemplative nuns, the People's Eucharistic League for the laity, and the Priests' Eucharistic League for parish priests.

Today, through the diligent efforts of laymen and clergy, Perpetual Adoration of the Blessed Sacrament is more and more being enthusiastically observed in churches and chapels throughout the United States.

Eucharistic Congresses

A Eucharistic Congress is an international gathering of ecclesiastics and laymen, presided over by a papal legate, for the purpose of celebrating and glorifying the Holy Eucharist and of seeking the best means to spread its knowledge and love throughout the world. The congresses are organized by a permanent committee consisting of clergy, religious and laymen from many countries, and representatives of national and international organizations. At the conclusion of each congress the committee prepares a volume giving a report of all the papers read, discussions held, sermons preached, addresses made at public meetings and details of all that transpired. The congresses are not intended as a display of numerical strength, and they have no commercial purpose.

The honor of being the originator of the Eucharistic Congress belongs to a pious lady, Marthe Marie Tamissier, who was born in Tours, France in 1834 and for the most part led a quiet and simple life. It was her idea that group meetings arranged outside the church, for the purpose of discussion and explanation of Church teachings on the Holy Eucharist, might overcome misunderstandings and encourage many who never attended church to hear about this doctrine. At her urgent and repeated request, Bishop Gaston de Segur organized a meeting and appealed to Mr. Philibert Vrau, an industrialist in northern France who was known as "the holy man of Lille," to support the endeavor financially. The congress, held at the University of Lille on June 21, 1881, was attended by thousands of the faithful who represented several nationalities. This gathering is regarded as the first Eucharistic Congress.

Bishop de Segur presided over this first gathering. In his opening address he explained the purpose of the movement in this way:

> It is quite evident that the great evils of the day, not merely in France but throughout the whole Christian world, are traceable to the denial of Jesus Christ. Secularization has been the watchword of the enemies of God and their purpose has been to keep religion and the supernatural away from the hearts of men. Our purpose is to open a way to man's heart for Jesus to enter, and this purpose can only be attained by means of the Holy Eucharist.

A second congress was held in Avignon, France in 1882 and was attended by 1,500 ecclesiastics and no fewer than 30,000 laymen. Thereafter with each observance the congresses grew with an ever-increasing importance and attendance.

After Pope St. Pius X expressed a wish for a Eucharistic Congress to be held in Rome, such a gathering was planned and held in 1905. The Pope added to the solemnity of the occasion by celebrating Mass at the opening of the session, by giving a special audience to the delegates and by being present at the procession that closed the proceedings.

In 1908, just three years later, a Eucharistic congress was held in London—the first held in an English-speaking country. At this gathering there were counted six cardinals, 14 archbishops, 70 bishops and a host of priests. This congress was proclaimed the greatest religious triumph of its generation.

Although a papal legate is usually appointed to oversee the proceedings, Pope Paul VI himself assumed this role, personally attending two congresses, those held in Bombay in 1964 and Bogota in 1968.

From the first congress, held in 1881, through 1985 there have been 43 international Eucharistic congresses. These have been held in many countries, including France, Belgium, Israel, Germany, England, Canada, Austria, Australia, Ireland, Philippines, Hungary, the United States (Chicago in 1926 and Philadelphia in 1976) and Kenya (Nairobi in 1985).

Sculpted loaves inscribed with a cross, representing the Eucharist. These were found attached to a tomb in the catacombs of St. Priscilla.

An example of a "Sacrament House," Cathedral of Regensburg.
Following two pages: Corpus Christi celebration in Freiburg im Breisgau, in the Black Forest, Germany. This is the last of the four outdoor altars along the procession route; it is situated in front of the cathedral, Our Lady of Münster.

Chapter 43

THE HOLY EUCHARIST
AND OURSELVES

The Church has been enriched throughout the years with pious associations and religious orders that have devoted themselves to increasing and encouraging adoration of the Eucharist. Likewise through the centuries the Blessed Sacrament has been honored by the introduction of various devotions such as Benediction, Perpetual Adoration, the Holy Thursday liturgy, Forty Hours Devotion and the feast of Corpus Christi.

But the most sublime act of worship is the Holy Mass itself, a service whose value we are unable properly to assess in this world. We who could not be present on Calvary are, at the Mass, given the privilege of witnessing Our Lord's unbloody immolation upon the sacrificial altar. And just as the Blessed Mother was present beneath the Cross, so too is she present during the Holy Sacrifice of the Mass, and according to sainted writers, angels surround them in adoring attendance.

St. Bernard tells us that angels also kneel at *our* feet when the sacred species is within us. With the Sacred Host within us, we not only give Our Lord reverence, but we also draw down upon ourselves manifold graces and blessings of various sorts. Among these blessings which we receive (according to our degree of fervor) is the diminishing of the temporal punishment due to our sins; furthermore, we gain merit that will redound to a heavenly reward. The Masses we have heard will be a great consolation at the hour of our death, and the souls in Purgatory, whose sufferings were alleviated by the Masses we offered for them, will in turn intercede for us.

The saints have repeatedly recommended frequent attendance at Holy Mass. St. Joseph Cottolengo recommended daily Mass for everyone and said that those who do not go to daily Mass practiced bad management of time, while St. Bernard said that "one merits more by devoutly assisting at a Holy Mass than by distributing all his goods to the poor and traveling all over the world on pilgrimage." Jesus once told St. Gertrude, "You may be sure that to anyone who devoutly assists at Holy Mass I will send as many of My saints to comfort him and to protect him in the last moments of his life as there will have been Masses which he has heard well."

It is also well to reflect here on the words of St. Anselm, a Doctor of the Church: ". . . a single Mass offered for oneself during life may be of more value than a thousand celebrated for the same intention after death." With this St. Leonard of Port Maurice concurs, as does Pope Benedict XV. But whether offered before or after death, the benefits of a Mass are inestimable.

A multitude of saints have been unsparing in their praise of the Holy Eucharist and in their suggestions that it be frequently honored and received. Among them is St. Francis de Sales, who wrote:

> If worldly folk ask you why you communicate so often, say it is in order to learn to love God, to purge yourself of your imperfections, to free yourself from your miseries, to console yourself in your afflictions, to support yourself in your weaknesses. Say that there are two kinds of people who should communicate often: the perfect, because being so well-disposed they would do great wrong if they did not approach the source and fountain of perfection, and the imperfect with the end of being reasonably able to aspire to perfection; the strong, that they may not become weak, and the weak to become strong; the sick that they may be cured, and the healthy that they may not fall sick; and that you, imperfect, weak and sick, need to communicate often with Him who is your perfection, your strength and your doctor.

St. Thomas More, when he was Chancellor of England, was reproached by his friends for going to Communion so often. They objected that this piety occupied too much time that should be applied to his other duties and responsibilities. The saint answered them:

> Your reasons for wanting me to stay away from Holy Communion are exactly the ones which cause me to go so often.

My distractions are great, but it is in Communion that I
recollect myself. I have temptations many times a day. By
daily Communion I get the strength to overcome them. I
have much very important business to handle and I need
light and wisdom. It is for these very reasons that I go to
Holy Communion every day to consult Jesus about them.

St. Bonaventure tells us that sinners must not stay away from the
Sacrament because they have sinned, since ". . . the more infirm a
person feels himself to be, the more he is in want of a physician."
We are also taught that the Blessed Sacrament produces sustain-
ing, healing and nourishing effects in the soul, much as material
food nourishes the body.

These saintly recommendations that sinners receive Holy Communion must not of course be understood to mean that those in the
state of mortal sin should receive Holy Communion. A person who
has committed a mortal sin must first make a good confession and
receive absolution in the Sacrament of Penance. The Holy
Eucharist must be received only in the state of grace. To receive
Holy Communion in the state of mortal sin constitutes another
mortal sin, a sacrilege, an act by which one eats and drinks judgment to himself. (*1 Cor.* 11:29).

In addition to all the benefits derived from the reception of Holy
Communion, as outlined by St. Francis de Sales and St. Thomas
More, there is still a greater reward, a promise given by Jesus
Himself. In the sixth chapter of St. John's Gospel, after the feeding
of the 5,000 with miraculously multiplied loaves and fishes, Our
Lord referred to Himself several times as "the bread that has come
down from heaven," and He promised eternal life in Heaven for
those who partake of Him. Our Lord tells us:

Labor not for the meat which perisheth, but for that which
endureth unto life everlasting, which the Son of man will give
you. For him hath God, the Father, sealed.

—John 6:27

For the bread of God is that which cometh down from
heaven, and giveth life to the world.

—John 6:33

This is the bread which cometh down from heaven; that if any man eat of it, he may not die. I am the living bread which came down from heaven.

—*John* 6:50, 51

If any man eat of this bread, he shall live for ever; and the bread that I will give, is my flesh, for the life of the world.

—*John* 6:52

Then Jesus said to them: Amen, amen I say unto you: Except you eat the flesh of the Son of man, and drink his blood, you shall not have life in you.

—*John* 6:54

He that eateth my flesh and drinketh my blood, abideth in me, and I in him.

—*John* 6:57

As the living Father hath sent me, and I live by the Father; so he that eateth me, the same also shall live by me.

—*John* 6:58

These biblical assurances indicate that not only does Our Lord endeavor to convince us by repetition that He is indeed present under the lowly form of bread, but He also pleads with us to receive Him in this Sacrament of love, and as an incentive He promises an eternal life of happiness in Heaven. While words are inadequate to describe this love and generosity of the Saviour, the preceding is ample subject matter for many meditations.

As to the dispositions we should entertain after receiving the Eucharist, St. Francis de Sales counsels us:

When you have received the Host, excite your heart to come and render homage to this king of salvation; speak to Him of your most intimate affairs; contemplate Him within you, where He has come for your happiness; finally, give Him the best welcome possible and behave in such a manner that by all your acts it may be known that God is with you.

It is sad to consider that such courtesies have not always been extended to Our Lord. It is also undeniable that countless receptions have been made sacrilegiously. Our Lord once said in a vision to St. Bridget: "There does not exist on earth a punishment which is great enough to punish a sacrilegious Communion." Holy Communion received with a mortal sin on one's soul has been likened to a Judas kiss, a slap in the Lord's face, a damnable insult. (Yet this sin is forgivable in the Sacrament of Penance.)

Those of us who struggle to reach some measure of virtue but are not gifted with supernatural favors, visions and heartfelt sentiments, should be consoled by an experience of St. Catherine of Bologna. Butler relates of her:

> . . . the devil would instill into her mind grievous doubts concerning the real presence of Jesus in the Blessed Sacrament. This caused her intense misery until at last, one day, God revealed the whole doctrine to her and so completely answered her difficulties that her doubts left her forever. He also assured her that if the conscience is pure the effects of the Sacrament are independent of sensible fervour . . . nor do doubts hinder its efficacy, provided no consent is given to them. Moreover, that those who are patient under such trials gain more by their Communions than if they were favoured with spiritual consolation.

In addition to attendance at Holy Mass and the reception of the Sacrament, there is another practice which is heartily recommended by the saints, and that is making frequent visits to adore Our Lord in the Eucharist. St. Alphonsus strongly encouraged devout souls to spend at least a quarter or a half hour in adoration, stating that:

> You must be aware that in a quarter of an hour's prayer spent in the presence of the Blessed Sacrament, you will perhaps gain more than in all the other spiritual exercises of the day.

The saint adds:

> They feel great tenderness and devotion who go to Jerusalem and visit the cave where the Incarnate Word was born, the hall where He was scourged, the hill of Calvary on which He died, and the sepulchre where He was buried; but how much greater ought our tenderness to be when we visit an altar on which Jesus remains in the Holy Sacrament!

St. Teresa of Avila tells us that in this world it is impossible for all subjects to speak to the king, and they must be content to speak to him by means of a third party. "But to speak with Thee, O King of Heaven, there is no need of third persons, for everyone that wishes can find Thee in the most Holy Sacrament."

The Church likewise has encouraged visits to the Blessed Sacrament, whether it is exposed or in the tabernacle, and has even rewarded a half-hour visit of adoration to Our Lord by granting a plenary indulgence, contingent upon the fulfillment of certain conditions: Confession within two weeks of the visit, the reception of Holy Communion and prayers for the pope's intentions; in addition, one must be free of attachment to sin, even venial sin. These conditions are few enough when one considers that a plenary indulgence removes all the temporal punishment (Purgatory time) due to sin and may be applied to a departed soul by way of suffrage.

If attendance at Holy Mass, the reception of the Eucharist and adoration of Our Lord in the Blessed Sacrament are of such inestimable temporal and spiritual value, there is yet another way in which these graces can be increased countless times during the day, and that is by the making of Spiritual Communions. A Spiritual Communion is an ardent desire to receive the Holy Eucharist when it is impossible to communicate sacramentally. It can be done by employing one's own words or by the use of various formulas which have been approved.

The Sacred Congregation of Indulgences on November 24, 1922 approved the following formula for a Spiritual Communion:

> O Jesus, I turn toward the holy tabernacle where You live hidden for love of me. I love You, O my God. I cannot receive You in Holy Communion. Come nevertheless and visit me with Your grace. Come spiritually into my heart. Purify it. Sanctify it. Render it like unto Your own. Amen.

St. Alphonsus de Liguori, a Doctor of the Church and the founder of the Congregation of the Most Holy Redeemer, wrote a book entitled *The Holy Eucharist*, in which he gives two prayers suitable for the making of Spiritual Communions:

> My Jesus, I believe that Thou art truly present in the Most Blessed Sacrament. I love Thee above all things, and I desire

to possess Thee within my soul. Since I am unable now to
receive Thee sacramentally, come at least spiritually into my
heart. I embrace Thee as being already there, and unite
myself wholly to Thee; never permit me to be separated from
Thee.

*   *   *   *   *

I believe that Thou, O Jesus, art in the Most Holy Sacrament! I love Thee and desire Thee! Come into my heart. I
embrace Thee; oh, never leave me!

One of the most ardent devotees of Spiritual Communions was
St. Mary Magdalen de Pazzi, who is said to have made at least 50
Spiritual Communions a day. She was once favored with a vision
in which Jesus held two chalices, one silver, the other gold. The
saint was given to understand that the silver chalice contained the
Spiritual Communions she had made, while the gold vessel held
her Sacramental Communions. In addition to this practice it is said
that she made 33 visits a day to the Blessed Sacrament in honor of
the years of Our Lord's life on earth.

Chapter 44

SPIRITUAL COMMUNION

(This chapter consists of an article written by Sister M. Barbara Anne, F.M.S.C. It was published in the magazine Apostolate of the Little Flower, *The Discalced Carmelite Fathers, San Antonio, Texas; July-August 1984, Vol. 52, No. 4, p. 24-28. It is reproduced here with the permission of the author and that of the magazine's editor, Father Louis V. Scagnelli, O.C.D.)*

Recently I referred to the making of Spiritual Communions in conversation and was confronted with the truism that "Our children do not even know what a Spiritual Communion is!" If such be the case, though hopefully not a universal one, need it stay this way?

I wager that the practice of Spiritual Communion arose from the intensity of love which the faithful bore for Christ in the Holy Eucharist. This is depicted in the lives of saints, too, such as Saint Therese of Lisieux, who like Saint Charbel Makhlouf pivoted her day about the reception of the most Holy Eucharist.

"Receiving Jesus 'to give Him pleasure,' Therese knows that at the same time she will receive from Him all that is necessary for her in order to live; this is the value throughout her life which she will attach to Holy Communion ... At the time of her last illness she overcame extreme weakness amid trials and sufferings in order to receive Holy Communion. 'I do not find that it is too much to suffer to gain a Communion,' she replies to a sister who reproaches her conduct. To communicate is to receive divine strength."[1]

In the life of Saint Charbel we note that the essence of his sanctity consisted in centering his entire life upon the most Holy Eucharist. For this purpose this Maronite priest preferred to offer his daily Mass at 11 a.m. It enabled him to spend a good part of the morning in preparation for this supreme act of worship and the rest of the day for thanksgiving.

In an official prayer for the public novena to Saint Rita, used for centuries, the faithful read: May every beat of my heart be a Spiritual Communion.

What then, in fact, is Spiritual Communion? The Catholic Encyclopedia, Imprimatured and prepared under the auspices of Cardinal Spellman in 1965, reads: "Those who attend Mass, and for some good reason are unable to receive Holy Communion, may do so in spirit and by desire. This is called Spiritual Communion. In order to receive Spiritual Communion one must have a lively faith and an earnest desire to partake of the Sacrament. These desires must be followed by sincere acts of faith, love and thanksgiving.

"The merits of Spiritual Communion, while not as great as in the actual reception of the Sacrament, are, nevertheless, abundant and fruitful. However, those who repeatedly receive the Sacrament spiritually, when they could receive it both spiritually and sacramentally, are depriving themselves of the great graces."[2]

Some may argue that this was for the Middle Ages when Holy Communion was received less often than today. They may even support the theory that they find Christ in their fellow human beings and the whole of creation, so why all the fuss about reverting to His real presence outside of the Eucharistic sacrifice and/or during it when impeded from actual reception. Lack of knowledge and love for the most Blessed Sacrament is all too prevalent today! Sad enough if it stems from ignorance of the fact that His presence in the Holy Eucharist far exceeds any other. It is His presence *par excellence*! [The consecrated Host actually *is* Jesus.]

In Father Faber's classic work, *The Blessed Sacrament*, he states: "Yes! it comes to this—that God vouchsafing to dwell in the Blessed Sacrament, it needs be His greatest work of love. O what was Palestine to this! He dwells there as our Father among His children, as our Redeemer to complete His work, as our Sanctifier to continue it, as our Glorifier impatiently anticipating our endless union with Him, and as our Creator perfecting, finishing and outstripping in Transubstantiation the most delicate processes of creation, which without it would be unfinished." He goes on to add that He who made myriads of angels, Adam and the whole of creation, is there, "His whole undivided ever-blessed self who is now in the tabernacle, taken captive by His own insatiable love of the creatures whom His mercy made!"[3]

"This food," says Saint Catherine of Siena, speaking of Our Lord's flesh and blood, "strengthens us little or much, according to the desire of him who receives it, in whatever way he may receive it, sacramentally or virtually"; and in her *Dialogue*, she proceeds to describe virtual or Spiritual Communion. In behalf of the same practice, Saint Teresa of Avila encourages her religious: 'Whenever, my daughters, you hear Mass and do not communicate, you can make a Spiritual Communion, which is a practice of exceeding profit, and you can immediately afterwards recollect yourselves within yourselves, just as I advised you when communicating sacramentally; for great is the love of our Lord which is in this way infused into the soul. For when we prepare ourselves to receive Him, He never fails to give Himself to us in many modes which we comprehend not."[4]

In the life of Maria Scholastica Muratori, a Roman lady, by Father Gabrielli of the Bologna Oratory, we read that she tried to make a Spiritual Communion every time she raised her eyes or drew her breath, so that, as she said, "Were I to die suddenly, I should die, as it were, inhaling my God." Another of her devotions was to make a Spiritual Communion in set form whenever she saw Communion given to anyone in the church.[5]

From these many considerations may we more fully appreciate this practice and keep it alive by speaking of its efficacy to those with whom we come in contact or those we have under our care.

That the Church encourages Spiritual Communion today is backed by the fact that in the latest listing of indulgences, entitled *Enchiridion of Indulgences—Official List of the Church*, a partial indulgence is granted for this laudable practice. Though it may take on "any pious form," a prayer is recommended to the faithful, which follows:

> My Jesus, I believe that You are in the Blessed Sacrament. I love You above all things and I long for You in my soul. Since I cannot now receive You sacramentally, come at least spiritually into my heart. As though You have already come, I embrace You and unite myself entirely to You; never permit me to be separated from You.[6]

In his book, *Living the Interior Life*, Father Wendelin Meyer, O.F.M. cites some of the virtues which flow from this frequent uniting of ourselves with our Eucharistic God. They are: jubilation of spirit, true charity, silence, joy in prayer and longing for God. He encourages religious to "value both kinds of Communion and communicate every day both actually and spiritually." He further stresses that "the one complements and deepens the other." Small wonder that he ventures to add, "Where actual and Spiritual Communion are often received, there floats the spirit of contemplation."[7]

In *Fruitful Activity,* Abbé Gaston Courtois devotes a chapter to the Eucharistic life and the apostolate. In it he proposes that we turn our thoughts continually to Jesus in the Host. He notes that "The intensity of your Eucharistic devotion" has a great bearing upon "the fervor of the souls to whom you have dedicated yourselves."[8]

It is precisely because Jesus Christ is there living in the Host that our Spiritual Communions become a tremendous asset to ourselves and others! St. Paul reminds us: "He is there to make intercession for us."

Christ is there ready and willing to help us when we are lost for words, as it were, to console a lonely octogenarian, or a drug-addicted teenager, a confirmed alcoholic, etc. Yet, He lets much depend upon your humble petition. That glance in His direction afforded by Spiritual Communion can make a difference. Try this direct line to the heart of Christ. It might be a habitual turning, as when the clock strikes the hour. Or, then again, it could be at that critical moment when the cross weighs heavily upon us or others. It is a way of responding to His invitation, "Come to me, you who labor and are heavy burdened, and I will give you rest."

Others have tried it before you. It was the Curé of Ars who said, "A spiritual Communion acts on the soul as blowing does on a cinder-covered fire which was about to go out. Whenever you feel your love of God growing cold, quickly make a Spiritual Communion."

—Sr. M. Barbara Anne, F.M.S.C

———

Opposite: Procession in 1978 with the miraculous Host of Alatri to commemorate the 750th anniversary of the miracle. This Host turned to flesh in the year 1228 after a young lady, in search of a love potion to attract a certain young man, had removed the Host from her mouth. The girl repented of her sin, as did the woman who had advised her to commit the sacrilege.

1. R. P. Victor De La Vierge, O.C.D., *Spiritual Realism of Saint Therese of Lisieux* (Milwaukee, Wisconsin: Bruce Publishing Co., 1961), p. 43.
2. *Catholic Encyclopedia for Home and School Use* (New York: McGraw-Hill Company, 1965). (Copyright 1965 by St. Joseph's Seminary and College, Dunwoodie, Yonkers, N.Y.)
3. Frederick William Faber, D.D., *The Blessed Sacrament* (Rockford, Illinois: TAN Books and Publishers, Inc., 1978), p. 326.
4. Faber, op. cit., p. 440-441.
5. Ibid, p. 443.
6. Sacred Apostolic Penitentiary, *Enchiridion of Indulgences—Official List of the Church*, translated by William T. Barry, C.SS.R. (New York: Catholic Book Publishing Co., 1968), p. 116.
7. Wendelin Meyer, O.F.M., *Living the Interior Life* (Cork, Ireland: The Mercier Press, 1963), p. 221.
8. Gaston Courtois, *Fruitful Activity*, translated by Sister Helen Madeleine, S.N.D. (Westminster, Maryland: The Newman Press, 1962), p. 35.

— SELECTED BIBLIOGRAPHY —

Abbott, S.J., Walter M., General Editor. *The Documents of Vatican II*. Herder and Herder Association Press. New York. 1966.

Anniversario 750 del Miracolo Eucaristico dell' Ostia Incarnata. Alatri. 1978.

Antonio, Juan. *Primera Parte de la Historia de la Ciudad de Compluto*. Alcalá de Henares. 1725.

Apostolate of the Little Flower. Rev. Louis V. Scagnelli, O.C.D., Editor. Discalced Carmelite Fathers. San Antonio, Texas. July-August 1984, Volume 52, No. 4.

Aradi, Zsolt. *The Book of Miracles*. Farrar, Straus and Cudahy. New York. 1956.

Auffray, A., S.D.B. *St. John Bosco*. Salesian House. Tirupattur, South India. 1930.

The Begijnhof. Amsterdam, the Netherlands.

Bevenot, Maurice, S.J., *Ancient Christian Writers*, No. 25. The Newman Press. Westminster, Maryland. 1957.

Brewer, E. Cobham. *A Dictionary of Miracles*. Cassell & Co. New York. 1884.

Bumpus, T. Francis. *The Cathedrals and Churches of Belgium*. Dodd, Mead & Co. New York.

Butler, Alban; Thurston, Herbert, S.J.; Attwater, Donald. *The Lives of the Saints*. 12 Volumes. P. J. Kenedy & Sons. New York. 1936.

Carducci, Luciano. *Il Miracolo Eucaristico di Offida e il Santuario*. Offida. 1980.

The Catholic Encyclopedia. The Encyclopedia Press, Inc. New York. 1912.

Code of Canon Law. Canon Law Society of America. Washington, D.C. 1983.

Concannon, Mrs. Thomas. *The Blessed Eucharist in Irish History*. Browne and Nolan Limited. Dublin, Ireland. 1932.

Conyngham, D. P. *Lives of the Irish Saints and Martyrs*. P. J. Kenedy & Sons. New York. 1870.

Corcoran, Rev. M. J., O.S.A. *Our Own St. Rita; A Life of the Saint of the Impossible*. Benziger Bros. New York. 1919.

Constantini, Sac. Ambrogio. *Rievocazione del Miracolo Eucaristico dell'Ostia Incarnata nel 750 Anniversario*. Diocesi di Alatri. Alatri. 1978.

Cruz, Joan Carroll. *The Incorruptibles*. TAN Books & Publishers. Rockford, Illinois. 1977.

Cruz. *Relics*. Our Sunday Visitor, Inc. Huntington, Indiana. 1984.

A cura dei Missionari del Preziosissimo Sangue. *Basilica di S. Maria in Vado*. Ferrara, Italy. 1971.

Danielou, Jean. *Origen*. Sheed and Ward. New York. 1955.

Daroca. Subsecretaria de Turismo. Zaragoza, Spain.

De Kruisbeuk. Hasselt. (Paper.)

de Robeck, Nesta. *St. Clare of Assisi*. Bruce. Milwaukee. 1951. Reprinted by Franciscan Herald Press. Chicago. 1980.

Dillis, P. Thomas Aquinas, O.P. *Das Wunderbarliche Gut*. Augsburg, Germany. 1949.

Documents relatifs a l'Apparition Miraculeuse, Le Miracle de 1822 a La Sante-Famille de Bordeaux. Bordeaux, France.

Donovan, The Reverend C.F., M.A. *Our Faith and the Facts*. Patrick L. Baine. Chicago. 1927.

Dunney, Rev. Joseph A. *The Mass*. The Macmillan Co. New York. 1925.

Englebert, Omer. *The Lives of the Saints*. Collier Books. New York. 1951.

Fatima in Lucia's Own Words: Sister Lucia's Memoirs. Sr. Lucia, O.C.D. Postulation Centre. Fatima, Portugal. 1976.

Fyot, Eugene. *Dijon*. 1979.

Gabriel of St. Mary Magdalen, O.C.D. *Divine Intimacy*. Desclee Co. New York. 1964.

Giordani, Igino. *Catherine of Siena: Fire and Blood*. Bruce Publishing Co. Milwaukee. 1959.

Grimaldi, Siro. *Uno Scienziato Adora*. Cantagalli. Siena, Italy. 1956.

Gritsch, Dr. Johanna. *Seefeld/Tirol: The Parish Church*. Verlag Schnell & Steiner. Seefeld, Austria. 1982.

Haffert, John M. *The World's Greatest Secret*. Ave Maria Institute. Washington, New Jersey. 1967.

Herbst, Fr. Winfrid, S.D.S. *New Regulations on Indulgences*. TAN Books & Publishers, Inc. Rockford, Ill. 1977.

Herval, M. René. *En Marge de la Legende du Precieu-Sang-Lucques-Fecamp-Glastonbury*. Fecamp.

Hoagland, Arthur N., M.D. *Miracle at Santarem*. (Paper.)

Holy Miracle of Santarem. The Church of the Holy Miracle. (Paper.)

Immaculata. The Conventual Franciscan Friars of Marytown. Libertyville, Ill. Dec. 1984/Jan. 1985.

Un Jubilé Eucharistique Dans L'Eglise Expiatoire, Très Saint Sacrement de Miracle a Bruxelles. Société de Saint Augustin, 1898.

Latini, Mario. *Attorno al Castello Di Morro un Giorno Lontano*. Morrovalle. (Paper.)

Liguori, Saint Alphonsus de. *The Holy Eucharist*. Redemptorist Fathers. Brooklyn, New York. 1934.

Lorente, Juan Francisco Esteban. *Apuntes Historicos de Daroca*. Daroca, Spain. 1982.

Macerata, E il Sangue Sprizzo sul sacro lino nella chiesa benedettina di Torresana. Macerata, Italy. (Newspaper article.)

Macerata, Una insigne reliquia nella Cattedrale. Macerata, Italy. (Newspaper article.)

Manna. The Society of the Divine Savior. St. Nazianz, Wisconsin. 1931.

Mansfield, Milburg Francisco. *The Cathedrals and Churches of the Rhine*. L. S. Page & Co. Boston, Massachusetts. 1905.

Mazille, M. L'Abbe. *Notice La Sainte Hostie De Blanot*. Blanot, France. 1981.

Merton, Thomas. *The Living Bread*. A Chapel Book. Dell Publishing Co. New York. 1956.

Merton. *What are These Wounds?* The Bruce Publishing Co. Milwaukee, Wisconsin. 1950.

Le Miracle de Faverney. M. Lescuyer & Fils. Lyon, France. 1958.

Le Miracle de 1822 A La Sainte-Famille De Bordeaux. 1954.

Il Miracolo Eucaristico Di Torino. No. 2 Edizione. Basilica del Corpus Domini. Torino, Italy. 1952.

Il Miracolo Eucharistico Permanente Di Siena. Santuario Eucaristico di Siena. Siena, Italy. 1962.

Miracoloso Corporale, Macchiato dal Sangue di Nostro Signore Conservato nella Cattedrale di Macerata. Macerata, Italy.

Mullen, Fr. Roland, O.F.M. Conv. *Miracle of Siena*. Siena, Italy. 1966.

New Catholic Encyclopedia. Catholic University of America. McGraw-Hill Co. New York. 1967.

Pastrovicchi, Rev. Angelo, O.M.C. *St. Joseph of Copertino*. TAN Books & Publishers. Rockford, Illinois. 1980.

Pio IV. *A Perpetua Memoria* (Bolla di Pio IV), 1560. Morrovalle.

Raymond of Capua, Blessed. *Life of Saint Catherine of Siena*. P. J. Kenedy & Sons. New York.

Ritarossi, Carlo. *La Vita Religiosa di Alatri e il Miracolo Eucaristico dell' Ostia Incarnata del 1228*. Cattedrale di Alatri. Alatri, Italy. 1965.

Rossetti, P. Felix. *Una Delle Piu' Grandi Meraviglie*. Edizioni Periccioli. Siena, Italy. 1965.

Samaritani, Antonio. *Miracolo Eucaristico di Ferrara del 28 Marzo 1171.* Stilia-Cesena. Ferrara, Italy. 1978.

Sammaciccia, Bruno. *The Eucharistic Miracle of Lanciano, Italy.* Sanctuary of the Eucharistic Miracle. Lanciano, Italy. 1977.

Il Santuario del Sacro Cuore. Pubblicazione Quindicinale Salesiani Bologna. Bologna, Italy. 1983.

Selon. *L'Histoire de Braine de Maxime de Sars.* (Paper).

Shapcote, Emily Mary. *Legends of the Blessed Sacrament.* Burns & Oates, Ltd. New York. 1877.

Sheppard, Lancelot C. *Don Bosco.* The Newman Press. Westminster, Maryland. 1957.

Staniforth, Maxwell. *Early Christian Writings.* Penguin Books. Baltimore, Maryland. 1968.

Stradella, A. Broccati. *Il Miracolo Eucaristico di Ferrara.* Periodico del Santuario del Sangue Prodigioso. Ferrara, Italy. 1968.

Tangen, Fr. Ronald. *Real Presence in the Eucharist.* Our Blessed Lady of Victory Mission, Inc. Brookings, South Dakota. (Cassette tape.)

Tanquerey, Very Reverend Adolphe. *The Spiritual Life: A Treatise on Ascetical and Mystical Theology.* The Newman Press. Westminster, Maryland. 1930.

Teresa of Avila. *The Life of Teresa of Jesus: The Autobiography.* Translated and edited by E. Allison Peers. Image Books. Doubleday & Co., Inc. Garden City, New York. 1960.

Il Tesoro Eucaristico, Nei Documenti Dell'Autorita Ecclesiastica. Santuario delle SS. Particole. Siena, Italy. 1969.

Il Tesoro Eucaristico. Periodico di Spiritualita Eucaristica. Gennaio-Febbraio, 1979.

Thurston, Herbert, S.J. *The Physical Phenomena of Mysticism.* Henry Regnery Co. Chicago, Illinois. 1952.

Van Tongerloo, Rev. D. *Guide to the St. Michael's Cathedral of Brussels.* Brussels, Belgium. 1975.

Vaudagnotti, Mons. Attilio. *Il Miracolo del Sacramento di Torino.* Torino, Italy. 1982.

Vincenti, A. *I Miracoli Eucaristici, Due pagine di Breviario intrise di sangue.* Vita Pastorale. giugno-luglio. 1969.

Wallfahrt Zun H. Blut Seefeld in Tirol 1384-1984. (Paper.)

Wils, Joseph. *Sacrement De Miracle De Louvain.* Louvain, Belgium. 1905.

Zayek, Bishop Francis M., S.T.D. *A New Star of the East.* Diocese of St. Maron. New York. 1977.

If you have enjoyed this book, consider making your next selection from among the following . . .

Prices subject to change.

Prices subject to change.

Prices subject to change.

At your Bookdealer or direct from the Publisher.
Toll-Free 1-800-437-5876   Fax 815-226-7770
Tel. 815-226-7777   www.tanbooks.com
Prices subject to change.

One of the most fascinating books ever . . .

THE INCORRUPTIBLES

A Study of the Incorruption of the Bodies of Various Catholic Saints and Beati

By Joan Carroll Cruz

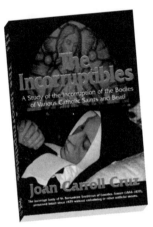

**No. 0199. 310 Pp.
PB. Impr. 33 Illus.
ISBN 0-89555-066-0**

16.50

Prices subject to change.

The stories of 102 canonized Saints and Beati whose bodies were found incorrupt long after their deaths, many of which remained fresh and flexible for years, or even centuries. Many endured abnormally adverse conditions in remaining intact, e.g., damp graves—or such as St. Francis Xavier's, which was buried in lime for quick decomposition. Also goes into heavenly fragrances, the exuding of holy oil and the flow of fresh blood several years after death. Includes St. Cecilia, St. Rita, the Curé of Ars, St. Bernadette, and many more. A fascinating, documented study which will reinforce one's faith in the Catholic Church—the only religion that possesses the phenomenon of bodily incorruption. Belongs in every Catholic home.

TAN BOOKS AND PUBLISHERS, INC.
P.O. Box 424 · Rockford, Illinois 61105

**Toll Free 1-800-437-5876
Tel 815-226-7777**

**Fax 815-226-7770
www.tanbooks.com**

NOTES

NOTES

NOTES

Joan Carroll Cruz is a native of New Orleans and is the educational product of the School Sisters of Notre Dame, to whom this book is dedicated. She attended grade school, high school and college under their tutelage. About her teachers Mrs. Cruz says, "I am especially indebted to the sisters who taught me for five years at the boarding school of St. Mary of the Pines in Chatawa, Mississippi. I cannot thank them enough for their dedication, their fine example and their religious fervor, which made such an impression on me." Mrs. Cruz has been a tertiary in the Discalced Carmelite Secular Order (Third Order) for the past 19 years; for eight years she served as Mistress of Formation (Novice Mistress). She is married to Louis Cruz, who is in the swimming pool installation and maintenance business.

Mrs. Cruz says that since her five children are now all young adults she has more time for writing, and she is immensely grateful for the invention of the word processor. Her books include *The Incorruptibles,* published in 1977 by TAN Books and Publishers, Inc.; *Desires of Thy Heart,* a novel with a strong Catholic theme published in hardcover by Tandem Press in 1977 and in paperback by Signet with an initial printing of 600,000 copies; and *Relics,* published in 1983 by Our Sunday Visitor, Inc. For her three non-fiction books Mrs. Cruz depended heavily on information received from foreign shrines, churches, convents and monasteries. The material she received required the services of several translators. Much to her relief, the research material for the book she is presently working on, and the book and booklet she has planned, is all in English. Her current project is a book about saints for laymen, as yet untitled.